D0787041

REVENGE of the NERD*

*OR . . . THE SINGULAR ADVENTURES OF THE MAN WHO WOULD BE BOOGER

A MEMOIR

CURTIS ARMSTRONG

THOMAS DUNNE BOOKS ST. MARTIN'S PRESS NEW YORK

THOMAS DUNNE BOOKS.

An imprint of St. Martin's Press.

REVENGE OF THE NERD. Copyright © 2017 by Curtis Johnathan Armstrong. All rights reserved. Printed in the United States of America. For information, address St. Martin's Press, 175 Fifth Avenue, New York, N.Y. 10010.

www.thomasdunnebooks.com
www.stmartins.com

Designed by Steven Seighman

The Library of Congress Cataloging-in-Publication Data is available upon request.

ISBN 978-1-250-11394-8 (hardcover)
ISBN 978-1-250-11395-5 (e-book)

Our books may be purchased in bulk for promotional, educational, or business use. Please contact your local bookseller or the Macmillan Corporate and Premium Sales Department at 1-800-221-7945, extension 5442, or by e-mail at MacmillanSpecialMarkets@macmillan.com.

First Edition: July 2017

10 9 8 7 6 5 4 3 2 1

To Elaine and Lily,
the loves of my life

Dudley Dawson —

Comes from a good, middle-class home. But from the sixth grade has been persecuted because of his height and the fact that he looked like a girl. The hurt and anger have built up, through high school, till he has taken refuge in cynicism, sloppy dress and obnoxious behaviour.

FOREWORD

What is a nerd?

For forty years I've been a professional actor, practicing my craft onstage, screen and television, building a career that many young actors have told me they envy, and *that* is the question—along with "Was that really you belching?" and "Did Bruce and Cybill really hate each other?"—I am most frequently asked these days. (The answers to those two other questions are no and yes, respectively.)

Not "How did you get your start?" or "Did you find the transition from stage to film and TV daunting?" or "How have you managed, against all odds, to achieve regular employment as a character actor in a brutal business in which barely making a living—let alone enjoying long-term success—seems like the elusive dream of a disordered mind?

Nope, none of those. The question I get is: "What is a nerd?" As if it's one of those large, metaphysical questions that most people would be unable to answer. Like when Lyndon Johnson met Louis Armstrong and said, with enormous weight and significance, "Louis, what *is* jazz?" Like he was expecting a big, heavy answer and what he got was Louis saying, "Pops, if you gotta ask, you'll never know." Funnily enough, I suppose that'd be a good answer to the nerd question as well.

Oddly, when *Revenge of the Nerds* was released in 1984, it wasn't a question I heard that much. In the 1980s, everyone pretty much knew—or thought they knew—what a nerd was. Certainly no one cared enough to ask.

Nerds were socially awkward outsiders: they may have been brilliant in math or science, but they could barely dress themselves. They never dated (and pretended that was a choice). Their skin was bad—this was nonnegotiable. They wore thick glasses/bow ties/and prescription shoes. Sports—or really any kind of physical activity other than running when being chased—was unknown to them. They collected comic books and subscribed to *Famous Monsters of Filmland*. They built and traded model trains, spacecraft, classic monster model kits and cars, and, if they were lucky enough to find another of their tribe in the neighborhood, they spent all their time in basements or garages together, deep in arcane role-playing games like Dungeons and Dragons, assuming the roles of characters who were not . . . you know, nerdy.

Some of them were brilliant academics and some were middling students. Some were "retarded," had learning disabilities or were abused or dyslexic. If they were lucky, they were ignored. If they weren't, they were bullied. A few became dangerous sociopaths.

But many went on to change the world in unimaginable ways, dreaming up ideas that would forever alter how we communicate, read, listen to music and send sexually explicit photos of ourselves.

They were the nerds, spazzes, dorks, retards and geeks. They were picked on, put down, beat up and ostracized. They were often lonely.

They were my people.

In a million years, they would never have been able to imagine a future in which the word "nerd" would have any kind of positive connotation. That "geek" could be something that highly paid government officials trained in foreign policy or counterintelligence would use to describe themselves; or that the adjective "adorkable" could even be a word in the English language, let alone that a highly successful, long-running television show could be marketed using it.

It's long been known that the etymology of the word "nerd" goes back to a man who could be considered a kind of Nerd Founding Father: Theodore "Dr. Seuss" Geisel. The first use of the word was in his 1950 book *If I Ran a Zoo*. Among the peculiar, bizarre and almost certainly socially inept creatures on display in Seuss's phantasmagorical zoo was a "Nerd." A year after the book's release, according to a report in *Newsweek* magazine, the term "nerd" had gained currency in Detroit, Michigan, as a derogatory slang expression for someone who was "square," or a "spazz."

And it was in Detroit, Michigan, at Harper Hospital, just two years later on November 27, 1953, where I was born, conveniently into the one town in America that had already coined the perfect word for some of its favorite sons to scream at me as they were pushing my head into locker room toilets.

The men in my family were bankers and auto company executives. The women were "housewives" except for my mother and aunt, who were teachers. I was to follow in none of their footsteps. I was on my way to becoming a sort of Nerd Founding Father myself.

I would accomplish that by going into a line of work as alien to my family's experience as migrant farm working. I did it by consorting for the rest of my life with a motley cast of actors, playwrights, misfits, radicals, alcoholics and English acting teachers. I would gain a solid professional reputation and secure a small place in cinematic history by indulging, for the amusement of millions, in antisocial, unhygienic behavior that my parents spent years teaching me never to do even in private.

I did it by dutifully playing second banana to universally acknowledged cool kids like Tom Cruise, John Cusack, Bruce Willis, Arnold Schwarzenegger and Jaime Foxx. I did it by marrying a woman with impeccable nerd credentials herself, writer Elaine Aronson, and eventually raising a nerd of our own, our daughter, Lily, thereby doing our bit to propagate the species. I did it by embracing my inner-nerd early, fully, publicly and with pride, to the point of creating and selling, with Robert Carradine, a hit comedy-reality television series called *King of the Nerds*, the entire point of which was to celebrate Nerd Culture in all its manifestations.

I did it by accepting the fact that to countless fans, the name

I had carried with pride for many years was not just unknown, it was completely beside the point.

So, the answer to the above question? What is a nerd?

I am a nerd.

My name is Curtis Armstrong. But you can call me Booger.

INTRODUCTION

There's a story my ex-wife, Cynthia, tells about when she and I first came to Los Angeles for film work after years in the theater.

It was 1984. I'd had a nice supporting role in a Warner Bros. movie, *Risky Business,* which had been released, and another nice supporting role in Fox's *Revenge of the Nerds*, which hadn't, but I had no illusions: I'd only just started to establish myself in New York as a stage actor and I wasn't expecting my arrival in Hollywood to shake the place up much, which turns out to have been a good bet.

But Cynthia had gone to meet her new West Coast agent and when she returned, I asked her how it went.

"Oh, fine," she said. "They seem nice. One of them mentioned you."

"Really?!"

"Yeah," Cynthia said. "I said I was married to an actor and

she asked which actor and I said Curtis Armstrong. And she said, 'Ah! Curtis Armstrong! The new Michael J. Pollard.'"

Now, maybe you need to know who Michael J. Pollard is to really appreciate the story. I guess it was the sheer unexpectedness of the comparison that surprised me. I would never in a hundred years have made that connection. I wasn't insulted, you understand. I like Michael J. Pollard. You'd just never think there could be *two* of him. I mean, Michael J. Pollard was short, a little dumpy, with a funny face, an unmistakable voice and an unruly mop of hair, and was known mainly for eccentric comedy roles, whereas I was . . . umm . . .

Okay, point taken.

And if that weren't enough, a few months earlier, *MAD* magazine had published their parody of *Risky Business*, and sure enough, in their treatment of the famous "What the fuck?" scene, there was young Tom Cruise, looking just like young Tom Cruise, and next to him, unmistakably, was Curtis Armstrong, looking just like a middle-aged Michael J. Pollard. Even *MAD* magazine couldn't tell us apart. There are probably still people who see me up on the screen and say, "Gosh, Michael Pollard's holding up well after all these years."

But getting down to this memoir business. Turns out I've written one and now here we are—I, shyly proffering the accumulated wisdom of a lifetime spent capering under hot lights for your amusement—and you, in a bookstore, perhaps, rummaging through the remainders bin, leafing through this introduction trying to decide if it's worth the buck and a half or whatever it's been marked down to, wondering if it might be good plane reading.

Well, let me tell you, this wasn't something I entered into lightly. In preparation, I have read a lot of contemporary memoirs written by various peers of mine. Reading these books was a humbling experience—not to mention expensive and, frankly, sometimes a bit of a slog—because it made me wonder if you are not *really* famous or wildly promiscuous or if you haven't wasted your best years waking up in a pool of your own vomit, is there really any point in writing a memoir? Obviously, promiscuity and alcoholic blackouts were always things I strove for, but is just striving really enough? In the harrowing-life-story department, there may be some areas I'm a little light in.

I was born in Detroit, which I know sounds promising, but it turns out not to have been the harsh, brutal Detroit of Eminem's youth, for example. Nearly four years of my childhood were spent in a foreign country, but not in a cold, heartless boarding school or anywhere I was made to eat dog. The country was Switzerland and it was clean and beautiful. (We did eat horse there, but it was always presented in such delicious sauces that we wouldn't dream of complaining.)

I was the product of a mixed marriage. My father, Robert, who spent a solitary adolescence buried in books, was a Nerd. My mother, the daughter of Italian immigrants, looked like Gina Lollobrigida. She fenced and taught judo to members of the Detroit Police Department. She was not a Nerd. It is a testament to their mutual love and devotion that they were able to bridge this significant cultural gap and remain a loving couple to this day. I have one sister, Kristin, who I never tried to sell into white slavery even when the opportunity presented itself. We've had our ups and downs, Kristin and me, for which I mainly blame myself. Certainly some of the constraint in our relationship stems from an ill-conceived prank I played on her when we were young. Having just seen Hitchcock's *Psycho*, I thought it might be a piquant thing to dress up in one of my mother's dresses, put on her wig and high heels, take a large butcher knife from the kitchen and then, just as Kristin was leaving the shower, leap in with the blade raised, shrieking, "REE! REE! REE!!" In retrospect, I realize this may have been the root of some long-term trust issues. Other than that, our childhood was the usual suburban mid-century American thing: she upstairs quietly playing with horses, me in the cellar trying to construct a torture chamber.

It may strike you that there are a fair number of school-related anecdotes herein, both in Detroit and Geneva. If so, that's because if we learn nothing else in school, it is usually the place where we first learn we are nerds. Depending on the person and circumstances, these can be difficult lessons, traumatic, even; or they can be glorious epiphanies, accompanied by a swelling soundtrack of celestial choirs. I think of nerd orientation as being kind of like sexual orientation. It's usually around age nine or so that people start being aware that something's up. Some are later bloomers and I guess some earlier, but school tends to be the great crucible of nerd self-identification. So I spend some time on it. If you want to skip ahead to the movies, be my guest.

I first appeared onstage as a professional actor in 1975, when I was twenty-three years old. For the record, it was in the role of Puck in *A Midsummer Night's Dream*, directed by Terence Kilburn, at Meadow Brook Theatre in Michigan. (You probably didn't see it.) I made my first movie, *Risky Business*, in 1983 when I was thirty years old. My first appearance on television was in 1987 in an episode of *Moonlighting*, when I was thirty-four. I'm writing this book now at the age of sixty-two, in 2016, more than forty years later. I held off as long as I could.

My goal from the start was to be a stage actor, and to that end I attended the Academy of Dramatic Art at Oakland University in Rochester, Michigan. I was trained in the classical English tradition (at least, that's what they told me it was and at those prices I expected nothing less). I began my career as a stage actor in Ann Arbor, Michigan, then moved to New York and, finally, to Los Angeles, where I still live to this day. All of this should be worth something, right?

The thing about show business is there's always a steady stream of optimists who are trying to break into it. Well, fine then! Some of them may be curious about what the business was like for someone who came before. Not a marquee name or an A-list celebrity, but a journeyman actor. One of those familiar faces with elusive names; one of those players who you figure must work all the time but they don't really; one of those character people who started by slaving away in the trenches and now, all these decades later, are lucky enough to find themselves still slaving away in the trenches. If that sounds like a joke, it wasn't meant to be. Unless you thought it was funny, in which case it was.

So all you sunny optimists, you thespians yet unsullied; you actors still brimming with ideals and passion; you uncynical masses still surging round the gate, looking for a way in—look no further! *Revenge of the Nerd* is just what the doctor ordered. Or maybe you're a civilian who has nothing to do with my profession at all, but who has a taste for this sort of rubbish and a long plane trip ahead of you—your search is over! This is a book for you.

Just to be clear, this is not a book that will try to teach you anything about acting. If you learn anything about acting here, it will be a fluke. It is, rather, a look back at a life lived while acting. Or, while not acting, as the case may be. Actors spend a lot of time *not* acting, which is why so many of us take up hobbies, like drinking. It might give you an idea what life as an actor would have been like for an actor in the last four decades, or at least what it would've been like if that actor were me. Or what it would've been like for an actor who looks just like me and had my exact career, without actually *being* me. (I'm hoping that last sentence will cover me in case any legal issues crop up.) Also I have, here and there, changed names in the book, though only those of people you probably wouldn't have recognized anyway. The famous ones are named and if they don't like how they're depicted they'll probably never speak to me again. Most of them haven't spoken to me in decades anyway, so who gives a shit?

One last thing: One night about twenty years ago I walked into a Mayfair Market in Hollywood at about one in the morning. It appeared to be completely deserted, but as I turned into an aisle I saw a man about halfway down standing very still, looking intently at a can he was holding. He wasn't just not moving, there was an aura of otherworldly stillness about the guy that was a little disconcerting. He was dressed in a green, shapeless coat, maybe an old army jacket. He had dark trousers, battered shoes and a tangled mess of hair and I knew the second I saw him that it was Michael J. Pollard.

I approached crab-casually, sideways, like I was scanning the aisle for something. He was just staring at the can he was holding and I was thinking, Here I am in a completely deserted grocery store with Michael J. Pollard! I felt like Robinson Crusoe finding Friday's footprint on the beach, only with Friday still in it. What to do? I had to say something, didn't I? What better than to share with him my ex-wife's story? What if I told him that years before an agent told me that I was the new him? And now here we are, the two of us at the Mayfair Market at one in the morning! My mind was racing as I tried to come up with the exact way of telling the story, but then I started having second thoughts. It was a great story, but as his role in it was, essentially, the punch line, would he see the humor?

Then again, taking a broader view, was the story really that funny in the first place? Maybe not. At that moment, I realized even I didn't find it that funny anymore. I knew too much. I had been an actor long enough to know how deeply even well-meant japes can cut. To this day I have scars myself and some of them are fresh.

I don't know what Michael was looking at so intently that night. It looked to me like a large can of Campbell's Tomato Juice, but he may have been seeing something entirely different. In fact, I'm sure he was. He certainly never saw me; the moment passed and I moved away.

If there's a moral of the story it's that character people are a resilient race. Michael J. Pollard is still around. And so am I. And in Hollywood, history is written by the supporting players.

DETROIT

I've said jokingly that I was the product of a mixed marriage, but there is more than a little truth in that statement. From a class, socioeconomic and even religious perspective, I was pulled in different directions as a boy. Detroit succeeded as a city because of the contributions and sacrifice of wildly disparate cultures. The ultimate clash and inequality of those cultures is what finally undermined it. Both sides of my family represent classic examples of American success stories, but they are very different stories. Detroit made my family and left a lasting imprint on me. But like the rifts exposed in the city itself, my family, the Italian Catholic D'Amicos and the upper-middle-class WASP Armstrongs, found that just interacting could be a fraught proposition.

I'll begin with the distaff side.

My maternal grandfather, Ovidio D'Amico, was born in the tiny village of Alfedena, in Italy. The D'Amicos, going back at least as far as Ovidio's great-grandfather, had been stonemasons in Alfedana and Ovidio's father, Antonio, had emigrated to the U.S. at some point, settling finally in Detroit, where he cut curbstones for the city's rapidly expanding street systems. Ovidio made the journey to join his father with his mother and three younger brothers in 1919. One of those brothers, Tom, later went to work for Chrysler, at their Outer Drive stamping plant. Emma, the youngest D'Amico sibling, the only D'Amico born in Detroit, worked her whole life for Goodyear tires, on the assembly line. Tom and Emma represented the only instances of the D'Amico family having a connection to Detroit's auto industry. As we'll see when we get to my father's side of the family, that connection was much stronger.

Ovidio's father died suddenly when Ovi was still in grade school. He dropped out of school at that point and went to work as a messenger for the Detroit Bank (later the National Bank of Detroit), where, over the years, he rose in the ranks to become a senior executive. My grandmother, the former Ida DeCesare, was born in Beverly, Massachusetts. Her mother died early and her father, feeling unequal to the task of raising two girls, packed her and her sister off to relatives in Italy, where, according to family lore, my grandmother made her village too hot to hold her; her wild-child behavior so appalled her keepers that they eventually shipped her back to the U.S., making her both a native-born American and an Italian immigrant at the same time.

From a fairly early age I was aware of the weird tension at work between the two sides of my family, the Italian-immigrant, working-class side, the D'Amicos; and the "executive class" side represented by the Armstrongs. It was only when I grew older that I grasped the racial and class hostility between the two families. By the time I had come along, the D'Amicos lived in the East Side neighborhood of Harper Woods, just off 8 Mile Road, in a small postwar house set on an enormous lot, which was taken up with their garden. They grew virtually all their fruits and vegetables, with Ida making her own sausage, pasta, bread, pizza and sauces. Dough was always placed to rise in heavy stoneware bowls on the floor in front of heat registers during the winter, wafting the scent of rising bread throughout their small house. Everything was kneaded by hand, and between the kneading and the gardening Ida had arms like an Italian communist. She canned and pickled obsessively. There was even a huge grape arbor, under which we would sit and eat in the heat of summer and where they harvested grapes for the wine my grandfather made in the basement.

To the extent that they socialized, they did so with an organization known as the Loyal Wing Society. This was an all-male Italian social club of which Ovidio was a member, but every now and then, during the summer, the women and children were invited to picnics in a local park in the heart of the Italian part of town, and it was during these afternoons that I came to understand the importance, and frankly, the otherness, of my Italian heritage. The women in floral dresses would sit in groups around the tables, fanning themselves, voluble and full of life. There were the other, older women, dressed in heavy black even in the hottest weather, as though in perpetual mourning, looking to me like crows among birds of brighter plumage. The men, meanwhile, in short-sleeved shirts, played bocce, smoking constantly, everyone speaking Italian. There was comfort in it and ritual, as well—a sense of timelessness and a kind of security in the knowledge that all was as it had always been and ever would be. That storied white American postwar sense of confidence that we'd gotten through the war and things would only get better from here extended to working- and middle-class Italians, as well, though the bitterness of the racism that had motivated my grandfather to ban Italian speech from the home during my mother's and her sister Elsie's childhood remained a problem for them. In the summer I would sit with Ovi on his porch at dusk as he smoked, mostly in silence, watching as the man across the street, a pigeon-fancier, released the birds for their evening exercise. They would fly, a small flock of them, in gentle circles above the street until, mysteriously summoned, they would return home. He also had a curious habit—this is Ovidio, not the man across the street—of sitting on the toilet with the bathroom door wide open, the light out, smoking cigarettes for long periods of time. At such times, all I could see of him in the darkened bathroom was the cigarette's glowing tip.

My mother, Norma, was not just glamorous, she was the older child with a fierce intelligence and endless curiosity, whose ambition to better herself equaled that of her father. How disappointed Ovidio may have been to have no male progeny is just a matter of speculation, but from an early age it was clear she was meant to be something other than an East Side suburban housewife.

The Italian-Americans were an isolated and insular society in those days. In school, we were always taught to take pride in Detroit's diversity of cultures, of its immigrant melting pot. But the Italians, like the Irish, Polish, Jewish, Greek, Arabic and—most significantly—black communities had their areas and stuck to them. It was only at this time, in the late fifties and early sixties, that we began to see a bleeding together of these cultures, to the disapprobation of Detroit's ruling white class, which was the class my father's parents belonged to.

I was a white child of privilege and I was raised under the influence of the automobile industry at a time when that really meant something. My paternal grandfather, Roy Armstrong, had been born in Herkimer, New York, and was an executive at General Motors, in the Fisher Body Division. Like Ovidio, his absolute opposite in almost every other respect, Roy never finished school, dropping out to join the navy, where he was small enough to earn the nickname "Pee Wee Armstrong." So underweight was he that, after one rejection from the recruiter, he devoured a dozen bananas in one sitting, returned and was accepted. His ship was the U.S.S. *Ohio.* He never saw a shot fired in anger and in one port got a tattoo that he spent the rest of his life regretting. He had used home remedies trying to rid himself of the thing, until it had become so blurred and smeared as to be unreadable. He caught me staring at it once. He held his forearm up to my face and said, "Don't ever do this. If someone tries to talk you into it, don't. Worst mistake I ever made." I once asked him what the tattoo had said, thinking it must have been something shameful, like "Roxy and Roy Forever" (my grandmother's name was Dorothy) or maybe "Kill 'em all: Let God sort 'em out." In fact, it was the U.S. Navy insignia.

And yet, tattoo notwithstanding, he was proud of his navy experience. He was an old-fashioned patriot. When we shook hands, often he would say, "That's the hand that shook four presidents's hands!" He would do an exaggerated, slightly comical salute whenever the words "United States of America" were spoken and would hold the salute until I returned it. The only real connection to "show business" in my family comes from Roy. As a youth, he played small roles in New York touring shows that would stop in Herkimer as a kind of cut-rate touring package. He was also part of a traditional, semiprofessional minstrel show. Blackface, banjos and everything. One of the jokes he used to tell onstage went:

"How's you feelin', Mr Bones?"

"Why, I'm feelin' like a dentist's forceps."

"How's dat?"

"Down in de mouth!"

He was a Mason, a fly fisherman, a duck hunter and a Protestant, though the last was pretty much in name only. He was a voracious reader and an autodidact and he owned books, more than I'd ever seen in a private home, housed in beautiful built-in bookshelves. My love of books was born in his den.

He liked to eat and drink, was loud and funny and brash. He was an Automobile Man.

Roy and Dorothy lived in a lovely mock-Tudor house in an area called Rosedale Park, on the West Side of Detroit. Unlike Ovi and Ida's house on the East Side—hot, treeless and very "new" feeling—Rosedale Park felt to me that it had been there forever, with quiet, well-appointed streets stretching out under the shade of cathedral arches of ancient elm trees.

Roy had married Dorothy Weekes, the diminutive daughter of George and Ivy Weekes of Smiths Falls, Ontario, Canada. She was in nurse's training in Utica, New York, when my grandfather met and courted her, a small-town girl who adapted quickly and decisively to life as the wife of a General Motors executive. She was a member of the Detroit Women's Club and wore white gloves when shopping downtown at Hudson's. Their house had a stained-glass window halfway up the stairs to the second floor and a formal dining room, reserved for state occasions like Thanksgiving and Christmas.

One Thanksgiving, we were all seated around the dining room table, I in my scratchy suit and bow tie. The candles were lit, and we were waiting for Dorothy, who was possibly a little lit herself, to make her entrance with the magnificent turkey on a Currier & Ives platter. Roy had just opened a bottle of champagne when the swinging door from the kitchen opened, and in swooped Dorothy with the turkey, to a round of applause. She was moving a little fast, though, or unsteadily, and the turkey soared off the platter, flying into the dining room and skidding across the floor.

There followed a moment of shocked silence, instant and absolute. Dorothy froze, expressionless, staring at the once perfect bird, lying upside down in a shambles on the floor. No one spoke or moved. Then, at an astonishing speed for a woman of her body type, Dorothy pounced on the turkey, scooped it up and disappeared back into the kitchen.

There followed a stage wait, during which no one dared look anyone else in the face. A moment later, Dorothy reappeared with the turkey back on the plate, as if nothing had happened.

"Thank God I cooked another bird," she said. So volatile was her temper that this palpable lie was accepted without comment and everyone dug in.

Roy and Dorothy had their own rituals, which included dining out at places like a private sportsman's club known colloquially as the Hunt and Grunt, Joe Muer's famous downtown grill, Carl's Chop House and the Top of the Pontch. They had cocktails every evening, and after a couple of my grandfather's Manhattans, my grandmother's stroppy side came out, sometimes with a vengeance. She couldn't do enough for her grandchildren, but she was a woman with a temper and a regrettable set of ingrained prejudices. Apart from the usual ones, including a notoriously short fuse with her husband, she had a particular aversion to Italian Catholics, especially when they tried to marry her son.

I became aware of racism in my city as something endemic to Detroit. It was a black versus white issue that had nothing to do with me and it was a shock to realize it was also a canker in my own family, to the point that Dorothy boycotted my parents' wedding, literally not showing up to the church until they had already started the service, and then only when she was forced to by Roy.

My father Robert was slight and short and looked years younger than his age, a family trait. No "Pee Wee" Armstrong for him, though. When he joined the navy, they nicknamed him, apparently without irony, "Army." He loved travel, good food and is, like his father was, irresistibly good company. He, too, was a book man. To this day, he enjoys a drink or two of an evening even if some of his other pleasures are lost to him. Until his conversion to Catholicism, following a chance encounter with the Pope at Vatican City, he was a Protestant. His ship was the U.S.S. *Topeka* and he also never saw action.

He started working for General Motors, switched to Chrysler and worked loyally for the company for the rest of his working life. Twice, at his request, our family was transferred overseas—the first time in 1964 to Geneva, Switzerland.

The second time was after I had left home, when my parents and sister were sent to London. This period between 1964 and 1978, when they returned to Detroit for good, is generally considered the Golden Age. My father, like his father, was an Automobile Man. And no matter how much they loved their lives in foreign lands, and they did, Detroit, with a hometown's grim, inevitable insistence, always dragged them back.

When I stayed with my mother's family, I felt like I was in the Old Country. When I was with my father's parents, I was in *Detroit*.

It may sound like a contradiction, but while I had no conscious desire to be an actor during the first decade of my life, I was obsessed with Robert Preston in *The Music Man*, the film version of Meredith Willson's acclaimed Broadway hit. Not just obsessed: it was my sole goal in life at that point to present a full production of this play in my basement. I, of course, would assay the role of the roguish con man, Professor Harold Hill.

This apparently contradictory reality—wanting to star in a production of *The Music Man* and having no desire to be an actor—can be explained when you understand my mother had a crush on Preston, which she actually talked about a lot. On a trip to New York a couple of years earlier, my father had taken her to see the Broadway production. She loved it and insisted on going backstage to meet the actor after the show. My father begged off and was waiting for her in front of the theater. Apparently, Preston invited her to come out for a late supper with him—an offer that she actually had to think about for a while before rejecting.

Therefore, my determination to play that same role would appear to have been more Oedipal impulse than legitimate desire for artistic expression.

I had my mother's copy of the soundtrack album to guide me and had been taken to see the movie in the cinema by my parents at least three times—the first time was my parents' idea. The subsequent viewings were all my own. I liked everything about this movie, which to this day remains the only movie musical I can say I have watched probably a hundred times.

I listened to the soundtrack constantly. When I saw a paperback novelization of the movie on a rack in a drugstore, I begged my mother to buy it for me and then proceeded to read it to pieces. One night I dreamed the entire film. I finally gathered every kid in my neighborhood into my basement for what I imagined was to be our first rehearsal. The only child I remember, for obvious reasons, was the one I had selected to play Marian the Librarian, my romantic lead. Her name was Yvette and I'd had my eye on her for a while. I'd say she was small and cute, but really we were all small and cute. She was smaller, though, and even cuter, and I suspected she might be French.

I filled them in on the story of *The Music Man* and what would be expected of them as my supporting cast. They would clearly not be doing this project for money, I said a little sharply in answer to one boy's question, and we'd probably have to work every day because the musical numbers alone might take weeks to perfect. I played them the complex patter number that opened the show, the "Rock Island Line." As it chattered its incomprehensible way through the tiny green speaker of my record player, they stared at each other blankly.

Finally one of them said, "Are you KIDDING? We can't do THAT!"

"Yes, you can!" I snapped, determined to quell this uprising before it spread to my other actors. "I know the whole thing. It's easy. I'll show you."

At that point, Yvette piped up, noticing the lack of anything resembling a female voice in the mix.

"Ah!" I remember saying. "You're not in this scene, but later, you get to sing a bunch of songs, including "Till There Was You," which is great, and we have a great scene on a bridge where we kiss."

"What?"

The soundtrack album was playing on, the rest of the cast were getting restless and I saw I needed to get Yvette on board fast or I'd lose everyone. I told her I needed to talk with her in the bathroom privately.

"Why?" she said, her adorable eyebrows furrowing with suspicion. She had a pageboy haircut and smelled of soap. I was sure she was French.

I took her into the bathroom and explained the situation.

"It's not like that all the way through," I assured her. "She hates Professor Hill at first. But then at the end she realizes she loves him and kisses him, but it's really quick!"

"I don't know," she said, glancing behind her, as "The Sadder-But-Wiser-Girl For Me" played on the other side of the door.

"Look," I said, with a sudden unexpected breathlessness, "it's just a small kiss. Like this."

And I leaned forward and gave her a chaste kiss on her chapped little mouth. For a moment, I felt my head was going to explode. There was a pause of several seconds. She appeared surprised at first but then almost thoughtful. She was clearly not rushing into anything. It was as if she were mulling over the pros and cons. It was an expression I would see for years to come on girls' faces after kissing me for the first time. Then:

"No." She walked out of the bathroom and out of my life. When I followed her out I found the rest of the boys had disappeared, too. The record had reached the end of the side and the arm bumped dully into the play-out.

As it turns out, I never played Professor Harold Hill. When you're eight or nine, typecasting doesn't really figure into your thinking. By the time I was acting for a living, I could've been considered for the role of Marcellus Washburn, the comic foil played in the film by Buddy Hackett. Perhaps.

But my formal debut as a performing artiste occurred in the autumn of 1963 at Swallender's Ice Studio on West Sixth Mile in Detroit. I was nine then and was finding myself on the cusp of significant changes. For one thing, our family was being uprooted. Within a few months my father, mother, sister and self were to be transferred to Geneva, Switzerland, leaving friends, loved ones and all that was precious and dear and familiar to me behind, for an indefinite period of years. Then, our beloved dog, Chloe, had been put to sleep after biting my cousin Dana. I protested vehemently, arguing that dogs were allowed three bites before being put to death *by law*, but was overruled when someone pointed out that wasn't true. And now, after the twenty-second of November of that year, my prized John F.

Kennedy impersonation, once greeted with howls of laughter from the adults in my family, had been absolutely censored and barred by those same adults on the grounds of Respect for the Dead. As impressions of dead people were my party piece at that time (W. C. Fields, Bela Lugosi and Humphrey Bogart were other popular favorites), I fell back upon ice skating as my only true means of self-expression. It wasn't something I could show off in the dining room after dinner, as in those carefree days prior to the assassination, but there seemed no alternative. My muse was stilled.

I would like to say that I was a natural ice skater, but I'm afraid that wouldn't be entirely true. Unlike my friends, for me success in areas such as baseball, football, skiing, swimming, dancing, singing, woodwork, gameplaying, cooking or pretty much anything else were always the product of long, laborious slogging away, rewarded usually with uninspiring results. In fact the truth is I've never been a natural *anything* in my life except maybe a reader. Reading is the one thing that took no effort for me to master. Reading I took to like a duck to water . . .

Why I embraced figure skating is anyone's guess. I had probably convinced myself that skating didn't qualify as a sport, thereby giving myself permission to succeed at it. I wasn't a bad skater, as long as I stuck to the figure kind rather than the hockey kind. These days, after a few drinks, when I start yarning about my skating days, people will just assume since I came from Detroit I must be talking about hockey, Detroit being a "hockey town." But even then I felt instinctively I had a better chance keeping all of my teeth if I stuck to figure skating, so that's what I did.

But I was talking about the night of my first public performance on ice.

Now, you may be thinking we would all just be doing figure eights and skating backward for the entertainment of the many-headed. Not a bit of it. There were production values in this show. Costumes, choreography, even drama. I mean, it wasn't *The Cherry Orchard*, but there was some suspense, some comedy and a resolution that left the punters feeling like they'd gotten their fifty cents worth. The evening was made up of several short "pieces," as we call them in the ice-skating game. Some of the least interesting involved the youngest children, who were sort of led around the rink on ropes, like tiny livestock at a county fair. The rope business hadn't been thought through, I noticed, because if one of them went down, the others tended to go down with them in a tangled mass of rope and recrimination; but even this rudimentary display was received with solid rounds of applause, making me suspect these kids had papered the house with supportive friends and relatives.

Now, my first appearance that evening was actually as one of a small knot or chorus of kids, including my sister, who were dressed as Chinese peasants. I have pictures of this and for the life of me I can't recall the point of the whole Chinese peasant motif. They probably had the costumes left over from some other show, *The Good Earth on Ice*, possibly, and just used them whenever they were stuck for a theme. Not an auspicious start, but I was a good sport because I could afford to be. What the audience didn't know was that in the very next "piece," I was going to do my solo bit, and all memory of this insipid bobbing

and nodding and grinning in our very best faux–Chinese peasant manner would be wiped from the collective memory.

Finally the rink was cleared and a new group of children
started surging around the entrance for the next piece, or as I
liked to think of it, My Turn. You could feel an almost electri-
cal thrum of excitement, of anticipation in the room. For you
see, everyone knew this was the last scene and the last scene was
almost always guaranteed to knock their eyes out.

Now I have to give you the scenario so you can appreciate
what happened next.

We had two instructors, a young man and woman who were
probably in their late teens, though they seemed impossibly sophisticated and worldly to me, especially the woman, who wore
tight sweaters that I admired enormously. At this point, the two
of them donned their costume for the scene, which was a large,
incredibly lifelike donkey suit. In the excitement of the moment, I don't honestly remember which of the two had the front
end of the suit and which the rear, but it didn't matter because
once they were suited up, I swear to God, they looked like a
real donkey. These people weren't fucking around. They *were* the
donkey.

So in this climactic scene, the donkey appears on the ice,
surrounded by a bunch of children, and then makes the first
of three complete circles of the ice rink, the children yelling
something, or singing—I forget, it's not really germane to the
story. Now the genius of this is that the three circles gave the audience plenty of time to admire the donkey costume, while the
children—who were not great skaters—were able to hang on to

the donkey and make it through the scene without falling over. Also, it gave me my first lesson in the art of building suspense, because after the first circle, the audience would be thinking, "Okay, donkey? Check. Yelling children? Check. Nicely done. But how do they top this?" After the second circle, they're getting restless. "Jesus Christ," you can almost hear them thinking, "the suspense is killing me!"

Well, I knew how they felt. As I stood there in the wings, I was thinking I had never seen a slower donkey in my life. These circles leading up to my entrance felt like they were taking years off my young life. Being an ice rink, it was always cold in there, but I felt a chill of excitement that went to the core of my being. I suddenly realized for the first time that ice *had a smell*! I inhaled, deeply, savoring it. In retrospect, I think it may have been me I was smelling, because I was really excited, but at the time I was only aware of the heightened state of my senses.

The donkey was rounding the final turn and it was my moment. As the donkey passed me this time, I was to let it skate a ways past before launching myself onto the ice—with the donkey's tail in my hand! That's right! I didn't mention this before, but one of the only things anatomically incorrect about this donkey suit was that there was a large patch of Velcro where the donkey's tail ought to have been. My role was that of the child, appearing like magic in the last moments of this oeuvre, who skates up behind the donkey and slaps the tail on the Velcro patch. Laughter, applause, exit, curtain!

As the donkey went past me, he glanced briefly at me and I heard a muffled comment from deep inside the suit. Probably saying, okay, you're on, or something. As they passed, I clutched the donkey tail to my breast, took a deep breath and flung my-self onto the ice, having forgotten to first remove the plastic skate guards on the blades.

I don't know if you've ever tried skating with skate guards on, but it's pretty generally regarded as something serious skat-ers should steer away from. Skate blade guards are excellent things for when you're walking around *off* the ice. But probably our first lesson at Swallender's included an injunction to remove the guards before skating. They tend to sort of stop the skater dead in his forward progress. It's the suddenness of the thing that makes it so unpleasant.

The fall was spectacular. The donkey tail went flying. Head met ice and for a second I sort of lost interest in the proceedings. The shame and embarrassment flooded over me in a wave. Then, through a dull fog of shock and despair, I heard the laughter and everything changed. All I could think was I've got to get this fucking tail on this goddamned donkey. Off came the skate guards. I scrambled to my feet, and snatching at the donkey tail, I charged off in a mad pursuit of the retreating animal.

The laughter increased, along with a smattering of applause. I raced up behind the donkey and smacked the tail on, to cheers from the audience. Couldn't have gone better if I'd planned it . . .

I believe that there is a natural human reaction to being laughed at by a crowd of people and it is a primal one. Like the ancient fight-or-flight response, our Neanderthal ancestors prob-ably felt it. There was always that one guy in the clan who would slip when they were trekking across the ice floe. The derisive, mocking laughter of others in his clan would turn him, un-knowingly, from the clumsy schmuck everyone made fun of to the comedian whose classic bit involved constantly slipping on the ice floe.

Not for the last time it occurred to me, if I could make people laugh by mistake that way, think what might happen if I really tried . . .

1964

THROUGH THE MAGIC DOOR

In the meantime, though, even a hunger for laughter and applause wouldn't get me on a pair of skates again so I retreated to my first love—reading.

I had never really left it, of course. From the very dawning of perception, books were vital to every aspect of my being. But 1964 was the year I turned eleven, and that was the year that two endless loves, unbidden, entered my life. When passions take hold of you at that age it never occurs to you that this is the beginning of one of the Big Loves, one of the loves that will never go away as long as you live. In early 1964 I was ten and when you're ten you're pretty much living half an hour at a time. But it is also around the end of one's first decade, as all nerds know, that we are first bitten by the things that will obsess us forever. It's then that we first realize we are nerds, around the same time that we start figuring out which gender we probably belong to. Both awakenings can be sudden and instantly life altering or they can come gradually, in fits and starts. But however they come, the result is momentous.

I don't think I ever had any thought about the gender question. Like many children, I didn't as yet realize there was a question to be asked. But as far as the nerd question went, this was the year of the Great Awakening.

It was significant enough that I'm taking a break in the chronology of my story to devote this chapter entirely to two of the extraordinary influences that made me a nerd, and which both occurred within that calendar year. And I should emphasize that what made this year a landmark was the fact that my love of books and music, which had been a constant in the most general way throughout my childhood, abruptly and unexpectedly became very specific indeed.

There were always books in my parents' house and in Roy and Dorothy's. Ovi and Ida, on the other hand, weren't readers. In their house, there were three books. Just three. One—improbably, given whom we are talking about here—was *The Selling of the President*, by Joe McGinniss, which must have been a gift to Ovi from someone at the bank; then, there was a battered copy of an old Edgar Wallace mystery, of the "Club of Men with Missing Feet" variety, which came from God knows where, but which I know he never read; and finally the great children's book *Stone Soup* by Marcia Brown. That was probably the first book I recall *possessing*. I mean possessing in the spiritual sense, as I wasn't allowed to take the book home with me. Ovi and Ida, I think, liked the idea of having a book on hand for me to read, though after a time, like, a decade, as dearly as I loved *Stone Soup*, it was a little light in literary calories and

I was forced to supplement it with my own reading material. But I read it constantly, and deeply, and read it with my daughter years later, to the point that I knew what the stone soup *tasted like*. To this day, I can savor the taste of it as clearly as any food I ever actually ate.

In addition to my family's books, I was a loyal devotee of the local Book Mobile, a little bus filled to the brim with books that would pull up every couple of weeks in front of Lockwood Elementary School, which had no library of its own. Stepping into the Book Mobile really was, in Conan Doyle's phrase, like walking through the magic door. It was a total sensory experience: the visual feast of old bindings on sagging shelves, the feel of the thick pages in my hands and of course the unmistakable, comforting yet heady scent of hundreds of old books in an enclosed space. I never wanted to leave. In a sense, I never have. The room in which I'm writing this now has the same scent.

I was probably part of the last generation for whom there was a canon of nineteenth-century books that were considered the essential reading for every boy. By the time I was nine or so, I had them all—Doyle, Poe, Twain, Stevenson, O. Henry, Jack London, Stephen Crane, Wells, Verne, de Maupassant. But even before then, there were books, titles and authors, forgotten now, that I slept with and ate with.

It was around 1960 or '61, I think, after an argument with my mother on some doctrinal point she was insisting on regarding television or homework, that I decided to run away. I stormed off to my room, pulled out a suitcase and started slinging my book collection into it. If I'd known any expletives I'd have been muttering them under my breath. By the time I was done, there were no clothes at all in the suitcase, just books, and they weighed about 160 pounds. I didn't notice. I dragged it into the living room and informed my mother that I was leaving. Her eyebrows went up in an appraising glance, standing there, one arm akimbo, looking even more like Gina Lollobrigida than usual. All that was missing were the sunglasses and a cigarette. Actually, in those days, Norma was so cool she made you believe she was wearing shades and smoking even when she wasn't.

"I'm leaving!!" I shouted, as I dragged the suitcase behind me.

"Okay," she said. "Don't cross any streets."

"I won't!" I snapped. And I meant it to sting.

She told me years later how she watched, bemused, as I pulled this massive weight down Kenwood Court, stopping approximately every two houses to rest. Sometime later, my kindergarten teacher, who just happened to be driving past, saw me standing with the suitcase at a corner, apparently trying to figure out how to continue my quest without crossing a street. She stopped and picked me up. Exhausted, I went along quietly.

My decision to run away from home with nothing but a bulging suitcase full of books was not just a phase that I was going through. My bibliophilia was a full-blown condition long before I even knew what a bibliophile was.

Books have been in my blood for as long as I can remember, but as I made the transition from child reader to adolescent budding bookman, I now realize that books were both the essence of my nerd being, and also my salvation and my refuge. Every nerd will eventually come to understand one of the Great Verities: that whether his or her obsession is mathematics, gaming, comic books or anything else, whatever it is that allows us to embrace whatever it is that sets us apart from others is what gives us the strength to persevere and overcome. As some might take to drugs or religion or gang life, I took to books.

Later, when my family was transferred to Switzerland, my love of books became a need. Cut off from American popular culture, with no television to speak of and too young by Swiss law to attend any new film that wasn't a Disney release, books and music were my sole source of entertainment. Fortunately, my parents had books, and there was an English-language library in Geneva. The library, though, was problematic. We lived outside of the town and the way I was burning through volumes at that point made it necessary to make twice-weekly trips just to feed my habit. I started raiding my parents' bookshelves, which contained the expected classics that any middle- or upper-middle-class college graduate of the time would be expected to have. And it was thanks to my parents' collection that the Great Detective, Mr. Sherlock Holmes, and his friend and associate John H. Watson burst into my consciousness like a couple of drunken uncles into a bar mitzvah, forever altering my reality.

Now, of course, more people are familiar with these characters through their modern doppelgängers in pastiches, on television and film, but even though Holmes had been regularly interpreted in all media for decades, he and I met as total strangers on an autumn afternoon in 1964, deep in an armchair in the Swiss countryside, and we met between the covers of a book.

For the uninitiated, the original Sherlock Holmes stories were written by Sir Arthur Conan Doyle between 1887 and 1927. They number a mere sixty stories but they are deathless examples of literature that outgrew their "adventure tale" origin. They're the best classic detective stories ever written. They are literature. They have become my church.

My father made the introductions. The story he picked was *The Adventure of the Five Orange Pips*—an interesting choice for several reasons, especially as it was one of the few cases where Holmes doesn't actually apprehend the criminals. That petty failing was as nothing to me. The atmosphere was dark and thrilling, the protagonist mysterious and fascinating, the murders baffling and the killers weirdly recognizable to an American in the mid-sixties (spoiler alert!) : they were members of the Ku Klux Klan!

From there, nearly panic-stricken with excitement, I moved on to the classic novel *The Hound of the Baskervilles*, and the die was cast. My utter absorption in the life and times of the Great Detective was such that by the late sixties my father became concerned. We actually had a couple of "talks." The kind of "talks" that other parents were having with their children when they thought they were becoming involved with drugs or free sex or communism. Nothing he could say, however, succeeded in releasing me from the thrall of Sherlock Holmes, and he eventually accepted the fact that there were worse pathways for his son to wander down.

And after all, it wasn't an entirely solitary pastime. As it turned out, Sherlock Holmes was responsible for introducing me to my first group of real, like-minded nerds. Sometime in 1970 I started subscribing to the literary quarterly the *Baker Street Journal*, which was the print organ of the legendary New York–based society the Baker Street Irregulars, founded by the writer Christopher Morley and assorted friends and drinking buddies back in 1934. In one issue I discovered with a shock of excitement the existence of a new scionist group of the Irregulars that had been established just miles from my home, and that it consisted entirely of young Sherlockians.

At this point, I had given up any hope of ever dating, let alone having sex with anyone, so my weekends were always wide open. I applied to join the group and was accepted. It was really the best of all worlds because I could indulge my love of Sherlock Holmes and do it in a social group consisting of both genders, which was all we had in those days. The group was called the Trifling Monographs, named for the scientific papers Holmes wrote for various journals in his day. The Monographs was founded by Susan Rice, a progressive, imaginative and sympathetic young woman who taught at the Kingswood School in Bloomfield Hills. Susan was my first and in many ways most important nerd mentor. Not just a Sherlockian, she was also my first feminist, and the breadth of her knowledge was intimidating. She read widely, traveled compulsively and was as eager to share with us as we were to be taught by her. I always envied those who were actually her students. Meetings were generally held at her apartment, and it was in this group that I first realized there were people like me, people who spoke a common tongue.

We represented a wide variety of Sherlockians with other things in common, like virginity, for example. In those days, forming "clubs" like the Trifling Monographs was a handy distraction for people who hadn't experienced sex yet. It kept our hands busy. One girl I took a particular shine to was not just a

Sherlockian, but also a Trekkie, which made her positively exotic. I never dreamed of approaching her, though, as I imagined there was probably some sort of Victorian code that would forbid our mixing Sherlockian business with that sort of pleasure. Not only was there no such thing, but she told me many years later that she had actually been sexually active at the time, just never with Sherlockians. Back then, it transpired, when she wasn't winning quizzes on Sherlock Holmes trivia like Name the Number of Dogs in the Canon, or What Type of Wine Was Watson Drinking When Mary Morstan First Came to Consult Sherlock Holmes in *The Sign of the Four*, she was dating a Detroit-area disc jockey.

I was shocked. "A disc jockey?!" I exclaimed, when she told me this. "A disc jockey?! What about me? I was in need! I was up in my Sherlock Holmes trivia! What did your disc jockey know? Could he name the three colors of dressing gowns Holmes wore in *The Sacred Writings*?"

"No, he couldn't," she replied. "That's why I was dating a disc jockey."

To this day I read, reread, discuss and write about the adventures of Sherlock Holmes with the devotion and commitment of the Talmudic scholar to his holy writings. I have even, thanks to Susan Rice, been inducted into that storied society, the Baker Street Irregulars, whose main purpose, aside from drinking, is the study, celebration and analysis of the Holmesian canon. Amazingly, I've been around long enough to have actually been witness to a kind of schism within the Sherlockian world. Some old-school Sherlockians of my generation, I'm sorry to say, are finding the Sherlock Holmes fandom of the younger generation unworthy of inclusion in their Holmesian world. These older, frankly bigoted Sherlockians consider themselves "aficionados" or "elite devotees," while younger, especially female Sherlockians are dismissed as "fans."

I had friends in both camps, but it wasn't difficult for me to pick the side I was on. I went with the fandom and I always will. I wasn't an elite devotee in the sixties and I'm not now. I'm a fan and I've never forgotten what that whole-souled, years-long immersion in Sherlock Holmes gave me in those early days. Here's a little story that will show you what I mean.

It was a particularly bleak winter in Detroit in 1969. We had returned from Switzerland and I was struggling to adjust to a teenager's life in suburban Detroit with mixed results. I had a few friends now, but Preferred Girlfriends shares were down in the cellar with no takers, as they would be for years. I was sitting in my room overlooking Wiltshire Boulevard, my fancy, as a young man's will, turning to thoughts of love. There was a girl I had fallen in love with at that time—her name was Jan—who liked me "as a friend" but who had a boyfriend who was a drummer in a rock band. The glamour quotient of this guy was off the charts, especially when compared to me, stuck as I was learning Woody Guthrie songs on my mother's old Gibson. While he was gigging with his band on the weekends I, thanks to one of those cruel coincidences that Charles Dickens used to write about, was babysitting his young cousins. Plus he was a really nice guy. How I hated him.

Anyway, I was thinking of Jan that evening, probably listening to some appropriately depressing music to help the mood along when I had a sudden idea. I had just reread *A Scandal in*

Bohemia, a Sherlock Holmes story that begins with Watson passing the well-remembered door of 221B Baker Street, where he had once shared rooms with Sherlock Holmes. He looks up and sees Holmes's shadow passing the blind and impulsively goes up to visit him. It was the beginning of a new adventure and it occurred to me that what worked for Holmes might work for me.

I had somewhere acquired a violin, cracked and missing strings, which I had in my room because I had some ridiculous idea I might get it fixed and then take violin lessons, because Holmes, you know, played the violin. So I should. By the same logic, I should also start injecting a 7 percent solution of cocaine when I was bored because he used to do that, too. (I was already smoking a pipe on the sly, usually in the bushes in front of my house.)

Anyway, having just read this story, and my eyes falling on this violin, I thought what if I were to draw my bedroom shade, backlight myself so that my silhouette is thrown dramatically on it and pretend to play the violin? When the object of my affection would walk past my house, she would naturally look up and see me there sawing away and think, "Hum. He's really a lot more interesting than I thought. Look at him up there, all solitary and brilliant . . ." and so on. And from there to the bed was just a few metaphorical steps.

I got myself set up and properly lit and got to business. Most of the time I just sat there, reading or staring off into nothingness until I would hear people talking in the street or a car drive by. Then I would desperately leap to my feet, grab the violin and start hacking away at it. Of course, Jan lived about a mile away and the odds of her ever driving or walking anywhere near my house were incalculable. Fortunately, math was never my strong subject, but I had more optimism and imagination than any fifteen boys of my age and weight.

I gave up eventually. She never walked by. She never came up to me with her eyes shining strangely to say, "Curt, I didn't know you were a violinist!" or, "I'm worried about you. You spend too much time alone!" Actually, I didn't. I continued to hang out with her and her boyfriend in the evenings at his house, while he practiced piano. (He played beautifully, of course.) We became very good friends, she and I, for years, even to this very day.

So pretending to be Sherlock Holmes may have been a poor strategy when it came to getting a girlfriend, but no one can say it didn't give me solid fanboy credentials.

And now, we return briefly to 1964 for a look at that second life-changing influence. This takes us out of the book realm and into music.

While it took a few years for me to find a community with which to share my love of Conan Doyle, the same can't really be said about my second obsession. You couldn't miss this community. It wouldn't have fit in Susan Rice's apartment. I was just one of millions swept up in the cultural slipstream. Like Sherlock Holmes, this is a passion that continues to be a source of joy and nourishment to this day.

One comment I've heard over the years in meeting members of fandoms—and I've met a lot of them—is that they appreciate my appreciation of their own obsessions. I have a sympathetic understanding for their love of something, whatever it is, whether

I share a love of that particular fandom or not. And there is an excellent reason for this.

As we've seen, I am one of them. For them it may be *Star Wars, World of Warcraft, My Little Pony* or *Supernatural*. For me it's Sherlock Holmes, P. G. Wodehouse, Washington Irving, the classic horror film cycles of the thirties and forties and Laurel and Hardy.

Or, arriving finally at the nub of this section, the Beatles, which was where my proclivity for fandom really began. It was there that the dormant fandom virus first turned into the full-blown disease. It started for me with the Beatles, in Detroit, in 1964. It was only months after the assassination of JFK, during one of those bitter winters where Detroit was beginning to feel like you imagine Pluto must feel; at just the point when you suspected that spring probably died in Dallas along with the president; just at that moment, if you were anywhere near my age in the U.S. with a radio or television nearby, at that moment everything changed, and changed splendidly.

It was February 9, 1964, and my family was in a state of sus-pended animation, still in Detroit, everything boring and typi-cal, as prosaic a suburban life as ever, but the clock was ticking down to our eventual departure for Switzerland and an unimag-inable future. The earth had been shaking for some time in the anticipated arrival of the Beatles to the former colonies, in a way that makes me wonder sometimes what it all would have been like with social media, God help us. On February 9 I was stretched out in pajamas staring at a small black-and-white screen, not much bigger than the one I'm writing on now, about to watch the

Beatles on the *Ed Sullivan Show* at 8:00 p.m. on Sunday night. And I was watching them under protest!

Yes, I didn't want to watch Ed Sullivan that Sunday night and I didn't give a shit about the Beatles. Amazing—I actually know to the precise date and hour the last time in my life I didn't care about the Beatles. Here's how little I cared: a couple of days before, my father came home with the paper, featuring a front-page photo of the Beatles on an airplane, bound for New York. My response?

"If there's one thing I hate," I said, to my eternal shame, "it's women who try to dress up like men." I was ten, but age is no excuse. For the first and last time in either of our lives, my father had to explain the Beatles to me.

My sister Kristin, like many girls her age, was tuned into the phenomenon before everyone else, by a kind of gender-based osmosis. People like Kristin hadn't even heard the music—they just *knew*. I, a clueless boy, fought to watch *The Wonderful World of Disney* but was overruled, and so the Beatles it was.

Looked at today, it's an indication of how the world has changed that there was a time when a man like Ed Sullivan would have had a television show at all, especially when there were only three channels and bandwidth was at a premium. Even more astonishing was the fact that his TV show—which had been a radio show before called *Toast of the Town*—was one of the most popular in the country.

He looked like somebody who *sold* televisions, not starred on them. But to say that he was the Simon Cowell of his day is not only incorrect but insulting to Ed Sullivan. Sullivan didn't create pop gruel for the masses. His shows were clogged with Borsht Belt comics, cornball puppet acts, lounge singers, magicians and god knows what, and are pretty much unwatchable now, but he did have an uncanny instinct for cultural shifts, and when something like the Beatles popped up on the horizon, he grabbed them. He was not a nice man, by some accounts, but he was The Man, nonetheless. Popular culture had the Ed Sullivan Stamp of Approval in the America of those days, or it wasn't popular. Or culture, for that matter.

So there I was, a pajama-clad, sullen ten-year-old, stretched out on my stomach, watching Sullivan doing his "And now, here they are, THE BEATLES!" introduction, as McCartney counts in the band and "All My Loving," a song I had never heard in my life, begins.

It took a few minutes—change is never instantaneous. At some point during that show, during which the Beatles appeared only at the beginning and the end, I began to feel . . . something. A widening of the eyes, perhaps, a breathlessness. And then, a curious . . . tingling in the loins. Possibly my first conscious erection, as feeble and pointless as it may have been. Certainly the first I remember. Was it them? Was it the frequent camera cuts to the young girls in the audience, many of them around my age, who were experiencing similar stirrings themselves? It was a little of both, probably.

It's hard to recount the moment when one's world changes forever. Now, the closest thing I could compare it to in its unforgettable, life-altering, immediate intensity is sex, and honestly, it was better than that. Sex took some time to get the hang of (in my case well over two decades) and to really enjoy properly. But this? This was Instant Joy. This was Right and Complete The Very First Time. Guilt-free and no mess to clean up afterward.

Music was something I had always known. We were a musical family. Pianos were played in our homes, and records—classical, jazz and easy listening, mainly. But the Beatles made music a vibrant, living thing for me. Listening to those early records never really made me want to be a musician, the way it did for many. Listening to it, delving into it, living within it: that was my glory.

Somewhere between *Meet the Beatles!* and *The Beatles' Second Album* I became a Beatles nerd.

In another even more important way they affected me. The first books I ever attempted to write were Beatles books. Modern fandoms know what I'm talking about. They were scrapbooks by definition, I suppose, but to me they were more. Whole biographical chapters, drawn from pop magazines, rumor and imagination, were my first stumbling attempts at writing something for the ages! I was translating my indefinable passion—what I would someday come to understand as a nerd's passion—into a form of literature. The Beatles have remained—together and apart—as much a part of my life as breathing, tea, food, books and Scotch. They have fed me when I was hungry, warmed me when I was cold. After fifty years they mean as much to me as ever and when I hear them sing, I am young again.

More than any other single thing, they made me the nerd I am today.

GENEVA

1964-1967

The Beatles were also, along with my collection of books, the only things I remember taking with me when we left Detroit for Geneva in 1964. I had the first three American albums, which were beginning their slow, agonizing Death by a Thousand Scratches from continual replaying on the worst battery-operated turntables the sixties could produce. All my friends, initially unimpressed that I was moving to Switzerland, were now thrilled beyond belief that we were stopping in London for several days on our way, certain in their belief that we would run into the band at some point during our visit. That trip to London, coming in conjunction with my Beatles fixation, planted the seeds of a lifelong indulgence of Anglophilia that, years later, even Margaret Thatcher couldn't extinguish.

Once I had recovered from the shock of displacement I came to realize that if Switzerland wasn't a perfect world, it was quite good enough. Our neighborhood, outside of Geneva, was called Chambesy and it was a quaint Swiss village, suburb, wilderness area and farmland combined. I made friends quickly: Americans, English, Australians, Greeks—no Swiss, oddly enough. I had a bike that I could ride all the way into Geneva, a route which took me essentially through the old Rothschild estate, whose abandoned, moldering family chapel we were able to break into and play in for hours at a time. We could stop and stare at the palatial embassy mansions around the United Nations.

If time were of the essence, I could ride into the village and take the train into Geneva and then cycle through the city, with regular stops at the Maison de Disques for the latest 45s or the English Book Shop for a new P. G. Wodehouse or Ian Fleming novel.

There was a forest down the road and some summer nights once the house was still, my friends and I would meet, go down to the forest and, alongside the stream that ran through it, build a fire and spend the whole night telling stories, roasting potatoes and trying to smoke cigarettes. I tended to blow on them instead of inhaling them, sometimes sending the lit tip shooting off into the darkness. My older friends tried gently to teach me the method but it was too much like work and I gave up on it.

So, basically, it was a Tom Sawyer existence, only in the middle of Europe instead of Missouri. There was an old walled-in graveyard, overrun with weeds with the headstones all broken and stained, listing to one side or the other, and until you've heard ghost stories told in a place like that at midnight, you've never heard ghost stories. We even stole apples by night from an old man's orchard down the road. In the States, he would've fired a couple barrels of buckshot at us. In Geneva, all he could do was loose his superannuated hound on us. Arthritic and short on breath, the dog's heart was never in it, but it was probably the only exercise he got. That was my life in the summer of 1965.

My first school in Geneva was the Collège du Léman. I have few recollections of the place but there are three memorable events that, in small but significant ways, shaped me.

For a while we were driven to school in the mornings, but after a while it was decided that we should take a bus like everyone else. So one winter's morning we walked the quarter mile or so through the bitter cold to the corner where the bus would pick us up.

This corner had a curious feature: a horse trough. A working one, for there were always horses about our neighborhood, with a steady stream of water trickling out of a pipe into the deep, bathtub-shaped cement trough. This first morning at the bus stop we had had a sharp freeze that had frozen the water solid. Well, of course, you'd have to be an idiot to not take advantage of an iced-over horse trough. It was for me the work of a moment to stash my book bag and clamber up onto the ice, skidding back and forth almost like the good old days at Swallender's Ice Studio. It was at that moment that the bus came over the hill and pulled up. I, of course, stayed on the ice long enough for everyone on the bus to get a good view of me just at the moment that the ice cracked and I plunged into the depths of the horse trough.

The shock of the freezing water was bad, but as I surfaced I at least had the comfort of knowing I had given my fellow students the laugh of their short lifetimes. I couldn't hear them because the bus was closed up, but their mouths were all wide with silent laughter, which added to the nightmarish feeling of it all. The other kids at my stop boarded, and the bus driver drove off without a backward glance as I started the long miserable walk back to the house, my clothes literally freezing as I walked.

Another vivid memory involved a curiously barbaric game we boys were forced to indulge in on cold winter mornings like that just described. Immediately after arrival at school, upper- and lower-school boys were herded onto the football field. The younger boys were handed white towels that we had to tuck down into the back of our trousers, like tails. Then, on a signal, we were to run, hell for leather, down the football field, through a small gate at the back and off the school property, down a pretty, winding road that went past the school. After a count of thirty, the older boys would be unleashed to run us down, retrieving the while tail as a trophy. The boy with the most tails before the end of the game won.

This is Switzerland, mind you. Not a country known for its blood sports.

There was a wood down the road we were running along. It was all kinds of spooky at that time of year. It was cold, sometimes bitterly so, and dark in the early morning. There was always a heavy winter fog blanketing everything. Often the only sound was that of the sleepy cawing of ravens in the treetops. That and the slapping of street shoes on the road and the rasping breaths of boys running frantically to escape the howling mob of sixth graders.

If you paused to catch your breath, you'd look back and for a moment all you could see was a bit of clear road that would disappear into an immense wall of fog. Then, nightmarishly, from out of the fogbank would appear the first boy. However big and threatening this boy would be normally, bursting out of the fogbank that way made him even bigger and scarier. It was a little like the climax of *The Hound of the Baskervilles*. The lust for the chase, the single-minded, bloody-eyed determination to hunt down these pathetic little boys, rip off their tails and knock them brutally into the nearest ditch—all free of adult supervision—had turned him and his classmates into a pack of ravening, baying predators.

We all instinctively headed for the wood. Dark, dripping and haunted-looking as it was, some instinct as old as Time drew us to it. It seemed, despite weeks of evidence to the contrary, to offer shelter from the mob, which, after their initial screaming, had fallen weirdly silent as they approached. The wood was thick, with low-hanging branches and masses of hellish thornbushes that ripped at clothes and flesh. We would stumble blindly into ponds, invisible under mats of dead leaves.

Reaching the woods in their headlong pursuit, the mob of boys would split into pairs or groups of three. Wherever you were, they'd find you, be all over you, wolf-like, then scuffle madly among themselves, barking and snarling for possession of the towel, while we, the prey, ran off into the bush.

Once I thought to out-general them by scrambling up a tree and hiding there, but some sort of animal instinct led one of them straight to me. He scrambled up after me, tore off the towel and then threw me out of the tree into the bush for my trouble.

At some point I had a kind of Darwinian epiphany. It may seem absurdly obvious to you, but one morning, surging through the gate into the road, it suddenly occurred to me if all they wanted was the towel, I'd give them the fucking towel.

A short way down the road, with the other young boys rushing past, I just stopped and waited. Before long, the first boy burst out of the fog to find me waiting for him, towel proffered. He didn't even stop to hit me—just snatched at the towel and went on his way. The others followed and I was left to take a leisurely stroll down the quiet country lane, eventually returning to the school, spotless and invigorated, in time for my first class.

The other experience at the Collège was even more significant. Unlike the sadistic morning exercise related above, which felt more like a sociological lab experiment gone horribly wrong or an outtake from *The Most Dangerous Game*, this was an event that gave me another nudging hint about how comedy could be more than just a laughing matter. As many nerds know from hard experience, humor can disarm our enemies.

This case involved a large boy. These things always seemed to involve large boys. This boy's name is lost to me now, but he was a brooding, silent, solitary type. My memory is that he was Russian, possibly a diplomat's son, but he never spoke so no one really knew for sure. He was like a great silverback gorilla moving slowly across the playground, his arms dangling from his shoulders, eyes shifting back and forth, as if looking for something weak or injured he could finish off slowly.

This particular day, I was over by the high-jump pit. Believe it or not, for someone my size, I had suddenly been taken with the idea of getting into high jump. When my father found out he almost wept for joy and immediately built one in my back-yard. The school pit was really nice, though, with its lovely, deep sand to dive into. I was on my lunch hour, doing a bit of high jump, when this junior KGB character shuffled up and started watching.

For a while he did nothing. I would jump into the sand, get out, raise the bar, jump again. After a few minutes, he made his move.

As I was getting up after a jump, I looked up and was startled to find him standing there beside me in the sand. It was like a shock cut in a slasher movie. Without a word or a change of ex-pression, he struck me in the chest with the back of his arm. I went down like I'd been poleaxed.

Even before allowing the stars to clear, I was back on my feet, only to be bludgeoned back down again. This time I lay there for a few seconds, considering my options.

They appeared limited. The kid was standing there like a mountain, as if he had been there since the beginning of time, massive and expressionless. He didn't dare me to get up but it seemed to have occurred to him that he had stumbled upon a potentially endless source of amusement and he wasn't going anywhere.

Neither was I, apparently. And strangely enough, this is when Dick Van Dyke popped into my mind.

In these early days, there was a small group of comic actors who were beloved heroes of mine: Laurel and Hardy, Jackie Gleason and Dick Van Dyke. Van Dyke's eponymous television show in the U.S. had been one of my favorites, and there was an episode of the show that I particularly loved and had already worked up an imitation of for friends and family back home. The story was Van Dyke's character, straightlaced comedy writer Rob Petrie, undergoes post-hypnotic suggestion. Whenever the phone would ring, he would instantly become falling-down drunk. He would snap out of it when his wife talked to him. His unsurpassed ability to go almost instantly from falling-down-in-the-gutter-drunk back into his normal upright self was unforgettable.

So, for some reason, Dick Van Dyke seemed to appear to me at this moment to show me the way. The next time I was hit, my fall into the sand was a pratfall. Then, again. And again. Every time this kid knocked me over, my fall was more exaggerated. Funnier.

There was now a curious crowd of students standing around the sand pit to watch. I'm not sure my tormentor was aware of them at first, but as my falls became more extravagant, people started laughing. The first laugh, I think, startled him. He was in mid-hit and he may have thought someone was laughing at *him*. By that time, I wasn't just falling funny, I was rolling around in the sand, struggling to get up, taking longer and longer, before planting myself in front of him for the next hit. And I was now controlling the hits! Instinctively! First lesson in stage combat!

The crowd got bigger and it was apparent that whatever else

was going on that lunch hour, this two-hander at the jump pit was the hot ticket. Now there was a slightly brain-damaged smile appearing on my bully's face as he realized he was actually a part of an act that was amusing all the children who would normally scatter in panic before him as he shambled across the yard.

In other words, we were a hit.

It was a one-off, thankfully. He didn't pick on me again and over the distance of all these years, I feel happy for him. It was his moment in the spotlight and for at least one lunch hour, he was popular. All of these kids were strangers in Switzerland, sometimes a little scared and lonely. Even though it had never been his intention, he had helped spread some laughter and joy in our little corner of a scary and uncertain world, and I like to think he felt good about that. As far as I know, that was the peak of his performing career. It was a lesson for me, too.

Many years later I had the chance to work with Dick Van Dyke and we spent an afternoon on the set. Mainly we talked about Stan Laurel, his close friend and the ultimate comic hero we both adored. But I also told him the story about how he had saved me from being beaten as a child and he was charmed.

"That's it!" he smiled. "You keep 'em laughing, you keep 'em off guard!" At the end of the day, I brought out my copy of the classic book on Laurel and Hardy by John McCabe, *Mr. Laurel and Mr. Hardy*, which included the eulogy Van Dyke gave at Stan Laurel's funeral. He made some self-deprecating comments about his writing and then signed it for me: *To Curtis— Keep 'em laughing! Dick Van Dyke.*

School in Switzerland was one thing, but it was there that

my comic education really took root, thanks to a tiny theater just at the edge of the Vieille Ville, next to the city's only department store, Le Grand Passage. This was the sort of thing you imagined only existed in Europe at the time: a cinema that showed only classic comedies and cartoons, all day, every day. There was no schedule that I was aware of, no logic to what was shown. But for a boy who had been given a steady diet of mediocre American television since birth, this was a revelation.

My parents started by dropping my sister and me at this place when they would come into the city to do a day's worth of shopping. They could take their time, eat lunch, come back hours later and there we'd be: besotted and beaming with pleasure, having gone through Laurel and Hardy, Chaplin, Keaton, Lloyd, Fields, along with classic Disney, Warner Bros. and Max Fleischer cartoons. I love to imagine the little mad man in the projection booth, almost buried among some of the greatest classic comedies ever, just throwing on one massive reel after another, barely able to hear over the clatter and rattle of the projector, the squeals of laughter and the patter of applause from the mix of pensioners, necking teenagers, military conscripts, drunks, ex-pat children and exhausted shoppers in the house. The theater had probably done service at different times as a legit theater, a music hall, an adult movie theater for all I know. What it became for me at that tender age was a graduate school offering degrees in pie throwing, pratfalls and the art of injecting, with the lightest possible hand, unexpected moments of grace, sentiment and friendship into a chaotic world.

I was raised in a warm, supportive, loving environment in which respect for conservative values was paramount. Because of our social and economic position, I was protected from much. Unfortunately, given our snipe-like darting about the world at the time, I never got the chance to fall in with bad company. Even as a child, I was young for my age. I would probably have developed at a normal speed had I remained in Detroit, but the combination of extensive travel, a total separation from everything familiar, exposure to children from other cultures and, with a near complete absence of pop culture via television and contemporary movies, a deepening reliance on books and music, the changes I went through between 1964 and 1967 were seismic.

Just the fact of living in Switzerland gave me a different perspective on the world. By the time I returned to the States I may have had opinions and experiences far beyond those of my schoolmates, but in other respects, I was a mere babe.

What I didn't learn in Switzerland was, in some ways, as important as what I did learn. Which brings me to masturbation.

I've been told masturbation comes naturally to babies and monkeys, but it was a mystery to me. I understood masturbation was something that was done. The problem was it was done by pretty much everyone but me. My father was almost boyishly eager to explain a kind of meat-and-potatoes variety of the facts of life—including oral sex—in surprising detail; but he left out any mention of any form of sexual pleasure that did not involve growing up, finding someone and getting married first.

I understood the overall idea of masturbation and certainly grasped the purpose of it. It was the mechanics of the thing that eluded me.

I had male friends who masturbated. They talked about it all the time, especially in my second school in Geneva, the Lycée des Nations. The Lycée was actually the original gatehouse of the Rothschild estate, though, being Rothschilds, they had done it on a grand scale. It was a mansion to us, with classes held in former bedrooms, and science classes in the horse stables.

At the Lycée, during recess, we boys would gather in groups and the conversation, which was never at a very elevated level anyway, would turn, almost inevitably, to masturbation. After all, it was Switzerland in the early sixties, and we were ten or eleven years old. Other than skiing, what were we supposed to talk about? And think of what an improvement this was over Detroit, where we wouldn't even have had skiing as an option. This was like an evening at Gertrude Stein's in comparison.

My friends would joke easily and at length about whacking off, but of course no one ever talked through how they actually did it. It was kind of like hanging out in a bar with a bunch of Masons hearing them joking about something funny that had gone on down at the Temple that week. They'd think it was hysterical, but if you weren't a Mason it didn't matter how good the story was, you just didn't get it.

And I felt instinctively that this wasn't a subject that I should bring up. I tried to imagine it: one of the guys finishing up a really good masturbation story and then, once the laughter died down, me saying, "Oh, Nicholas, man, that's really funny!!" (Beat.) "But, how do you do it, exactly?"

You see the difficulty. Once I came up while one of them was talking about having whacked off with a pillow. Everyone was laughing. This was so frustrating. If I'd come up two minutes earlier, he might have let something drop that would've given me some clue as to how it all worked. Out of desperation I very uncharacteristically just slapped this guy down.

"Bullcrap," I snapped, in the heat of the moment not even caring about my language. "A pillow? A PILLOW? Come on!! I don't believe it!" I thought at that point, Derek or whatever his name was would get all defensive and say, "No, I swear! It really works! You get a pillow . . ." And then he'd spell out his method and, like magic, I'd know how to masturbate.

Instead, of course, all the boys just stared at me for a moment before one of them started talking about cricket or something and the moment passed.

There was almost a culture of masturbation at the Lycée des Nations. A lot of the boys were English, after all, and to hear them tell it, English schools in the sixties were just places where boys went to play rugger and cricket and toss each other off. The headmaster of our school was English. He was young and hip. He was married to the young French teacher, who was French and hot. He was also a teacher, but he didn't like that part of his life. In class he had to be the thing he hated, and he resented it. He had no patience for those of us who didn't grasp things immediately. "Armstrong, it's a simple concept, really absurdly simple!" An intolerant teacher, as many of them were, but when he was being headmaster, he was in his element. He remade the whole idea of what a headmaster was, essentially re-creating it in his own image. He loped insouciantly about the place, running his fingers distractedly through his hair, and dressed like a young poet with a private income. He liked the Rolling

Stones and he played the bongos. Not in a band or anything. He played solo bongos, which made him, if possible, even cooler; or, if you were musical, even more irritating.

There were eyebrows raised when he allowed the sixth-grade boys access to the cellar of the old mansion that was our school. This was to be, as it were, a clubhouse for the upper-form boys. It was cold and dark and smelly. Perfect for sixth-grade boys. But no one other than sixth-grade boys were allowed down there under any circumstances, so of course rumors sprang up about what was really going on down there. One story, the gospel truth according to the classmate who passed it breathlessly on to me, regarded a ritual that any new kid had to endure in order to be allowed the right to sit in a dank cellar with a bunch of stupid boys.

All light was extinguished. The boys would kneel in a circle around a piece of bread. They would then whack off, there in the darkness, onto this piece of bread. Then the light would suddenly come on and whoever had not yet come on the slice of bread would have to eat it. Inevitably, it seems, the new boy would lose.

(I've told that story to men repeatedly over the years and they always say something like, "Oh, yeah. The cum on the bread thing . . ." So this would appear to be a more common hazing ritual than I imagined at the time. Maybe it's just me, but it is just this kind of thing that makes me hate boys. Some are okay, I guess, but in numbers they really bear watching. As P. G. Wodehouse might've said, they call into question the whole idea of Man as God's last word.)

Weirdly, the headmaster would sometimes go down there

with the boys. He'd take his bongos and disappear into the cellar with the sixth graders. We would be in class when the ghostly sound of bongos would start coming up through the ventilators. We'd all exchange meaningful glances. *He is down there again,* the glances would say. With the sixth graders . . .

He was something of an eccentric, this headmaster. In chemistry class—for he was also our chemistry teacher—he was bragging about how he knew the exact ingredients to make the kind of gas that the Germans used to kill people in World War I. And then prepared to show us.

"Yes, it's quite simple, really." He mixed some chemicals in a beaker and then held up a bottle of something else, the stopper removed, and held it over the other beaker.

"Now, if I were to mix this with these other ingredients, that would be . . . oh!" Then something happened. I don't know if he absentmindedly added this other chemical, or if it slipped out of his hand or what, but the next thing I knew I felt my chest constricting alarmingly. Everyone was screaming. He was carrying one of the girls out, yelling, "Outside!! Outside!!! Everyone!!!" We all somehow made it out and collapsed under a tree, coughing and choking and vomiting until finally our lungs cleared.

The headmaster was eventually let go due to some kind of arcane contractual dispute and not—as you might think—for the German-death-gas incident.

But one final thought on masturbation. I did finally discover masturbation some time in high school. It coincided with the first time I got really drunk. Not blackout drunk, because I somehow managed to get myself into my pajamas and into bed.

That was the night I was, in a manner of speaking, introduced to myself. Sometime in the middle of the night, in a smelly, sweaty, cotton-mouthed haze, I awoke to find myself taking advantage of myself. It was a revelation. It was like I'd been doing it forever. As my old headmaster might have said, "Quite simple, Armstrong, once you grasp the fundamentals!"

Unlike at the Collège du Léman, I was never bullied at the Lycée des Nations. I guess there were just too many better targets. Two of them haunt me to this day. I have no idea whether they are alive or dead. I have always wished I had been able to apologize to them. I was not one of their tormentors, but I never came to their defense either, which makes me just as culpable. One was a student named Angela.

Angela had been dealt a shitty hand. She suffered from what appeared to be a variety of birth defects, including a cleft palate, which made understanding her difficult; bad eyes, which necessitated extraordinarily thick Coke-bottle glasses; and one leg that, I guess, was shorter than the other. She had one prescription shoe to try to remedy the problem but she still suffered from a strange, rolling gait. This girl had the worst imaginable type of target on her back, and the children were ruthless, especially the boys.

Angela had already been the target of bullies before arriving at the school, and had developed a hostile attitude to everyone as a result. While it was not obvious at the time, it seems to me now that this was a pure defense mechanism, but it had the worst possible effect on those who didn't need an excuse to bully her. She would be verbally abusive to everyone indiscriminately, in a futile attempt to lash out before being hurt herself.

She needn't have bothered. I don't know if this child had a single day without pain or humiliation during the entire time I knew her. I had conversations with my mother about her, and Angela and I did have a few hours together once as an attempt to find some common ground away from the other children, to whom I was usually so busy trying to endear myself. It was unsuccessful. She had no experience communicating with boys at all and I was being my usual awkward, uncomfortable self. She went back to her own private hell and I went back to the few friends I had. My attempt at communication hadn't only not worked, for all I know, it had made matters worse.

The other victim of this kind of nerd persecution was actually one of the teachers. He was English, slightly pudgy, delicate, and clean shaven. He was terribly awkward in his dealings with everyone and, especially, the older sixth graders, whose instinct for the jugular was amazingly well developed. They had him spotted as a "fairy" from the start and some of them were unafraid of calling him one to his face. Horrible notes were left for him on his desk or tucked into his books. Complaints to the powers that be went unaddressed, I suspect because they thought it was all rather funny.

The taunting of this man started with the sixth graders but when it became clear he was too weak to fight back, it trickled down, in a slightly less lethal form, to some of the boys in my year. He had milk poured on his head from the windows above as he entered the school. Boys would draw obscenities on the chalkboard for him to see as he arrived for class but no one would admit to being the culprit. One Christmas, the older boys left a wrapped Christmas present for him on his desk containing a brassiere.

We finally broke him, I guess. He became reduced to a screaming, incoherent wreck by something someone had done in our class one day, I don't even remember what it was. He left the school in tears, prompting the Scottish maths teacher to burst into our class almost speechless with anger at our treatment of this man.

"If I'd done that when I was a lad," he cried out in a strangled rage, "I'd 'ave been caned, I would!!"

The teacher never returned to school and the word was he'd had a nervous breakdown and returned to England.

Our age was no excuse. Regardless of who did what, we were all guilty and I still bear the mark.

In Geneva, my friends were from other cultures, which was invaluable. Most of them didn't even attend my school. Two of the most important were English brothers, Jon and Tom Higgins, the sons of a member of the English diplomatic service. Jon was the oldest, tall, lanky, with hair he was continually pushing back out of his eyes. He was truly sophisticated and experienced; he played cricket and smoked and remains probably the coolest person I ever met. His brother Tom was my age and he was the funniest person I had ever met. I know the two of them to this day and they haven't changed that much. One of the things these boys did for me was to introduce me to the books of P. G. Wodehouse. If they had done nothing else, that was a gesture for which I will be forever grateful.

Switzerland was also important because, being so centrally

located in the continent, it gave my family the freedom to travel extensively. Aside from France, just minutes away, we traveled through Italy, Germany, Spain, England, Portugal, the Middle East and North Africa. We were in Greece just before the coup, Florence just after the flood, Beirut before the Six-Day War. In Morocco we saw unimaginable poverty and in Egypt we crawled through the Great Pyramid of Cheops. We swam in the Dead Sea and the Mediterranean. I danced with men in Jerusalem, took a ferry from Tangier to Lisbon when fog had grounded air traffic and tried—and came to love—every sort of food imaginable. And all this at a time when these places remained still untainted by American fast food and popular culture. The years I spent there remain probably the greatest gift my parents ever gave me.

1967

A SEAT AT THE SPAZZ TABLE

I had left Detroit right after the Beatles' first appearance on *The Ed Sullivan Show* and I returned to it just after the release of *Sgt. Pepper's Lonely Hearts Club Band*. The Beatles weren't the only ones who had changed during those watershed years. Though young, I had seen something of the world, and felt a growing sense of confidence. That was soon to be slapped out of me but I didn't realize it at the time.

Detroit had changed, too, and not necessarily for the better.

During the few short years we had been away, Detroit had gone from what may have been considered its peak as a city that exemplified the dreams and possibilities of the industrial Midwest to a troubled and increasingly violent place. That was the summer that the Detroit riots swept the city, altering it forever.

We were far from the center of the violence, having bought a house on Wiltshire Road, in the northern suburban town of

Berkley, just two blocks from Woodward Avenue. My sister attended the elementary school on Catalpa Road, while I started doing my stretch in what I referred to as the Big House: Anderson Junior High School.

My reentry into the suburban Detroit public school system was bumpy. I personally made certain of that the very first day, during orientation.

It was one of those marathon days where you do fifteen or twenty minutes in one class, then on to the next—a break for lunch in the cafeteria—then another class and so on. Having come from the Lycée des Nations, it was a little intimidating. The Lycée was a house. You could've fit twelve Lycées into Anderson Junior High School. There was no cafeteria or gymnasium at the Lycée. There was no organized sport at the Lycée. If we wanted to play cricket, or baseball, we had to rip a picket off the fence in the backyard and play in the clothes we were wearing. It was kind of like going to school in Kenya compared to Anderson.

My orientation had gone pretty well and I had begun to feel something approaching confidence when I walked into the classroom where we were to meet our gym teacher, Mr. Jordan. Mr. Jordan was like a high school gym teacher from central casting. Well-built, abundantly muscled, bald-headed, probably an ex-marine. He was dressed in matching gray sweats, with a whistle around his neck on a string. He needn't have bothered. He wasn't going to break a sweat talking to us in a classroom, and the whistle was just rank affectation. He entered the class after we were all seated and swung up onto the desk. All the other teachers had done orientation either standing at the blackboard or seated at the desk like human beings. Not Mr. Jordan. Desks were for sitting on. I got the feeling that desks were kind of beneath his contempt. They were things pussy intellectuals sat behind. He was sending a message to the boys: "I'm a goddamned drill sergeant in my gym. I'm your worst fucking nightmare. If you bring in a note from your mommy excusing you from push-ups, I'll make you eat the note. And then do twenty push-ups. If you start whining during track that you're sick and can't run anymore, I'll crush you like a fucking bug." He might not have used those exact words, or really anything at all like those words, but that was the message he was putting out. The one I got, anyway. He was terrifying. He wasn't just a gym teacher, which was bad enough. He was a fucking *guy*.

You could feel the other boys in the class relax the minute they saw him. They'd started slumping down in their desks, smirking at one another—you know, the sort of thing they'd never try to get away with in civics class. They knew it was okay with Jordan. Desks were beneath their contempt, too.

Jordan launched into his slightly bored recitation, with that "This is bullshit, but it's what those eggheads on the school board expect me to say" attitude. He was telling us what was required, apart from absolute obedience on our part.

"We will supply towels for showers. You will shower at the end of every gym class without exception. You need gym shoes. You will not be allowed in gym class without them. You will need clean gym shorts and tees year round. You will need one set of clean sweatpants and shirts in the winter. And of course, you will need a jockstrap. Any questions?"

And this is where I made my first mistake.

"Please, sir," I said. "What's a jockstrap?"

Looking back, I see there were really two problems here, and it's hard to say which was the biggest: the question itself or the twee little Lycée-inflected "Please, sir" which preceded it. It was an honest question. Partially I think I wanted to show him that I was paying attention and, since no one else was asking questions, if I asked one it might endear me to him. It was also, I'm afraid, a genuine request for information. Towels and gym shoes I was clear on. Gym shorts and tees I understood. "Sweats" was not a problem. But a jockstrap was, to my ears, an expression in a foreign language I did not speak.

It was at least a minute by the class clock before the dust settled. There was one boy, I recall, with tears streaming down his face with laughter. Another fell from his desk, then stood up, laughing, and banged his desk repeatedly on the floor. These boys were howling, screaming—gasping—with laughter. Jordan looked down at the floor from his perch at the desk, knowing that there was no point in trying to regain control of his classroom for a while. And the laughter rolled over me like a great wave . . .

Finally, once Mr. Jordan could be heard over the general hysteria, he said, "Okay, okay, come on, knock it off . . ." The boys settled down and he continued, in a surprisingly gentle voice. "A jockstrap, or athletic supporter," he added, as if its official name might be more familiar to me, "is a strap you put on in gym to protect your balls."

This set the crowd off again as I felt that tiny thrill of confidence I had felt earlier in the day shrivel and die inside. The bell rang, we were dismissed and I was the proud possessor of my first school-wide nickname: "Jockless" Armstrong.

I suppose that sort of thing was to be expected, but it didn't end there. Verbal abuse in a place like Anderson was like a gateway drug to the hard stuff. It became pretty much open season on "Jockless" Armstrong after that and I found myself subjected to the occasional beating by my greaser friends. I was also mocked and persecuted by their girlfriends, who gave me another nickname: the Swedish Faggot. (I'd heard their blowjob skills were unsurpassed, but geography confounded them. I corrected them over and over, saying, "No, it's Swiss Faggot. Not Swedish. Swiss!," but it never seemed to sink in. "Faggot" was appended, I guess, because I could form sentences and didn't use stray cats for batting practice, like their boyfriends did.)

Greasers were interesting, sociologically. The subculture was unknown to me. Before I had left for Switzerland, I was in elementary school, where bullying was not an issue, or at least there was nothing about me that stood out to the point that I deserved it. About the worst you could say about me in those days was I thought the Beatles were women, which apparently didn't warrant corporal punishment. Middle school was different.

And I probably shouldn't generalize about their girlfriends' blowjob skills. Some may have been more accomplished than others, but I was obviously not in a position to judge. I understood what a blowjob was only in the vaguest sense, but the fact that blowjobs were something these cretins got on a regular basis was information I picked up one day during an otherwise routine bullying session from some guys in metal shop. They were all gathered around one of their lockers, huddled around something one of them was holding. As I passed by, one of them leaned across, knocked my books out of my hands and then kicked me over as I scrambled to pick them up. As I rose, I saw they were all facing me and one of them said, "Hey, Faggot. Look at this!"

He showed me a photograph of his girlfriend—whom I recognized—with her mouth closed delicately around his massive, engorged penis. He and his pals snorted and butted each other like gleeful bison as I blushed and stammered, unable to take my eyes off the picture.

Somehow, I said, with a desperate attempt at casual interest, "Huh. Cool."

His face lit up. "Oh, you like blowjobs from girls, too, Faggot? I'll ask her, if you want. Maybe she'll give you one!"

I gave a sickly laugh—you know, just a little blowjob banter between the guys—and made my escape. I discovered later that this guy, whose name I long ago wiped from my memory, had at some point kicked out the back wall of his locker, revealing a space behind it large enough for him and his friends to get a little oral sex from their girlfriends at lunchtime. I didn't believe it but then one day, during lunchtime, I was walking down the deserted hallway when his locker door opened from the inside and he and two of his friends and their three girlfriends emerged, like clowns tumbling out of a VW.

This guy was one of my regulars. I've forgotten his name; we'll call him Dan. Picking on the nerds at Anderson wasn't just some kind of random thing, by the way. There was a kind of code among the abusers at that school. It was really kind of civilized almost: once one of these thugs found someone they felt comfortable brutalizing, the other guys tended to back off. For a while, it was open season on Curtis. Having come to Anderson from Switzerland, I was a particularly attractive target to these characters, and some days you could see them, hands twitching, waiting patiently in a line to have a crack at me, like senior citizens at a deli counter. But once Dan settled on me, it was a done deal, and the other guys respected that. Sometimes a new greaser might come into the school and just start hammering me at random, but the other guys would take him aside and explain the situation. "That's the guy Dan beats up," they'd explain. "Pick another one. There's, like, hundreds here just like him." And you know, the new greaser was always cool with that. Only when your regular bully dumped you—usually without so much as a phone call—would you be considered open game by the other guys. Kind of comforting, really. I went through several of these weird arrangements during my time at Anderson.

For example, there was Ralph. Ralph was a big boy with a round face, pink cheeks and ham-like hands. His approach to dealing with kids smaller than he was to come up from behind and hit them very hard in the back of the skull with his heaviest textbook. He never said much. He wasn't adept at verbal abuse. He preferred to let his textbook do the talking, and it was always effective. Ralph was the reason my mother decided to send me to judo classes on the weekend.

Not knowing much about this ancient art of self-defense, I jumped at it. I figured I'd get a couple of easy suggestions on how to commit mayhem on other boys at my school and that would be it. I was horrified to discover that judo was a discipline that took time and trouble to learn correctly. Weekend after weekend I would attend classes to find myself thrown and battered by boys and girls years younger than I. I was also finding it difficult to imagine how I could induce my greaser friends to stand in front of me long enough for me to place myself properly to carry out my vengeance.

In time, I became discouraged enough that when I noticed I was breaking out in a mysterious rash, I told my mother that I figured I was allergic to the grass mats at judo school. I don't think for a moment she actually believed me, but she relented.

On my last day, I had a little farewell talk with my teacher.

"Well," he said, when I said I was leaving, "that doesn't surprise me. Not really cut out for it, are you?"

"Not really, no," I confessed, with a frankness stemming from my certain knowledge I would never see this guy again.

"What made you want to take the class?" he asked, knowing the answer. I told him I was being bullied and I thought it would help.

He nodded thoughtfully. Then he said, "Okay, here's a couple on the house. If someone is beating you, try to hook your index and middle finger in his nostrils. Like this, okay?'" He stuck two fingers into my nose. "Then pull back, hard. It'll totally incapacitate him. If you pull hard enough, you can actually rip his nose off that way, so you shouldn't do that unless it's really an emergency. If you can't get into their nostrils, just go for the eyeballs. That always works."

I've never forgotten his advice, though thankfully I haven't had to use it. Strangely enough, having just received these pearls of wisdom from my instructor, I reached a moment of truth with Ralph.

I was walking down the hall, when I felt the now familiar blow in the back of my head from Ralph's textbook. And something happened. I experienced a second of blinding rage, threw my books to the ground, spun around, leapt into the air (Ralph was quite a bit taller than I) and hit him in the jaw with all my strength, with a closed fist.

Ralph just stood there for a moment, the mindless grin wiped off his face like chalk off a blackboard. In the corner of his mouth was a small strip of saliva that had been knocked out by the impact. He stared at me without expression. Then, to my horror, I saw his eyes well up with tears.

He was struggling to keep them back and unable to say anything in response to this wholly unexpected development. He was hurt. Not physically, of course. I doubt that even my most powerful hit would really have hurt him. It was something else. I realized at that moment that the constant shoving, kicking and head bashing had been Ralph's way of showing affection. It would never have occurred to him that I would ever hit back.

"I'm sorry," I stammered. "I'm sorry." I *was* sorry. "Are you okay?" He nodded and moved away. My guilt at having made this thoughtless bully cry was such that it wasn't until years later that I could begin to see the irony. I want to make it clear that I'm not saying that violence solves all of our problems, though I know that's the way it reads. Two things happened as a result of this: (a) Ralph never laid a hand on me again and (b)

I took every chance I could to say hello to him. He started re-ciprocating and before long we became friends. Maybe "friends" is too strong a word. But we enjoyed each other's company for short periods of time.

Considering most of my relationships in middle school, that made us practically Damon and Pythias.

After a few experiences, I made sure to stay clear of the show-ers after gym class. I was forbidden to eat lunch with the general population and was banished for many months to the Spazz Table. The Spazz Table became my cafeteria safe haven. This was where all the "retarded" children ate, supposedly, but I remember it as my introduction to nerds. Not brilliant, pop-culture literate computer geeks, who didn't really exist as a culture yet. These were the real outcasts, the misunderstood, the bullied, the not-to-be-tolerated. A couple of them had eye-glasses so thick they made *my* head hurt. They were kids who moved oddly, smelled a little past the use-by date and dressed in mismatched stripes and checks, decades before any of that was fashionable.

Obviously, no one who ate at the Spazz Table called it the Spazz Table. That was a designation bestowed upon us by others. It turned out, to my innocent surprise, many of my lunchmates were not technically spastics at all. As one of them patiently ex-plained to me at the time, "We're not retarded. We're just slow."

I'm not certain they were even that slow. They were quiet, though. No ever one talked much at the Spazz Table and it was there I developed a lifelong horror of egg salad sandwiches, but these people were accepting and tolerant and always made room for me.

Like any oppressed minority, they had learned the value of keeping your head down and not drawing attention to yourself when outnumbered in occupied territory. That's actually a pretty good life lesson, and it would come in handy during my time in Hollywood years later. I came to school one day in a pair of bell-bottoms so tragically ill-conceived that someone shouted over the din of the crowded hallway, "Hey, Armstrong! Where'd you get those pants? Omar the Tent Maker?!" As a sally, it was actually an improvement over the usual stuff and I turned to see who was responsible. To my amazement it was actually one of the teachers. It had come to this. I switched to plain slacks.

Into the nerd hell of bullying, verbal abuse and loneliness that was middle school one day appeared, looking like a kind of hip Greek god, Will Young, the new speech and drama teacher. There was a smudgy picture of him on the front page of the school newspaper in an article announcing his arrival. Looking resolutely unlike any other teacher in the school, impossibly handsome, with long, perfectly tousled hair, Will Young stared into the lens of the staff photographer with the quiet confidence of a man who knew where all the Minotaurs were hiding and, furthermore, intended to slay them all without breaking a sweat.

But first, he needed to introduce me to my destiny.

The little blurb under the picture heralding his arrival, obviously penned by a member of the Journalism Club in a state of feverish arousal, advised all the other female members of the student body not to faint, but this—THIS—was the new speech and drama teacher! If heart and unicorn emoticons had existed at the time, they would've been sprinkled all over the page. Anderson Junior High, as it was known then, may have had a speech or drama teacher already at that point—they may have had a dozen—but their existence was unknown to me. As a life raft to a desperate boy who had found nothing to keep him from slipping under the surface for the last time, they were less than helpful.

Will Young changed everything. No one taking his speech and drama course emerged the same. Everyone discovered the performer rubbing up against the underside of their skin. People who took the class because it was an easy grade found themselves subtly changed. Some of my very worst tormentors in the halls and locker rooms came into Young's class anticipating a midmorning nap, from which they would awake much refreshed; but before they realized it, they found themselves at the front of the class doing a three-minute storytelling mime exercise. It's difficult to effectively bully smaller people after they've seen you pretending to be a poor homeless guy, begging for money on a street corner in the middle of winter. And then been applauded and praised for your performance, however rotten it may have been.

Whatever purpose it may have been intended to serve, Will Young's speech and drama class turned out to have been a great social leveler.

One particularly tough character who wound up in Will Young's class was Joey. Joey was tall, lanky, with shoulder-length blond hair and incongruously thick glasses. They were the kind of glasses kids at the Spazz Table would be teased about. Not Joey. Nobody teased Joey. This was a guy who made his own hunting bow in shop class. He was the sort of redneck brute that was very thick on the ground in the northern Detroit suburbs in those days. Ted Nugent owed his livelihood to characters like Joey. Though not a jock in the classic sense, he was still pretty much a pitiless thug when I first met him. But he wound up being one of those rare souls that, with a proper introduction to drama, found to his unutterable astonishment, that there was a little glimmer of immortal light inside of him. His friends on the lynching team might not have noticed the difference, but I did. He'd still knock me around the locker room after gym class, but now there were little differences, things only a regular victim like me would notice. Now there was a kind of twinkle in his eye as he knocked my head into a locker door. Or the way he would make sure the toilet had been flushed before sticking my head into it. They were small gestures, but I appreciated them.

A couple of years later, while attending Will-O-Way Apprentice Theatre, a kind of theatrical day care center for rich people to dump their kids on the weekend, who should suddenly appear as part of the crew but my old nemesis Joey. The theater had proved to be as much a calling for him behind the scenes as it had for me centerstage. Letting the dead past bury its dead, I hailed him genially. After all we were now, as it were, brothers in the world's second-oldest profession.

He didn't even recognize me. I couldn't believe it. Frankly, I felt a little used.

I tried to jog his memory.

"Oh, come on, you remember me. It was only a couple years ago! You gave me my first wedgie!"

He shrugged noncommittedly. Clearly he had given so many boys their first wedgie, he couldn't be expected to remember all of them.

"And that time I was climbing the big rope and almost made it to the top even though I was terrified and you suddenly grabbed the rope at the bottom and started to swing it around to try and throw me off?"

True to form, his mind was a blank. But the fact that Joey and I were even having that conversation—if you could call it a conversation—was a kind of evolutionary miracle that I attribute without question to the drama course in general and Will Young in particular.

But getting back to Mr. Young himself. One of the things about the man that kindled my imagination was that he was an actual actor. He wasn't an American history teacher who had drawn the short straw and was stuck directing the school play that semester. He was the real thing. He had trod the boards. He knew the bitterness of rejection and the thrill of a great first night. He had sipped from the Cup. Will was the Gatekeeper.

Everything that happened thereafter happened because of him. He was the one who gently pushed me into the National Forensic Society, where, for the first time, I seized the spotlight and never relinquished it.

The National Forensic Society was basically an educational organization that recognized excellence by students in public speaking. There were numerous categories, such as declamatory speaking, current events, poetry and my choice, dramatic interpretive speech. The competitions started with one in the school itself. You then went on, in whichever category you had selected, to a local competition, district, then a regional, then a state final. What started out as a lark when you were just competing against the idiots you were going to school with would gradually become a heart-squeezing, breath-stopping agony of dread—less a friendly competition among fellow nerds and more like a difficult medical procedure than anything else.

I underwent this torture a number of times. I never made it past the regional competition. The time I reached that, I faked illness to get out of doing it. My choices were predictably those of a boy who lived in books. One was Captain Ahab's speech to the crew of the *Pequod*. Once I tried poetry and chose a poem virtually impossible to recite, Poe's "The Bells." But my masterpiece, the reading that established my reputation (such as it was), the piece that was so popular that I was requested to do it for classes all over the school, was my interpretation of Edmond Rostand's *Cyrano de Bergerac*, Scene 4, in which Cyrano humiliates those who mock the length of his nose by mocking it himself, brilliantly, for two pages. It was my mother who suggested I try it and, remarkably, there was a copy of the play on our shelves at home.

It is a tour de force for any actor lucky enough to play it. After it became my signature piece I saw it truly performed in a production at the Hilberry Theatre in Detroit with Cyrano played, unforgettably, by actor John Sterling Arnold. I can hear his voice in my head to this day.

For an outsider in middle school who was regularly picked on and mocked, and for whom revenge was always just out of reach, the power, the sense of self that Cyrano gave me wasn't just gratifying, it was a revelation. "Acting," as I thought of it at the time, gave me the self-confidence that all the martial arts in the world wouldn't have done. I don't know whether, when she made the suggestion, my mother understood the significance of the choice, or whether Will Young did as he worked with me to shape it. But there is probably no funnier or more tragic romantic nerd character in the post-Elizabethan canon. My discovery of Cyrano and John Sterling Arnold's performance marked the moment my decision was made, positively and irrevocably, that I would make my living as an actor.

The biggest immediate change was largely a symbolic one: as I found my niche, I started eating at a table with the drama kids. The Spazz Table became a thing of the past, a reminder of the dark days. I don't remember the transition. One day I was with my fellow exiles, the next I was gratefully elsewhere. My former luncheon companions still sat at the old table, stolidly munching away in silence, serene, or at least philosophical, in the knowledge that people like me would always come to them when they needed a refuge but were guaranteed to disappear when they got a better offer elsewhere. I don't recall any of their names.

I still blush to think of it.

1971

THE NERD EMERGES

Woodward Avenue, which begins at the Detroit River and runs far out through the northern suburbs and beyond, is the drab, utilitarian road separating East and West Detroit. As teenagers, the section of Woodward from 9 Mile to Long Lake Road was the legendary "cruising" area, as carloads of desperate suburban boys drove slowly up and down, seeking cars full of available girls, hoping for that one flustered, overheated grope that would give the lucky would-be cocksman sexual bragging rights over his friends. Cruising was something everyone did, but I don't think I ever knew anyone who actually scored doing it.

I certainly didn't. My friend Ron Merkin and I would cruise Woodward every weekend, always with an optimism that remained undiminished in the face of constant failure. Ron was one of my best friends, a guy I looked up to for several reasons. One, because of his extensive experience with women (much of that completely invented, as he has admitted since). He was also an old hand at Will-O-Way Apprentice Theatre, that center of theatrical learning to which I aspired. And Ron drove a white Roadrunner, for God's sake. A new one, with an FM radio and those race car things stuck on the back. If you couldn't pick up girls in a white Roadrunner, we figured, you just weren't trying. Ron even installed a telephone receiver—just the receiver, you understand, not the phone itself—so that if we drove up beside any likely prospects, we could pretend to be talking on the phone. Incredibly, even this didn't work.

The only time that anyone even noticed us was the night two very promising types with big hair came up beside us at a red light. Ron and I both scrabbled for the phone while trying to remain cool. After giving us a once-over, one of them rolled down her window, pointed at me and shouted to Ron, "Hey, is that a girl?" The charm of "cruising Woodward" paled considerably for me after that.

I really hated cars. I still do. I didn't care that, in the broad, abstract sense, cars put food on the table, clothed and educated me. By the time I was old enough to drive them, I wanted nothing to do with them. My friends had cars and we were usually going to the same places. In a pinch I'd take buses.

In Detroit in those days, driver's education was a part of every high school student's life, like everywhere, only being Detroit, even more so. It was a part of the curriculum, unless you were Amish and could opt out on religious grounds. One of our driver's ed teachers was an alcoholic, and once the students were actually out behind the wheel, we'd have to go on quick runs to the liquor store. This was fine by me. The actual mechanical driving of cars was never a problem for me. But then it would come time for the written exam and I would absolutely go to pieces. I could not—or would not—pass this goddamned test.

I amused and amazed friends and family alike by failing the written driver's education exam not once or twice but three times. Finally, in despair, my parents sent me, secretly, to take the course taught by a seedy character who rented a filthy room in the basement of Northland Mall whose name, he claimed, was Fashman. He was paid in cash, there was no sign on the door and you had to knock to be admitted, so the whole process felt like a drug deal. It was clear even to me that this was where they sent real idiots to drive.

There really was a sense of shame in the whole thing; kind of how parents would send their pregnant daughters to give birth out of town so no one would know. I never told a soul that I was matriculating at the Fashman School of Driving or whatever it was called. It took me forty years to find out that my best friend in high school also took driver's ed there. He never told anyone either.

But by the 1970s, everyone my age either had their driver's license or had lost their virginity, or both. Lots of people only got their license *in order* to lose their virginity. It was a rule.

For people with big families, the car was literally the only place they had any privacy at all. I had loads of privacy. My parents spent a lot of time out of the house and my sister was often with friends. I had the house to myself. The only thing missing was the other person.

Anyway, to everyone's relief, I finally passed my test and became an adult in the eyes of the state of Michigan, if not exactly my own. The sex thing was still some ways off, but this was a start.

The night of the day I passed, I stood with my father next to the car he didn't care so much about, which was, by unspoken understanding, the one I would drive. I remember it so well. A late autumn evening, the musk of burning leaves hanging in the air, the first chill heralding a long Michigan winter. It was kind of a big moment and we both knew it. As he handed me the keys to go out for the first time on my own, he had a word of fatherly advice. It wasn't "Don't drive drunk," or "Remember to drive defensively, there are some crazy people out there." No. His sole piece of advice in the driveway that night was, "No copulating in the car."

No copulating in the car? Who did he think he was talking to? Was he joking? I give you my word, until that moment, the thought of copulating in the car had literally never entered my mind. Beds, certainly. Beaches, zoos, beside railway tracks, in woods, in airplanes, absolutely. When you're not having sex, pretty much anywhere sounds like a good idea. But in *cars*? I couldn't even imagine how you would do it. But of course, thanks to my dad, from that moment on, all I could think about was copulating in the car.

Never did, of course. Which brings me to a recounting of my adolescent romantic history, a subject that has the advantage of brevity if nothing else. I have said that I couldn't get dates in high school, which is mainly true, though that didn't stop me from having girlfriends. Far from it: I had, by a rough estimation, dozens of girlfriends between the end of middle school and high school graduation. The catch was, none of these young women actually knew she was my girlfriend.

This was the peak of my Imaginary Girlfriend stage.

To clarify, the Imaginary Girlfriend is not the same thing as a crush. It isn't just not being able to take your eyes off someone. It isn't someone you want to be with if you could only get up the nerve to ask her. It isn't even the one you fantasize about when you're masturbating, assuming you know how to do that.

No, an Imaginary Girlfriend is one who you may or may not know, who maybe knows you; who might even be your friend, in the strictly platonic sense. She can even have a boyfriend. She can even talk to you about problems she's having with her boyfriend or boyfriends, because as her friend, you are safe. Only, while she's talking and you are listening sympathetically, you are thinking about what's going on in your Imaginary Relationship with her.

In this Imaginary Relationship, you can actually have memories about this girl and you can think back to that time when she first admitted, shyly, that she loved you. She never did that, but you have the memory of it and no one can take that away from you. As long as you know this girl, your actual relationship with her—if you have one—will run whatever course it's meant to. But your Imaginary Relationship runs in its own Space Time continuum. You may have only known her—oh, let's give her a name. She's Kim. You may only have known Kim for six months, but in your Imaginary Relationship, you are already through college—you both went to the Sorbonne because she got in first and you couldn't stand the idea of long-distance relationships so you went too.

So in your real relationship, there the two of you are—you and Kim—in the cafeteria or the library. Kim's talking about whatever and in your Imaginary Relationship, you and Imaginary Kim are apartment hunting on the Left Bank because you both decided to stay in Paris rather than return to Detroit. Neither of your families are very happy about your decision, but it's not up to them, it's up to you. Everything goes beautifully for a while. You're writing a novel and have mastered the art of French cooking. She speaks perfect French and translated for a while at the IHO but she's really good with numbers so she's got a job in finance, or whatever. The sex is ridiculous. Suddenly, out of the blue, the two of you are sitting one night by the Seine and she breaks the news. You didn't see it coming. She dumps you. She moves to Holland with her lesbian lover. You keep the stray cat the two of you took in, which will probably outlive you. End of story.

Which is the problem with having Imaginary Girlfriends. With a fantasy girlfriend, it's simple. Suddenly the girl is naked in your bed. Everything leading up to that moment is unimportant. From there on, it's just the two of you with as much as you can remember from *Lady Chatterley's Lover* to keep you going. It's the same every time. Never fails. But you can't control an Imaginary Girlfriend. It's a lot more complicated and a lot of the time it ends badly.

Fortunately, you and Real Kim are still friends, and Imaginary Kim's dumping you has loosened you up for an Imaginary Relationship with Michelle, who is another friend of yours who's having trouble with her boyfriend. There's a better than even chance that this Imaginary Relationship is doomed, too.

So what's the point in having an Imaginary Girfriend? In lieu of actual experience, it was excellent practice.

HIGH SCHOOL

DETROIT 1969–1972

My unexpected and determined commitment to a life onstage could easily have been undermined once I reached high school if it weren't for the embarrassment of riches that the Berkley school system possessed in their drama department at the time.

Will Young had done what he could for me at that point and passed me on to the high school with a firm injunction to try to get into Duane Thompson's drama class. And lo and behold, here I discovered yet another professional actor who, due to the exigencies of a family to support, had left the stage and taken to teaching drama. It's hard to imagine two such people teaching in the same district today. The high school also boasted a speech teacher, Peggy Metzger, who along with Thompson embraced and encouraged me for the next three years. Though my parents didn't realize it at this stage, the hope they had entertained that this acting thing was a passing fancy died the day I walked into the Little Theatre.

There were two theaters at the high school then, but to me only one counted. There was the big stage in the gymnasium, which was mainly used for the big spring musicals, which were directed by yet another drama teacher, Margaret McQuaid. Musicals didn't interest me for some reason. Maybe there was a deeply suppressed bitterness from that whole *Music Man* fiasco from my childhood, with Yvette refusing to kiss me. Who knows? Mrs. McOuaid directed me in the first full-length play I had ever done, called *Auntie Mame*.

In the bowels of the Berkley High School, however, was a tiny space that was Duane Thompson's domain. He was in charge not only of acting classes but also of the Technical Theatre Workshop, where the real theater nerds held sway. Thompson always directed the fall production, which was usually some form of supernatural story. Each production was introduced by Thompson himself, in Rod Serling mode, standing in a spotlight, preparing the audience for the creeps to come. It was his production of *The Innocents*, based on Henry James's *Turn of the Screw*, that gave me my first lead, as Miles, in a full-length play. My sister Kristin played my character's sister Flora, and revealed for the first time her own talent as a budding stage actor, which was considerable. The once and future Imaginary Girlfriend Jan Puffer played the haunted governess, Miss Giddens.

Like Young before him, Thompson had an eye for those of us who showed even a glimmer of talent and determination. But we were children and very few, if any, were seriously thinking of becoming actors some day. But people like Jim Richards (a year ahead of me) and Jan in my year were exceptions to the rule. We were in it for the long haul. Within a couple of years, we would find ourselves at Oakland University's Academy of Dramatic Art together.

In the meantime, I was busy burying "Jockless" Armstrong and the Swedish Faggot—and burying them four fathoms deep. What Cyrano had started, the constant working on plays, scene work and monologues had finished. I spent all of my time in the Little Theatre working with kids who loved it all as much as I did. When working on final scenes and monologues, my selections were as eccentric as ever. For one monologue I picked the Creature's final speech over the body of his creator from Mary Shelley's *Frankenstein*: the ultimate outcast character. I chose a scene from Woody Allen's play *Play It Again, Sam*, in which I both played the ghost of Humphrey Bogart and directed. My Orson Welles passion coming into full flower, I became a triple-threat: directing and adapting a scene from James Goldman's screenplay of *They Might Be Giants*, as well as starring as Justin Playfair, the famed jurist who has a mental breakdown and believes he is Sherlock Holmes.

Peggy Metzger, the speech teacher, eventually turned me completely loose. With another boy in class, Dave Stroud, I embarked on a series of comedy pieces that had nothing to do with speech and everything to do with amusing ourselves. The series became known as "Dummy and Stroud." I would draw two lines on my chin on either side of my mouth and sit on Dave's knee (Dave was about 6'3" in his socks) and be the dummy. It was really just a parody of a bad ventriloquist act, during which Dave would drink a glass of water while I would sing, but it amused the class and gave Peggy a break from time to time. While the rest of the students had to give assigned speeches, I was basically allowed free range. At one point, she discovered there was a radio station at another high school that was looking for people to create their own shows. To create *The Baker Street Theatre*, in which I adapted the original Conan Doyle stories, broken up into fifteen-minute weekly episodes, all characters played (naturally) by me, was the work of moments. It ran for months.

If there's one thing these choices showed it was my insistence on having my acting work reflect all my nerd obsessions of that period. They are pretty much all there and accounted for: Sherlock Holmes, Woody Allen, Humphrey Bogart and classic horror: all of which, save Woody Allen, remain obsessions to this day. Truly, the nerd is father of the man.

By this time, I was a long way from the Spazz Table. I had a circle: Cindy Van Loon, Cheryl Waskin, Cathy Frederik, Jan Cutlip, David Weinberg, Jay Schwartz, Val Kinunen—many others, but all of us jetsam from different ships, keeping each other afloat until finally washing up on the same beach.

But the last piece of my nerd jigsaw puzzle fell into place the day I met Elliott Milstein. It was a Pan edition of Ian Fleming's *Dr. No* that brought us together. I was still carrying around books bought in Europe and Elliott was bibliophile enough to recognize that my edition of the Bond book was unavailable in the U.S. This started a relationship that was cemented when we discovered a shared love of tea, chess and the great P. G. Wodehouse.

I was a Jeeves/Wooster devotee and he a Blandings Castle aficionado, and neither of us had much patience for the other's saga, but we patiently guided each other, Anglophiles both, through Wodehouse's entire ouvre. We both joined the International P. G. Wodehouse Society, Elliott eventually becoming the president and making him, at least in the Wodehouse department, an even bigger nerd than I was. (But he lost a lot of points for having lost his virginity before we graduated, so I still win.) We have remained friends, traveled, quaffed, dined, listened to music, gone to films and plays and read our way through our lives, even when the road was bumpy, and all of it was made possible by a dog-eared Pan paperback, which I still own, by the way. In this case as in many before, books have proved a sustaining force.

COLLEGE

My parents were the first generation in my family to make it past high school, if that far, so naturally, it was a forgone conclusion that I would go to college. The logic escaped me, especially since I already had my future completely planned out: I was to be a great stage actor like John Sterling Arnold or my new hero, George C. Scott.

No one else seemed to see it that way. My family seemed to have nothing better to do than to throw up roadblocks to my dream. It was dangerous, they said. It was unpredictable. I'd never make a living. I'd be consorting with communists, alcoholics and pederasts. Any reader who has expressed a similar goal to their families may have gotten a similar response, even in these more accepting times, but in those days you could pretty much expect nothing else. Their opposition to my career choice was at that point rigid and inflexible.

My family was being transferred back to Europe at that

point, this time to London. My immediate future was a matter of some moment. What made it all the more fraught was my growing obsession with the Academy of Dramatic Art. The year before, the previous golden boy of Mr. Thompson's Little Theatre company had been accepted. In our last year of high school, Jan Puffer had also been accepted. Negotiations, arguments and desperate deal making went on for months, so long that I missed the auditions for the following autumn semester. On the eve of my parents' departure it was agreed that I would attend regular college for one year. If I was still committed to this mad idea at the end of that time, I could audition for the Academy.

Western Michigan University, in Kalamazoo, drew the short straw and I started my single year of higher education in August of 1972, my curriculum heavily weighted with literature and theater classes. Two theater professors, Drs. Flieshacker and Grandstaff, became my mentors, featuring me in productions of Sheridan's *School for Scandal* and John Guare's *House of Blue Leaves*.

There was a black box theater, too, where I did a trilogy of avant-garde pieces written by graduate students. And it was this production that led to an important change in my fortunes. My parents had come back to the States from London on a brief visit, which coincided with this production. In one of the plays, *The Prometheus Riddle*, I played a young Nazi, of all things, who addresses the audience in long, intimate monologues. It was, my parents said later, the first time that they thought I had what it took to be an actor. My mother was convinced, though my father remained reluctant. "We will lose him," my mother warned him. He finally acceded. Their resistance to the Academy faded and they gave me their permission to audition for the following year.

That finally settled, I really buckled down to make the most of what remained of my freshman year: binge drinking and learning to play pool. I continued to write, bad plays and short stories primarily. In short, my first year at college was remarkably similar to a lot of people's. Right down to finally losing my virginity to a lovely young woman who admitted afterward that she had slept with me because she really liked my Malcolm MacDowell impression. Decades later I worked with Mac-Dowell and told him that his performance in *A Clockwork Orange* was responsible for me losing my virginity.

"Well," he said modestly, "you probably would've lost it sooner or later anyway."

THE ACADEMY OF DRAMATIC ART

At 11:00 a.m. on April 28, 1973, I drove to Oakland University to audition for the Academy of Dramatic Art. I must've been nervous, though I remember very little of the day. I was signed in for the audition by a young woman in a floral dress who was a member of the second-year class named Jayne Houdyshell (now a toast of Broadway; then, like the rest of us, someone from elsewhere taking a gamble on an improbable dream).

I was told to prepare three audition pieces: a dramatic, a classical and a comic. The first was Jaimie Tyrone, from *Long Day's Journey Into Night*; the classical was Arthur from *King John*. For the life of me I can't remember what the comic piece was. Possibly I pulled out old Cyrano again. I remember nothing of the questions or comments made by the faculty, arrayed before me there in the studio theater along a table. I do remember the endless wait for the verdict. It was weeks before the postman delivered my parents' worst nightmare in a beautiful, fat envelope.

The Academy had been founded years before by an Englishman, John Fernald, who had come to Oakland University in Rochester, Michigan, to assume the position of artistic director at Meadow Brook Theatre, a well-regarded regional theater located on the campus. While he was at it, he began the Academy and brought over with him an imposing group of actor/teachers from the Royal Academy of Dramatic Arts (RADA) and other schools in London and Canada.

It seems hard to imagine now, but there was a time when people spent a great deal of time, effort and money to become a "trained" actor, whether the training came from RADA or the Neighborhood Playhouse. In the case of the Academy, it was the sort of training that taught you the difference between a sixteenth-century bow and an eighteenth-century one. It taught you how to move, how to fight on stage, how to use your voice properly. Recitation, improvisation, yoga, dancing, singing, sword fighting, neutral mask, commedia dell arte, pantomime blanche, clown work and, of course, Basel Carnival mask technique, later popularized by the Swiss mask troupe Mummenshanz. We studied the Greeks, Shakespeare, Arthur Miller, Harold Pinter. I'm not sure that sort of training can be found in the U.S. anymore, because this period, the early seventies, was probably the last one in this country in which the stage was not just considered a stop on the way to a career in film or television, but an actual goal in itself.

The irony that, after all this esoteric training, I finally would become famous for belching and picking my nose is not lost on me.

By the time I auditioned, the Academy was in a state of flux. Some of the original acting teachers were returning to England and were being replaced by Americans, trained either in the U.S. or, in the case of our mask/commedia teacher, in the Lecoq school in Paris. The white-haired, soft-spoken Paul Lee was replaced by brash New Yorker Al Ruscio. It was kind of as if the role usually played by Alec Guinness was now being played by James Gandolfini. The message being sent by the school was now less strictly that of the English classical tradition and more a mélange of traditions. Still, Alex Gray, Elizabeth Orion and Kate Fitzmaurice continued to represent the old school, while James Tompkins and Jessica Woods, Ruscio and Kate Williamson brought a variety of disciplines to the training.

Regardless of which school one related to, it was all training and it was an intense physical and emotional workout, occasionally brutal and, provided you didn't weaken and quit (or weren't weeded out by the faculty, as many were by the end of the first year), everyone came out of the experience better than when they went in. Some of the most lasting lessons for me came from the English contingent. Liz Orion, in midsentence, suddenly stopping, looking at us and saying reflectively, "You know, much of what we're teaching you here will be of no use at all once you graduate."

And Alex Gray, giving me a review at the end of the first year, saying, "You know, Curtis, you're an amazingly glib actor."

"Great," I said, swelling a little with pride. "Thanks!"

"No," he said, patiently, "that's not a compliment. You can be glib or you can be good. That's entirely up to you." Nothing I ever learned at the Academy has haunted me quite like that statement.

Varner Hall was where we lived for the two years we were at the Academy. We all had homes away from there, of course, but we seldom saw them. Classes from early in the morning to late in the afternoon became rehearsals that would go on into the night. One verity, pretty much whoever your teacher was, involved the stripping away of "bad habits." Not bad habits as in sex, drugs or alcohol. Both students and teachers—and some-times students *with* teachers—grasped at those bad habits like drowning people would grasp life rafts. In this case, bad habits were bad acting habits, physical, vocal and emotional. This process entailed peeling away bits of you until your ego was exposed and then peeling away that. It involved bringing you to a kind of natural state, from which you could be built up again to their idea of what a good actor was.

Not that they necessarily agreed on what a good actor was. But generally, each student would have his or her partisan. If not, those students disappeared. At the end of each semes-ter, some would be shown the door. Others left of their own volition.

An example of the latter occurred one day when we were rehearsing a class production of *Detective Story*, our class final. It had been droning on forever, until the moment one actor was to make his re-entrance. Stage wait. No actor. People called down halls, checked the green room, toilets, but couldn't find him. Finally on an impulse, I checked the parking lot. His car was gone. He had, after months of struggle, realized that nothing was worth this. As he had exited the stage in the previous scene, he just kept walking. Out of the building, into his car and back to Kansas. We never saw or heard from him again.

It was probably ungenerous of me, but my first thought was that this fucker had upstaged everyone. It was an exit nobody could ever top. I remember everyone standing there in the hall, absorbing it. It was like the sailor falling from the masthead into the ocean in *Moby Dick* and being swallowed up without a ripple. One minute he's there, the next it was as if you had just imagined he was there. It felt ominous, almost, like it portended bad luck for the rest of us. We reacted the way actors would— some crying, some laughing uncontrollably.

He was just the first, though. We had started with thirty students and by the time we had graduated in the spring of 1975, there were fewer than twenty of us, and we were so close we couldn't imagine life without the others. But it's been years, even decades since I've spoken to any of them. I don't imagine a day passes, though, that I don't think about them.

By the time I left the Academy in April 1975 as a member of the Studio Company, I had performed in plays from Eugene O'Neill to Ben Jonson; from Arthur Schnitzler and Chekov to Shakespeare. I was a passable stage fighter, proficient in mask work of all kinds, had created my own clown—whose name was Sharkey, and who I never found particularly funny—and was actually something of an expert in commedia dell arte. I had gone into the Academy completely unable to dance. I left the same way.

But I had also met Terence Kilburn, the associate dean of the Academy and then artistic director of Meadow Brook Theatre. Terry had been a child star on radio and in Hollywood and I had recognized him instantly as the original Tiny Tim in the classic Reginald Owen *A Christmas Carol*, and from the Robert Donat version of *Goodbye Mr. Chips*. He has also been featured as Billy, the very wise and tactful page, in the 1939 Basil Rathbone and Nigel Bruce version of *The Adventures of Sherlock Holmes*. He was a gentle, kind man with a welcoming presence, and a world of stage and film experience. I liked him instantly and he was to prove instrumental in the next step in my journey.

MEADOW BROOK THEATRE/ROADSIDE ATTRACTIONS

1975–1976

Sometime around the middle of our second year at the Academy, one of my classmates and I hatched a plan to form our own theater company after graduation. The core company would consist of those of our class who chose to join us. Others would be welcomed in after undergoing an abbreviated form of that which we had undergone. It would be called Roadside Attractions and would be itinerant at first, performing at art fairs, Renaissance festivals and anywhere else that would have us, for nothing. Eventually, the dream went, we'd have our own theater, where we would perform a combination of new plays and classics, modern and ancient, which would be directed by the very teachers who had just spent two years directing and instructing us. What could go wrong?

As it happened, nothing did. We were driven and inspired by that sixties/early seventies spirit of independent and political action, which often found expression in just this sort of hand-to-mouth theatrical adventure, from Steppenwolf to the San Francisco Mime Troupe. Our teachers agreed to direct and, in some cases, continue to teach workshops, for free. Some of our company chose to go their own way, but around half of the class joined us. We were all just brimming with confidence and idealism. We had our youth and health and strength and were confident that, if nothing else, starving together would be better than starving alone.

Lavinia Whitworth was my co-conspirator in this scheme. While we were technically co-founders of Roadside Attractions, there was never any question who was the real brains of the operation and it was Lavinia. She was several years older than most of us, far more experienced in life and art. She was funny, knowledgeable, bawdy and driven. A good actor but probably even a better director.

Lavinia and I spent our last few weeks at the Academy scouring downtown Detroit for our theater. We came up empty. Even downtown, the rents were out of our league, enough so that we realized we didn't really have a league to start with. Eventually we decided to take a chance on the overall-more-arts-friendly city of Ann Arbor. We had no better luck there, until one day we were hired—actually hired—to do a clown act for children at a run-down suburban mall called Arbor Land, located halfway between Ann Arbor and an adjoining college town, Ypsilanti. It had been built in the 1950s with all the design touches that miserable decade had to offer. It was an outdoor proposition, with absolutely nothing whatsoever to commend it except that in the very center of the place were a set of steps leading down to a storage/meeting room area, which we felt would serve us very well as a lobby and black box theater.

It had probably, at one time, been an air-raid shelter. The walls were made of metal, there were no wings, the acoustics were horrible, it probably sat fifty people on metal folding chairs. It was hot in the summer, freezing in the winter, impossible for audiences to find, and we would have to take all of our belongings with us at the end of every day, props, costumes—even the *set*. But it was rent-free. It was perfect.

We took possession immediately and began work on our first "main stage" production, a revue based on the cartoon strips of Jules Feiffer. There was a similar revue already running in small theaters around the country, but it had played New York and we knew the royalty payments would be out of the question. Rather than do it anyway, and trust that no one would ever find out, we assembled a completely new set of strips and gave it a new title: *Feiffer in the Flesh*. I wrote a letter to Feiffer's representative at the time, told him what the deal was and could he give us a break on the royalties. He wrote back giving us permission to use the material saying only that, in return, Jules would appreciate a letter thanking him and telling him how it all worked out.

(A couple decades later, I contacted Feiffer again, asking for an original strip of his choosing that would be sold at a fund-raiser for the Fund for the Feminist Majority, a feminist organization based here in Los Angeles that I've long been associated with. The strip arrived practically return mail, with no conditions—even a thank-you letter—attached. They don't make them like Jules Feiffer anymore.)

Everyone took what part-time jobs they could get to sustain themselves. Aiming high as always, I started as a day laborer, down around the railroad tracks. A bunch of us would gather there before dawn, glowering at our shoes, smoking cigarettes and grunting monosyllabically, waiting for someone to show up with an open truck to take us someplace to do something. We were paid in cash and it was just enough to keep us in cigarettes.

Then I became a janitor at a little art gallery/framing store on Main Street, but as you can imagine, there wasn't a lot for a janitor to do in an art gallery, so I got another custodial job at a women's clothing store at the new mall just off the 94 freeway. I can't recall the name of it, but a women's clothing store gave me a chance to express myself. In no time, I had gone from cleaning toilets to dressing and undressing the mannequins in the window. This was handy because at last I was able to figure out how the snaps on brassieres worked. It wasn't really practical experience, though, as the mannequin wasn't trying to undress me at the same time and I wasn't doing it in the dark.

We all roomed together in various houses and apartments around Ann Arbor, and one of my most memorable was a room at the top of a condemned house on Fifth Street just off the railroad tracks that boasted a wider variety of vermin than I'd ever seen. The wall-to-wall green shag carpeting extended into the kitchen and had, on close inspection, not been cleaned since the Eisenhower administration. The resulting rich mixture of cooking grease, smoke, rodent feces and generations of food and alcohol ground deep into the pile made up an aroma better imagined than lived with. The constant rumbling of the adjacent trains made sleep a theoretical concept, and appeared to be literally shaking the house down around us. The last straw for me came one night when I arose from my mattress in the early hours for a drink of water. I heard a crash that shook the house and on returning to my room found a large wall unit had crashed onto the bed.

I moved into Lavinia's unfinished basement, where I slept on a mattress. During rainstorms, a sort of young river flowed past my bed, gathering in a still lagoon at the far end of the room. There were no lights, and I used an oil lamp when writing, which added to the sense of mid-nineteenth-century squalor. In Ann Arbor, as Sherlockians might put it, it was always 1895.

We had set out to do eclectic theater, and eclectic we were. After the Feiffer show, we went on to Carlo Goldoni's commedia play *The Servant of Two Masters*. But at this point, fate intervened in the person of Terry Kilburn of Meadow Brook Theatre.

Kilburn had planned to open his 1975 season at Meadow Brook Theatre with *A Midsummer Night's Dream*. Of Shakespeare's fairy band, the part of Oberon was given to the flamboyant audience favorite, Eric Tavares, that of Titania to New York actor Susanne Peters, and the part of Puck to me.

This period of late summer 1975 marks the real beginning of my acting career. I had just finished two years of intense technical training and was only months into the establishment of Roadside Attractions. Being offered a role like Puck at a regional theater like Meadow Brook may sound like watered whiskey to some, but to me it was utter intoxication.

Our production of *The Servant of Two Masters* had actually

garnered some attention in Ann Arbor. One night we were seen by a local man who was looking to open a dinner theater in his nearby restaurant, the Spaghetti Bender. He decided, bless his heart, that a bawdy, partially improvised eighteenth-century Italian Renaissance commedia dell arte production was just what his patrons were looking for and booked us. So just months into our existence, we were being paid to perform an original production in a dinner theater.

I was playing the lead in *Servant*, the titular wise and unscrupulous servant, Arlechino. The part was physically demanding, like doing a combination of dance and stand-up for two hours a night. With *Midsummer Night's Dream*, my weeks became ridiculously full.

Since I was technically a "local hire," Terry Kilburn was under no obligation to put me up in the theater's housing, so I was still sleeping, if you can call it that, in Ann Arbor. *Midsummer* didn't open until the beginning of September, but we had full rehearsal days six days a week for almost a month. So I would get up in Ann Arbor in the morning, drive two hours to Rochester to start rehearsals at 10:00 a.m., work until 5:00 p.m. and then drive to Ypsilanti for curtain at 7:30, then drive back to Ann Arbor for bed. Then up again to do it all again until our contract at the Spaghetti Bender finally concluded just days before the first night of *Midsummer Night's Dream*.

None of the actors in the Meadow Brook productions were stars. Most of them you have never seen or heard of. Many of them, though, were known all over the country in the regional/repertory and summer theater circuit. This web of small-to-medium-sized theaters and opera houses was the bread and butter for stage actors of the time. Even small towns and universities had them, professional and semi-professional houses that booked union actors for one show, or six, paying them a sustaining wage, if not a living one. Many New York–based actors never set foot on a Gotham stage, because they were too busy traveling: doing productions in Cincinnati, seasons in Fort Lauderdale, from Rochester, Michigan, to Rochester, New York, from Providence, Rhode Island, to Fayetteville, Pennsylvania—any town that boasted a stage, a bed and paid Equity minimum. If you had the talent and the luck and the commitment, you could go months, even years, working regularly, if not constantly. When you weren't working, thanks to the union, there was unemployment compensation. It wouldn't be much but it would help hold you over until the next theater called.

Here are some names: Eric Tavares, Cheryl Giannini, Robert Grossman, John Peakes, Jim Corrigan, Fred Thompson, Peter McRobbie, Richard Riehle, Bill LeMassena, Booth Coleman, G. Wood, Jeanne Arnold, Susanne Peters, George Gitto, Paul Barry, Michael Allinson, Michael Egan, Kevin O'Reilly, Jack Aranson, Ian Stuart. I wanted to *be* these people. Well, some of them I didn't really want to be, but I wanted their lives, their stories and their experience.

I was able to romanticize their lives even as I saw the loneliness, bitterness and jealousy that absorbed some of them. I was consumed with wanting a life like theirs even when I saw aging ex-soap stars furtively consuming flasks of alcohol during shows; hearing wonderfully funny anecdotes about third, fourth, even fifth marriages shot to hell. Even while seeing, and occasionally indulging in, sexual liaisons rooted in boredom, sadness or even contempt.

And the drinking, to one degree or another, was an indelible part of the culture. Most of us managed it well enough but during one production at Meadow Brook years later, I got a bleak lesson in one of the road's most insidious traps.

One of the actors I worked with during those years was an American, but one who had numerous credits in London and Dublin as well. His marriage—which one or to whom I can't recall—had ended and his daughter, maybe fourteen at most, lived most of the time with her mother. This man was a drinker, and a world-class one. None of us objected because usually he was wonderful company when he was drunk. Which was, like many of us, most of the time he wasn't on stage.

Then his daughter came to visit for a few days. He was on his best behavior during her stay. He'd go back to his trailer after the show with his sweet girl and was basically the perfect dad. Didn't even have a drink in his room. Until about two o'clock one morning when he cracked and showed up at my door, pale, shaking and begging for a bottle. Not a drink, he said, a bottle. To go. And behind him, stricken, with tears in her eyes was his child, looking imploringly at me, shaking her head and mouthing, "No. Please."

Some times were harder to romanticize than others.

It would be a few years before I could truly claim to have joined their ranks, but this was the world I aspired to. Not the sodden, broken alcoholic side, nor the side that saw the future as an endless series of lonely hotel rooms, broken families and missed opportunities. For me there was nothing but hope in my future. Meadow Brook was the first brick-and-mortar stage that I would call home but it wouldn't be the last. Just a whiff of the unmistakable backstage scent would brighten my eyes and flood endorphins into my brain. I already had a work ethic, but working with these people taught me a thing or two about onstage discipline, at least. Thanks to them, I learned what "professionalism" really meant. It was a lesson that many young actors who got their start in film or television never had the chance to learn, but you couldn't survive in the theater without it.

As important as my teachers like Will Young and Duane Thompson were; as valuable as Russell Grandstaff and Dan Fleishhacker had been at university; as essential as Liz Orion and Alex Gray, Jessica Woods and Jim Tompkins and Al Ruscio and Ron Mangravite, Kate Williamson and Kate Fitzmaurice had been at the Academy, it was the people I started working with at Meadow Brook and many other theaters who were to be my most important mentors.

I went back to Roadside Attractions with the same passion and determination I had had from the beginning, but Meadow Brook had proved a watershed moment. It would be two years before Terry hired me again, by which time I had moved to New York and already started performing in showcases and small off-off-Broadway productions. But once he did, I started working regularly, for money that mostly paid the rent. There were national tours on the horizon and bigger theaters. Regional theaters and summer theaters and repertory theaters. The theater had ceased being something possible I played with and had become something definite I had chosen. Fortunately, it had chosen me, too.

I would eventually become a member of the Colonnades Theatre Lab, where I was featured in a well-received Wolf Mankowitz play, *The Irish Hebrew Lesson*. I would do a national tour of the Pulitzer Prize–winning Hugh Leonard drama *Da;* then a pre-Broadway tryout of the Colonnades cult sensation *Moliere in Spite of Himself,* with the great Richard Kiley, which closed out of town. With each of these, the auditions got bigger. In time I was reading for Broadway plays, though managing to avoid being cast in any of them. Some of these, like the one-on-one with playwright Peter Shaffer on the Broadhurst stage to replace Tim Curry in *Amadeus*, were so exhilarating I didn't even care about losing the part.

I loved the theater past expression. I loved it with the irrational fullness that made the prospect of being even in a "quality" motion picture seem like the worst kind of selling out. As for television, well, there existed in the U.S. no TV show fine enough for *me* to appear in. And commercials were things that we "trained actors" didn't even acknowledge. That's the kind of theater fundamentalist I had become.

A period of about three and a half years took me from the Academy of Dramatic Art, to the co-founding of Roadside Attractions, to the move to New York. My future as a stage actor appeared written in indelible ink, its arc an inevitable thing.

Except, it wasn't.

ENTR'ACTE

My decision to leave Roadside Attractions and start my career in New York in earnest was made scientifically: by taking a 1976 calendar, closing my eyes and jabbing my finger down on an arbitrary date. It was August 11.

I must have really wanted to go. Money was still tight, but I had at least the potential of a growing career as a regional stage actor in Michigan. Roadside Attractions had suffered from chronic income deficits and some internecine conflicts, but there were discussions of moving to an actual theater in Detroit, which was promising. There were a lot of reasons to stay.

And yet it was on August 11, 1976, that I arrived, friendless, in New York, a city I had never so much as visited. My way had been smoothed somewhat by Susanne Peters, who had played Titania in *A Midsummer Night's Dream*. Susanne lived in a sixth-floor cold-water apartment on Sullivan Street in the Village, with a bathtub in the kitchen and a toilet in the hall outside. She was going on a tour for over a year with the John Houseman Company and needed someone to sublet the place and look after her cat. Nevertheless, despite having a roof over my head, I'm not sure I could've made the move in cold blood.

I arrived at LaGuardia on a beautiful summer afternoon and took my seat on the shuttle to Grand Central. As I looked out the window, a man with the largest penis I had ever seen was peeing on my bus. Tourists were taking pictures of it. The shock of seeing an appendage of that size caused the symbolism of the act itself to elude me completely.

At Grand Central I got a cab to take me to Sullivan Street. My cabbie was a young black man, born and raised in Manhattan. He was cheerful, voluble, full of information about places to go and neighborhoods to avoid. The Village was still festooned with brightly colored banners in honor of the Bicentennial celebrations the previous month. He helped unload my luggage outside the apartment building, and as he turned back to his cab he gave me a smile I'll never forget and said, "Welcome to the Big Apple!"

I got through that first day on a cocktail of excitement and dread. But by the time I was lying in my loft bed sweltering in the August heat, all that was left was the dread. In the street below I could hear the faint screaming of two men in dispute mingling with the alien music of a New York summer's night. As the hours crept by I could hear the sinister skittering of the rats in the walls and the gentle rustlings of the cockroaches in the cereal boxes from the kitchen below.

It's common knowledge now that New York in the seventies was a far dirtier, more dangerous and more dysfunctional city than today. Nevertheless, it's possible to overstate the peril in which we walked in those days. In the eleven years I spent in New York I was only mugged once, and that was when I was in Pittsburgh. Once, when walking down Forty-second Street by Ninth Avenue, I felt my checkbook being dexterously lifted from my outside pocket. I was on the verge of spinning around and pursuing the guy when I recalled there were no checks in the book. Discretion being the better part of valor, I kept walking. Suddenly there was a tap on my shoulder. I turned to see the man holding my checkbook out to me.

"Excuse me, sir," he said. "I think you dropped this." I thanked him and we went our separate ways.

My apartment was burgled only once during that period, but it was by a junkie named Pietro, who lived on my street. Somehow, the fact that the guy lived in the neighborhood took some of the sting out of it. He was about my size and mainly took clothes. I realized he was the culprit when, some weeks later, I saw him wearing a sports jacket I had valued rather highly.

"Nice jacket, Pietro," I said.

"Oh, thanks, man!" he replied, revealing a mouthful of unspeakable teeth in a genuine smile. "Have a great day!"

For a while my story became every actor's story: a blur of uncertainty and fumbled auditions. I needed to work for food and rent, but never waited tables. Instead, I found myself peculiarly adapted to working in—and eventually running—mailrooms for Manhattan companies of all sorts, in buildings from the then new World Trade Center to Columbus Circle (including, strangely enough, the mailroom for the company that would one day publish this book).

Acting jobs came at what seemed like a snail's pace but looking back I realize what a deceptive mistress memory can be. The point was, they came. When I was finally cast in Hugh Leonard's *Da* in 1979, it was a turning point in more ways than one. I was in a national tour—an extensive one—of a Tony Award– and Pulitzer Prize–winning play that was to prove another step up the ladder professionally. Personally, it was even more significant.

It was during *Da* that I met and fell in love with one of my costars, Cynthia Carle. The affair began on the road, as they often do, but this one was different. By the time we were done with the first half of the tour, we were besotted. Back in New York, during a long hot summer with no work, the two of us wound up in her apartment with a pack of cards. She asked if I'd like to play some poker. I admitted it was a game I'd never learned.

"You've never played poker? *Poker?*" It was clear, she said, that my education had been lacking in a significant detail and she proceeded to teach me poker there and then.

As with most games involving that part of my brain—or any part of my brain, really—I was a little slow on the uptake, but finally got the hang of it. After a few hands of five-card draw, she said, "Of course it's more interesting when you're actually betting."

We were flat broke at that time, but an idea occurred to me. "How about," I suggested, "we try it this way. One hand: if you win, we stay as we are, living in our separate apartments. If I win, we get married and move in together."

We looked at each other for a long moment. This was my

idea of a marriage proposal. Some women might have been of-fended. Not Cynthia. She shrugged.

"Okay," she said, and started shuffling the cards. We played the hand. I stared at the cards, the blood draining from my face. "Okay," I said, putting as bright a face on it as possible. "I guess we stay in our separate apartments."

She looked at me with a slow smile. "Um, no. Actually," she said, arranging the cards so I could see them, "you won."

Ten days later, we were married at Manhattan City Hall. Our honeymoon was the completion of the seventy-seven-city tour of *Da* . . .

That all came much later, though, long after my first solitary arrival in New York. There were certainly adventures ahead, but when I woke up, exhausted, from my first night at 71 Sullivan Street, I could see no future at all. I wandered out into the street, bought a paper and a cup of coffee. I had no idea where I was, but like a salmon traveling upstream, I headed north to Washington Square. I sat on a bench there and took it all in. Aging commu-nists playing chess; couples in the first flush of love, taking dogs for obligatory walks before going back to bed for the day; drunks lying in fetid heaps, steaming in the sun; dark-eyed Puerto Rican boys streaking past on skateboards.

Day One.

RISKY BUSINESS

CHICAGO, 1982

I auditioned for movies before *Risky Business*, but usually I found these fairly cut-and-dried experiences: get the audition, do the audition, get rejected. You could pretty much set your watch to it. For different reasons, only one or two stood out.

One of my earliest auditions in New York was for the Milos Forman film of the Broadway musical *Hair*. It was a general audition, a cattle call, for which some hundreds of us showed up at a space in Times Square, shuffling defensively through a stark hall, with resumes and sheet music for a song of our choosing. I had never sung on a stage and had no agent or anyone else to advise me at the time, so I chose "As Time Goes By," a poor choice for a rock-and-roll musical but so *me*. Forman and various casting people were at a long table, shuffling papers and consulting audibly throughout the process. He never looked up. The pianist charged through the song with a kind of reckless abandon, as if he were competing for a Guinness World Record for getting through a ballad in the shortest time. I was trying to sing like Nilsson while my accompanist played like Carl Stalling.

Another standout was reading for the lead role in *Lady Hawke* for the director Richard Donner. I entered the small office where the man himself was seated, looking like he didn't have a friend in the world. An aura of dejection and ennui settled round him like a toxic cloud. Without preamble, I went into my piece, which was fairly lengthy, and I figured I should get out as much of it as I could before he could stop me and go blow his brains out in the men's room.

Surprisingly, this did not happen. I was aware early in the reading that he seemed to perk up. Something about me or my choices appeared to have gotten his attention. He sat up straight. His eyes were focused on me intently. When it was over, he said, "You committed."

"I what?" I asked.

"You committed. The lines. You committed the lines to memory. No one does that."

"Well," I said, a little awkwardly, "that's kind of my job."

"You would be amazed," said Donner, "how few actors seem to understand that. I liked the choice you made with the character, too. That was really excellent. Very good. Thank you!"

I went out in a daze. No one had ever been so lavish with praise for an audition of mine before. This job, I imagined, was in the bag.

And it was, but for Matthew Broderick. And I never got the chance to read for Richard Donner again.

But good, bad or indifferent, the audition process was generally swift. There are seldom appeals in this business. Once you've presented yourself, the verdict is fairly swift and pitiless. That wasn't the case for *Risky Business*.

It started in the usual manner. I had the sides, including the "what the fuck" scene. This appeared kind of light and rather banal as a statement of philosophy, but I figured it should probably be delivered as though the character, Miles Dalby, truly believed it. Actually, while there are always exceptions, believing what you're saying when acting is usually a pretty good rule of thumb. In this case, it was only part of what got me the role.

Months would elapse before that was official. In the meantime, I'd been offered a summer of repertory at the New Jersey Shakespeare Festival, including roles in *Henry IV* parts 1 and 2. Work tended to dry up in New York during the summer, and NJ Shakespeare was one of the plum jobs for young actors at the time. It would start in May and run into September. But could I commit to it when there was a good role in a movie in the offing? A movie that, by the way, I didn't want to do anyway! Because I was a stage actor, you remember, and even though the movie would presumably pay much, much better, well, that's just crude mammon, isn't it, and you get into that kind of habit and you cease being an artist at all and become nothing more than a stooge in pursuit of great wealth for evil influence. And that way lay the worst kind of debasement and self-betrayal. The choice was obvious: I passed on the New Jersey Shakespeare job and took my chance on the movie and in doing so opened the door to a very different future.

I had agonized over this decision, and as the weeks crawled by I cursed myself for it. It turns out, the delay had been due to difficulties in the casting of the lead, Joel Goodson, and the beautiful young prostitute who comes into his life. Paul Brickman, the writer and director, had a very clear sense of *exactly* how this film would go and the casting of these two roles was essential. At that point, he had seen most of the big or promising young actors around. Actors Brian Backer and Megan Mullally were two early favorites, as were Tom Hanks and Linda Hamilton, among many others, but the perfect combination of costars had remained elusive.

During this interminable period our casting director, Nancy Klopper, was generous and dutiful in keeping my agent up to date and assuring her that I was still being considered. This assiduous attention to a mere supporting actor I now put down to her youth and inexperience. Most casting directors at that point wouldn't have bothered.

After a few weeks, Paul and the producers flew into New York to settle on the rest of the cast. I read for them on my own and with two of my eventual costars, Bronson Pinchot and Raphael Sbarge, as well as with Brian Backer. Weeks passed. While in this limbo, I punished myself by rereading the script and actually working on scenes that I might never get a chance to play.

I was no expert in judging the quality of screenplays. I'm still not. Years later I even turned down an audition with Quentin Tarantino because I found the screenplay of *Reservoir Dogs* revolting. But the *Risky Business* screenplay spoke to my deeps. In 2015, I asked Paul Brickman, with thirty years of hindsight, what he'd had in mind in 1982.

"The whole intent of this movie, before there was a story, before there was a theme—actually the story came last—but the intent was the style. I wanted to do something in a stylized way that had never been done before. I wanted to combine elements in a way that had never been done before, certainly for a teenage film. I wanted a very stylized, romantic look that had sexuality, darker themes and humor. How would that mix? That was the challenge. I wanted to make a film that I would've wanted to take a date to in high school. It was kind of ass-backwards, it's easier to do the story first. Then I was working out the themes. The whole idea of capitalism, what a myth it was, how it was being romanticized, how it was not really true, that it takes its toll. Some people suffer enormously from this. And then add to that mix a character who's beside himself because he's so full of fear about his future."

The road to the making of the movie was an all-too-common one. Paul was writing it as part of a two-picture deal for Warner Bros. The other film, for which he was only writing the script, was the black comedy *Deal of the Century*, eventually directed by William Friedkin (a movie Brickman utterly disavows). The second film Brickman was contracted to do, he was to write *and* direct, and that was *Risky Business*. But the unexpected success of another teen comedy gave Warner's cold feet.

"*Risky Business* was at Warner's," Paul told me, "but they put it in turnaround: they got the script, but they didn't want to make the movie. They didn't think it was funny enough. They wanted it to be more like *Porky's*. Jon [Avnet] and I started shopping it around, we were thinking, how hard can it be? It's fresh material, wouldn't cost a lot to make. But we were turned down everywhere. We could not get this movie made. But then when Geffen wanted to do it, it was back on, and it went back to Warner's, because that's where his deal was. So they were doing *Risky Business*, even though they didn't want to have anything to do with it."

Finally, Paul had his stars and they were worth the effort and then some: Tom Cruise and Rebecca De Mornay were his Joel and Lana. I got the word at last, and I was off to Chicago to make my first movie. At that point, it almost seemed anticlimactic.

I recently came across a scrap of paper with the scribbled information I received during a phone call with my agent the day I was told I'd be doing *Risky Business*. I kept it at the time because I felt it was, in a small way, historic. It documented my first day as a film actor! Why I have kept this scrap for three decades but at the same time managed to lose an ounce of pure gold I inherited from my paternal grandfather, I'm at a loss to say.

As a historic document it doesn't amount to much. It's the usual sort of stuff—where we were shooting (Chicago); for how long (eight weeks!); what my income would be (considering I was on unemployment at the time, it was princely); the names of the screenwriter and director (Paul Brickman); the producers (Jon Avnet, Steve Tisch and David Geffen); and finally, the star—"Tom Crewes," as I wrote it down on that day. I was told later that it was actually spelled "Cruise," which struck me as improbable. I remember thinking that was a mistake, and he might want to consider changing it for professional purposes. Later, I found out he already had.

Tom Cruise's worldwide superstardom is now such an article of faith that it's hard to recall a time when he was just kind of a goofy, slightly awkward and insecure kid at the start of his career, still playing roles that any young hunk could play. Basically, before he became "Tom Cruise." I think I'm safe in saying that *Risky Business* was the last time he was just "Tom." The people around him, I've always thought, knew better where he was going than he did. But he was not a naïf. His eye, as much as anyone's has ever been, was fixed upon the prize.

The first time I met him was at the production office the day I arrived in Chicago to begin working on *Risky Business*. He smiled on seeing me, giving me my first glimpse of those extraordinary chops, all white and straight and sharp and in perfect alignment, which instantly made me feel self-conscious about my own teeth. He appeared so . . . clean. He gave me one of those handshakes where the arm starts almost perpendicular to his body and arcs around—slowly—until his hand grasped mine, which was already open, just hanging there expectantly. Then he called me "Miles." He always called me by my character's name. At the time, I thought it was part of his process. It could be he just didn't know my name.

He was nineteen, about to turn twenty, and I was twenty-eight, which made me the grand old man in that cast—which included people like Bronson Pinchot, Raphael Sbarge, Joe Pantoliano, Shera Danese, and the beautiful, inscrutable Rebecca De Mornay. Except for Tom, who had done several films at that point, we were all fairly new to film. But everyone, including Tom, was unknown to me. In any but the most superficial of respects, he remains so to this day.

If Cruise's unprecedented success was a surprise to me, the perpetual rumors regarding his sexual orientation were utterly mystifying. At least at that time, there was no question which side of that particular fence Tom stood on. It's no secret that Tom engaged in an intense affair during the shooting with costar Rebecca De Mornay—who, as a woman, managed to maintain her inaccessible sexual mysteriousness under any circumstances, unless you could catch her in a joke, at which point her mask would drop as her eyes lit up and she would burst into a full-throated laugh.

Their romance was some time aborning. Part of the delay was caused by the presence of Harry Dean Stanton, who was involved with Rebecca during this period. During the hours she worked, Harry Dean—an affable man and great actor—spent his days swimming slowly the length of the hotel pool, literally for hours at a time. My room overlooked the pool and usually, on rising, I'd see Harry Dean churning his solitary way through the water with a black bathing cap and goggles. I'd go out for breakfast, come back to my room and there he was, his folded towel untouched, still swimming. I'd go to the set, shoot a scene and by the time I returned in the late afternoon, Harry was still in the pool, stroking away. The man's stamina was extraordinary, which I suppose it would have to have been if he was dating Rebecca De Mornay. By evening, he would be found parked at a Pac-Man console at just outside the hotel bar, low-ball within reach, playing endless hours of the game with the same focused, unhurried concentration he brought to his swimming. It got to the point that if someone asked where the bar was, they would be told, "Go that way till you reach Harry Dean Stanton, then turn." I liked and admired Harry Dean immensely. He is a genuinely nice and generous character. He even took my father under his garrulous wing one afternoon when Dad came down from Detroit for a few days and I was stuck at the set.

I suspect that most of Harry Dean's great qualities were lost on Tom, who I think was beginning to regard him as a guest who was overstaying his welcome. It must have been a little galling to have your heart set on fucking your costar, and just when you think you're starting to make some headway, her significant other comes popping up out of a trap like a lanky, amiable Banquo's Ghost. This was a man who, in the eighties, seemed to turn up in every film released. He was ubiquitous, the envy of character men everywhere. You would think a career that hot would require him to be back in Hollywood, busily stealing scenes from entire casts and yet he appeared to be *in situ* indefinitely. "Can no one," I imagined Tom thinking, like a modern-day Henry the Second, "rid me of this turbulent actor?"

In the meantime, though, Tom kept busy. As an actor, he was disciplined and serious about his work and also about where he was going. When I think about it now, Tom may have been the first person I ever knew who possessed an absolute and voracious ambition. It wasn't something he discussed in those terms. There was, though, an aura around this good-looking but otherwise unremarkable teenager that suggested that anyone who stood in his way, or underestimated him in any way, did so at his or her own peril.

Tom wasn't fucking around.

Actually, I take that back. He was. With Rebecca inaccessible, he started cutting a wide swath through the local talent.

Not that I noticed right away. He self-identified as a born-again Christian and the rumor was he had actually considered shepherding souls for a living. I could believe it. As I've mentioned, when away from the set, initially, Tom made straight arrows look like corkscrews. One evening I recall him giving me, a feminist ten years his senior, a stern lecture on why the Equal Rights Amendment was bad for America. (His basic argument? "Hey, my mom worked!")

Missing from my journal was the exact moment that Tom ripped off his beard and revealed himself to be a little less than the born-again Christian he made himself out to be. Or, at the very least, revealed a born-again Christian who was keeping his options open and then some.

I would ask him at the end of the day if he would like to join us in the bar for a drink.

"No," I recall him saying, "got an early call tomorrow. Got to work out still, study my lines. And then I like to read the Bible a little before bed."

I laughed. He didn't.

"Ah," I said, cutting off the laugh at the pass and nodding wisely. "A little bit of the Good Book before bedtime, eh?"

"Yeah," he said. "Just a little at night. Keeps me on the right track. You know?"

But then returning late one night from some jollification, I found three or four young girls—late teens, I suspect—lined up in the hall outside of Tom's room. I remember thinking, *It's late; Tom's going to be really upset if these hot girls interfere with his Bible reading.*

So I asked them, with all the stern gravitas of my twenty-eight years, if there was something I could do to help them.

They just stared at me and at that moment, Tom's door opened and another girl came out, adjusting her hair and took off down the hall, while the first girl in line slipped into Tom's room and the door closed.

"Aha!" I said to the remaining girls. "Right! Carry on!" Tom, it appeared, had everything under control and didn't need my assistance after all. This was a young man who knew something about time management, and understood how to successfully juggle Bible study and blowjobs. That's a gift and one not given to everyone. I went to bed alone that night thinking it served me right for not being religious.

I've said that Tom wasn't a naïf, but he was nineteen and maybe a little gullible. An example is the Louis Armstrong story. The immortal jazz icon had died in 1971, having changed music forever a couple of times, and had been a personal musical hero of mine from an early age. Satchmo's recordings were among the first I remember hearing being played in my home and when I went away to college, I took some of my parents' Louis Armstrong records with me. I adored him. It actually had nothing to do with the fact that we shared a last name.

But for some reason, around this time, when certain people—usually youngish white men—heard my last name, they would say, "Oh! Any relation to Louis?" It was a joke, apparently. They always found it funny and always delivered it with the same smug certainty that no one had ever thought to say it before.

One night Tom, Bronson and Raphael and I were in the

hotel bar when Tom said, "So, Armstrong. Any relation to Louis?"

It was late, I was almost certainly drunk and here was the fucking joke again. So I said, "Yes, actually. I'm his grandson."

All three started to laugh, but I had said this with such seriousness they stopped. Still smiling uncertainly, Tom said, "Yeah, right."

"Dammit," I said. "Look . . . never mind. Forget it."

"What do you mean?" he said.

"Oh, look, seriously," I said, "I should know better than to talk about it. Just forget I mentioned it!"

"What?" Tom said. "What are you talking about?"

I sighed. Deeply.

"Okay," I said, "but this is something you have to keep to yourself. I don't like talking about it, okay? No one must know!!"

"Okay, okay!" screamed Bronson. "Tell!!"

I looked around and lowered my voice. They leaned forward.

"A lot of people don't know this," I said, "but Louis's son married a white woman. They had two children, my sister and me. And through some weird genetic anomaly, she wound up with all the black genes and I got all the white genes. No one ever believes it when I tell the story and I just wind up having to explain it over and over and it's just really frustrating, so please, just keep this to yourselves. Okay?"

"Okay." Tom said, eyes twice their normal size. "I promise!" They all promised. Solemnly.

A few days later, the cast was taken to the Playboy Jazz Festival in Chicago to see Ella Fitzgerald, who burned the place down, with the great Duke Ellington Orchestra. Afterward, Tom sidled up to me. "So are you going back?"

"Going back where?"

"Backstage," he said. "Haven't you met her before?"

"Who, Ella Fitzgerald?" I said. "Of course not. How would I kn—"

"Well, she worked with your grandfather," he said, like I was some kind of idiot for not catching on.

"Oh! Right!" I said, having forgotten all about the Armstrong story. "Well, you know, that was long before my time. And keep it down, okay? I don't want to have to keep talking about the Louis Armstrong thing!"

"I know. Look, I did tell my parents. Hope that's okay, but they're huge fans of your grandfather . . ."

The first scene that we would be shooting was the opening poker game in the basement of Joel Goodson's house, and that scene was rehearsed often, as I noted in the diary I kept at the time:

June 31
Today, our rehearsal consisted of sitting around a table, playing poker, smoking foul cigars and improvising into a cassette. I'm a little slow picking up the game but Bronson, bless him, hasn't a clue. A lot of cards will have to be played in the next week in order to smooth it all out. One improv started heating up when Barry (Bronson) called Joel a "slut-fucker." Tom got angry and said, evenly, that he didn't fuck sluts. Bronson said he imagined actually that he, Tom,

*had fucked several. I thought it was funny, but Tom didn't
and it got very tense, with Bronson finally whining, "Joel,
don't do this to me!!"*

And then:

*Went out with Bronson for dinner, but he smoked a two-
dollar cigar on the way to the diner and was very sick. Half
the time we were there, he was outside, hanging over a
newspaper box like a pair of discarded overalls. The other
half was spent in the bathroom. His face was a pretty green
and his hands were actually translucent.*
     "So much for sensory work," he said.

Bronson and I became fast friends on the film, and it was a
friendship that would last for years. We both loved books and
music—though, strangely, he had never heard the Beatles. I
mean he did not know their music at all. Named for the Tran-
scendentalist Bronson Alcott, to whom he was distantly related,
he had been brought up to higher things than pop music, apparently, and had studied art history at Yale. He was elegant,
flamboyant and screamingly funny. But he went through life
without a single unexpressed thought, which got him into trouble more than once. He was a wit, though, in the eighteenth-
century meaning of the term. I don't like to think what that
summer would've been like without him. We were both based
in New York and both moved to Los Angeles around the same
time. Eventually, we even took holidays together, once going to
London and then driving all over Scotland together. We were

a strange pair, in retrospect. I think people were kind of expecting us to open an antiques shop together.

Meanwhile, the days of hanging out on the company dime were beginning to wear me ragged. We started doing further rehearsals with the first of our three directors of photography, Peter Sova, which helped, but I desperately wanted to get to work. My insecurity with the idea of working in films for the first time was affecting me. And trying to get a handle on our star wasn't easy. Tom was truly something of a conundrum.

July 1

Tom's an interesting character. Can't really make him out. He would appear to be on the brink of a great career. But when it comes to doing things with him—socially or professionally—he's not terribly reliable. Always late, very casual with other people's time. But he was kept waiting the other day by Kevin (Anderson) and he threw a fit.

He seems to be infected by the old star trip, too, at times. For example, a few days ago, he and Bronson had arranged to see a film in town. This entailed arranging for a driver, which Bronson did. The driver shows up, Bronson's there but no Tom. So Bronson calls up to his room and wakes him up.

"Let me," says Tom, "just take a thirty second shower."

"But the driver's waiting," says Bronson.

"That's his job," snaps Tom.

He finally ambled down about twenty minutes later and said, "Let's go to the bar." No movie.

But in spite of it all, it's difficult not to like him. Though

it's early days, the rehearsing I've done with him has gone
smoothly. No arrogance or selfishness there. Yet. We'll see.

In the meantime, I got a call from someone in the production office, wondering whether I was over twenty-one, for liquor-buying purposes, since some of our cast was underage. I assured her I was, indeed, twenty-eight; she thanked me and then said, "And so, you're Louis Armstrong's grandson, right?"

"Oh," I said. "That's gotten around, has it? Who told you?"

"Raphael told me, but I thought he was pulling my leg."

"Well," I said, seriously, "no. It's the truth, but, honestly, I'm trying to keep it quiet, because people tend to ask embarrassing questions. You understand."

"Oh, I get it," she said, earnestly. "I'll keep your secret. He was really great, though."

"Yes," I replied. "Yes. He was a wonderful man. Now, if you don't mind, I'd rather not talk about it anymore."

I was beginning to realize how difficult it was to be related to really famous people. No one likes you for yourself, you know?

July 2
A long poker session today, followed by a blocking session
with Paul and Peter Sova. We blocked the scene with Joel
and Miles with the sex newspaper. Looks good, apparently.
Sova was delighted, anyway. "Too bad it wasn't in the can,"
he told me. "It was wonderful." This started me wondering
again. Is it possible I'm actually going to be good in this

*film? Will people notice me? Will it lead to other things? I
wonder. Still haven't a clue what it's all about . . .*

*This evening's poker game was something of a bust, as
most of the principals got so loaded we kept forgetting the
rules. It says something when I say I was the soberest of the
lot, save Bronson who drank nothing but tonic water, bright
boy. Tom alone demolished half a bottle of vodka and I did
my usual half bot. of scotch.*

Once he let his hair down, Tom could be one of the lads.
While we had been brought into town a week early for rehearsals, the "rehearsals" themselves would've appeared to most
people just like five young guys hanging out together during the
last summer before going off to college. Which was, of course,
just what our characters were doing in the film. Tom, Bronson,
Raphael, Kevin and I looked the part as we were shuttled around
the tony suburbs of Chicago's North Side to cafés, bars, bowling
alleys and the mall. We spent, according to my journal, an
amazing amount of the time at the mall. The record store was a
regular stop, but a lot of time was spent just doing nothing. Sitting around on benches looking at women consumed the better
part of several summer afternoons. This was something that I,
at twenty-eight, and the others some eight or ten years younger,
would never have thought of doing but Paul Brickman insisted
upon it, and a better way for us to get to know one another would
be hard to imagine.

Then as now, Bronson Pinchot enjoyed his own unique view
of how to waste time, and the first time we were left on our

own at the mall, he proposed an ugly shoe contest. Tom started laughing in spite of himself.

"Barry," he said, in keeping with his policy of only using character names, "what?!"

"An ugly shoe contest," yelled Bronson, who could be heard from blocks away when in a state of heightened excitement, which he usually was. "You've never done an ugly shoe contest?! It's so FUN!! So, what we do is," he said, suddenly switching gears and speaking in a serious, normal tone of voice, "we split up and find shoe departments. We find the ugliest pair of shoes there and then we SMUGGLE one of the shoes out of the store and bring it back here. Then we vote on the ugliest shoe, based on applause, and the winner collects the pot!"

I swear to God there was not even a discussion as to whether this was a good idea or not. No question of what would happen if we were caught shoplifting and had to call the production office to come and bail us out. Anyway, Bronson assured us, we weren't really stealing since part of the game was returning the shoes after the contest. Everyone put a quarter—25 cents—into the pot, which I held as Bronson had determined that I, as the oldest, should judge. He counted off and the four of them ran off in different directions in search of shoe departments. That's right, Tom Cruise, future embodiment of the male action film ideal, was on the afternoon of June 30, 1982, in some Buster Brown shoe store in a suburban shopping mall looking for what he determined was the ugliest pair of shoes he had ever seen, and he was doing it for a dollar.

And he lost. Raphael Sbarge, with his really sublime gold, red and clear plastic entry, took home four shiny quarters.

Coincidentally, during the same summer we were shooting in Chicago, Sean Penn was also in town filming *Bad Boys*. Tom and Sean knew each other from the film *Taps* and had bonded closely during filming. Around the time principle photography began on *Risky Business*, Sean dropped in to say hello and basically never left.

Sean seemed to spend any time he wasn't needed on his set hanging around ours with Tom. Sean had already acquired the reputation of a volatile, unpredictable man, one who submerged himself deeply into the characters he was playing. *Bad Boys* was no different. When shooting *Fast Times at Ridgemont High* the year before, people had talked about how totally Sean lived the role of the genial, sweet-natured Spicoli. In *Bad Boys*, Sean was being . . . well, a bad boy. In addition to occasional explosions of temper and general "difficult" behavior, he told me he had a picture taken of himself dangling from a twenty-story hotel room balcony, which he then sent to the bond company insuring the picture. He thought it was funny. He was also widely rumored at the time to be engaged to Bruce Springsteen's sister, which only added to his glamour.

Tom admired him enormously. He admitted to me that he was intimidated by Sean's talent and even then, in 1982, believed him to be the greatest actor of his generation—which became a pretty widely held view as the years went by.

But even the two movie stars in the making had their own idol to worship. Both Tom and Sean sincerely revered Timothy Hutton, the star of *Taps*. According to them, it was Hutton who inspired and guided them both as actors and men. By their account, Hutton ruled that set. There was no question of who the star was: it was Hutton, and this was a movie that costarred George C. Scott. I was privy to countless reminiscences about working with Hutton, hearing endless stories as they quoted him or reflected on what Tim would think of this or that. They were shocked when I admitted I was unfamiliar with his work. I wasn't really; I was just tired of talking about him all the time. Unfortunately, I didn't succeed in changing the subject. Instead, I just caused these two men—future Oscar nominees and arguably two of the most influential actors of our time—to believe there was something actually wrong with me. They weren't angry. Just very, very disappointed.

Sean would hang out on set with Tom and actually appears in the movie in an "uncredited cameo," driving Joel's Porsche out of the garage. Why this was done escapes me. Sean probably just wanted to drive the Porsche. And Sean tended to do what Sean wanted.

I spent a fair amount of time in Tom's room and was always struck by how neat and well kept it was. Whether this was usual for Tom or whether he was doing it as a Method thing (because Joel Goodson's room was probably really tidy), I wasn't sure. But going into the room just a couple of days after Sean's arrival was a revelation. It looked like someone had blown up a convention of rising young eighties actors. There were clothes literally covering the entire floor. By which I mean there was no carpet visible—just clothes. There was a heady scent to the place, too. A rich musk of dirty laundry, cigarette smoke, alcohol and young white male. The curtains were drawn against the light no matter what time it was. The two of them, like as not, would either still be in bed or lounging in underwear. It looked like a Calvin Klein ad. My regular suggestion that they should be playing outside on a beautiful day like this was usually not dignified with a response.

Over the course of filming, I became something of an awkward-older-brother type that seemed to routinely overstay his welcome (regardless of how short the visit). One day I was having lunch with Sean and Rebecca, and Sean asked me what sort of music I listened to.

"Oh, Beatles, Nilsson, Stones, Creedence—"

He cut me off with a sneer. "Oh, yeah, I forgot. You're twenty-eight."

I wound up in the bar later with Rebecca, who told me she was giving Tom a bottle of perfume for his birthday.

"Perfume?"

"Well, you know," she said, "we're going to be spending a lot of time together. I want him to smell nice."

"Ah," I said. "A present for you, then."

Finally, on July 7, the five of us sat around the poker table as the cameras rolled on *Risky Business* for the first time.

It was rugged going at first . . . the first try was a master shot which felt terrible to me and Tom, I know, felt the same way. We then shot it a few other ways but the actors didn't click until the three-shot (Tom, Bronson and me). Everything came together then and it stayed cooking for the rest of the afternoon.

All told, each of us smoked ten cheap cigars apiece. Before lunch, mind you. We were nauseous through a good portion of the day. But Paul and Jon were happy. And believe it or not, by the end of the day, I was feeling pretty good, too.

Six and a half hours later, we shot the brief scene where Joel sends Miles and Glenn away because Lana won't leave his house. And, as we were ahead of schedule, we shot another scene, just with Joel . . . But we're over the hump. My first day in front of a camera is over.

I don't think we got ahead of schedule again after that. If I had any real concerns about my performance thereafter, though, they weren't reflected in the journal. Rebecca, though, was uneasy.

July 9
Talked to Rebecca for quite a while in her dressing room today. She seems to value my opinion quite a bit. She's uneasy about her first day of shooting (yesterday). Paul, it seems, is asking her to deliver her lines at machine-gun speed. Sounds like a terrible idea to me. During our read through the other day, she took her time and was really splendid. She's not getting that time now and it bothers her. If this is true it doesn't surprise me.

She talked with a call girl before she came here. Apparently, this woman talked in real life exactly the way Paul

wants her to talk! Not the same thing, I said. Told her
there was a difference between real-life speed and theatrical
speed. She jumped on that theatrical speed gag. Hope she
uses it. She really is perfect in this role if she's left alone.
(Isn't it wonderful how one day on a movie can turn me
into an expert on film acting?) She told me what Paul had
told her about me in L.A. "We have this guy for Miles
who's never made a movie before. But I wouldn't think
about not using him because he reads the lines the way
I wrote them."

Shera Danese, who played Rebecca's coworker in the film, was a constant source of entertainment during off hours. There were few things I wouldn't do in those days for a laugh, but Shera was tops when it came to general misbehavior. She and I often led the others into adventures they regretted the next day. She was like a cross between Judy Holliday and someone out of *The Sopranos*. Most intriguingly, for me, was discovering she was married to the great actor Peter Falk.

July 17
Peter Falk came to town today to visit Shera but they're
staying in Chicago. Wise move. He wouldn't be able to move
around here without getting mobbed. Interestingly, Bronson
and I were in Chicago today, too, on a secret mission. Love,
it seems, has come to Bronson Pinchot. His Dark Lady of the
Sonnets is Sarah Partridge, who plays the babysitter that
Joel fantasizes about in the film. He has arranged a lunch
with her but insists on my accompanying him to fill in

*any long, awkward pauses during the meal, should any
arise.*

*So the three of us were sitting in a window at Harry's
Café when who should walk by but Shera and Peter.
They didn't see us, but were obviously looking for a place
to eat and wound up walking right into Harry's. Shera
saw us and brought Peter over to introduce him. He was
charming but no matter how many times this happens,
when I meet someone I really admire I am genuinely
speechless . . .*

At dinner after Peter had gone back to California, I admitted I had been terrified to meet him.

"Huh?" Shera said, fork arrested halfway to her mouth.

"Oh, my God, yes! I've been a fan my whole life. I mean, the body of work! The ability to be brilliant as a dramatic actor and also have this phenomenal comic talent . . . I mean, as far as I'm concerned he's one of the best American actors we've got! He's an inspiration!"

"Really?" she said, incredulously. "That's amazing, 'cause to me he's just a pain in the ass."

July 18
*A crisis has arisen. My father called and said he's coming
down in a few days. You realize what this means to the
Louis Armstrong Story?! To paraphrase Ray Charles,
another legendary black musician I wasn't related to, I was
busted. I have five days to figure out how to get out of this.*

*The problem is my father, normally a good-natured soul,
completely disapproves of this little jape so I can expect no
help from that quarter. Now what? After several days of
quiet, during which time I figured the rumors regarding
my being one of Satch's descendants had died down, I was
reminded that these kind of things never go away. Our set
photographer, the only black member of the Chicago crew,
had come on the set the other day, spotted me, grinned and
said, "Heeey, Brother!"*

I did eventually find a moment to explain to Tom and
Rebecca. Rebecca was in the lobby when I took her aside.

"So, you may have heard this rumor that I'm Louis Armstrong's grandson," I said.

The sunglasses came off.

"Yeah," she drawled. "I heard that."

"Well," I said, "it's not true. No relation, really."

"Yeah, I thought it was bullshit at first," she said. "But then
I thought, well, your hair is awfully curly . . ."

I broke it to Tom around the same time. He just stared at
me for a moment and then started giggling uncontrollably.

July 23
*When I got back to the hotel this evening, I headed for the
bar like a stag thirsting for cool waters. Tom, Shera and
Rebecca were drinking in the bar. I joined them for three
bottles of $100.00 Champagne. Peter Sova joined us and
invited everyone up to his room for a party. Peter has been*

*trashing the film in general and Paul Brickman in particular
quite a lot, which I'm trying to not let bother me. Tonight,
though, he was in fine fettle. A great impromptu Bacchanal,
where much ice was thrown and many drinks consumed.
Tom and Rebecca necked for hours, it seemed. Shera and I
necked, too, but it was for their benefit and they didn't
notice, so we stopped.*

*July 30
A six p.m. call. We drove out to do the "what the fuck?"
scene. Tom and I rehearsed it a bit in the afternoon and we
were well prepared. The scene was done in three takes; then
Tom's single and then mine. I was less than ecstatic over mine
but by then it was about two o'clock in the morning so who
knows. Paul and Jon and Tom all seemed happy. Later we
did the end of the car chase ("Porsche. There is no substitute.")
My tag line ("Fuck you.") was put in at the last minute.
Hope it's used. Dawn broke and Tom, Rebecca and I were
driven home. Got back at six. The phone rang. Rebecca.
We talked for over an hour. Then I had a few restless hours
of sleep.*

One of the little mysteries of this diary: after spending twelve
hours on the set together, we come back to the hotel, exhausted,
and Rebecca calls me up and we talk for an hour. About what?
I have no idea. I'm sure at the time I thought I'd remember
forever.

Some few hours later, though, my father arrived. We spent

some time out at the pool, swimming, reading and talking. The Louis Armstrong situation was studiously avoided. As we headed back into the lobby on our way back to the room, we ran into Tom and Rebecca.

"Oh, Tom, Rebecca, this is my father, Bob," I said, introducing them.

"Hi," said Rebecca.

"Hello, Mr. Armstrong," said Tom politely, shaking his hand.

And then my father, straight-faced but in a startlingly effective vocal imitation, roared out, "Hey, Jackson!!! How's it goin', Pops?!"

After a few weeks, I hit a long patch where I wasn't needed. The days became endless and the nights worse. The exhilaration of working long hours on my first film and being thrown into the rambunctious company of my fellow actors wore off quickly with no one around, and a prolonged front of boredom and loneliness set in with unusual severity. The journal reflects this, with page after page filled with maudlin scrawls of self-pity. Judging from this it's apparent that there was a good deal of drinking and drug taking going on, and distressingly, more and more of it alone. Cocaine was, of course, easily available and relatively cheap in Chicago and was supplied round the clock, care of some of the borderline hoodlums we found ourselves associating with. I had too much time on my hands and it seemed like I was spending most of it poisoning myself.

At one point I knew they were shooting the party scene: a huge set piece in the film where the hookers take over Joel's house. Miles Dalby is the only one of Joel's friends who doesn't go, because, as he says, "I don't have to pay for it." So everyone on the film was shooting at that location for days at a time without me. I couldn't stand the loneliness another minute and drove over to the set.

Anyone who's seen the film remembers what it was like: apart from Rebecca and Shera, there were about a dozen gorgeous young women and truckloads of teenagers. It was a rich mixture. I'm not sure when the idea occurred to me but at some point I thought the thing to do would be to dress up in drag, get completely made up and costumed, and then sneak onto the set and try to make an appearance in the film as a hooker.

I went straight to wardrobe and asked if they could help me out. Everyone was running on fumes at that point and this idea struck them as funny as it did me. They started selecting an appropriate hooker outfit while I went into makeup and hair. They went into a kind of gleeful overdrive and within an hour or so I was transformed into a working girl.

Everyone was on their lunch break, but right after everyone was called to the set by Jerry Grandy, our first assistant director, I sashayed over and slipped unnoticed into the dining room set with the rest of the girls. Jerry was well into placing background for the shot when he got to me.

"And, ahhh . . ." He froze for a moment. "You . . . CURTIS!! Out!! What are you . . . get out!!"

The place exploded. Jerry laughed for probably the first time in weeks.

"Give me a chance," I said. "C'mon. Put me in deep background. I don't care! Just give me something to do!" My pleas fell on deaf ears. I was allowed to stay on the set only long enough to pose for a few snaps with the actual actresses and then I was unceremoniously escorted off the set.

But on my way back to base camp, I got the idea that I should be introduced to Tom. It was not uncommon for him to be introduced to potentially generous young women on the set and I had seen for myself the lines outside his hotel room. Tom was still napping after his lunch, but I had the A.D. knock on the door and when he answered, tousled and still half asleep, the A.D. said in an undertone, "Tom, there's someone here who's been begging to be introduced to you. You're not going to be called for a while, so I thought . . ."

Tom brightened right up. It was apparent that as far as cute blondes were concerned, his trailer was Liberty Hall. He gave a sort of an old-world gesture of welcome as I came around the open door and stepped into his trailer. He closed the door and turned to me.

"I thought you were so hot in *Endless Love*," I told him.

And if you can believe it, he threw me out without a word and went back to sleep. I gave him a golden opportunity and he turned me down flat. Sometimes I think I was the only really great piece of ass who didn't get to screw Tom that summer.

August 2
Today was bad. Very bad. We shot the scene at the Drake
Hotel. And I sucked. I just couldn't get control of myself. My
concentration was shot. Tom and I signed autographs for

about twenty minutes afterwards and I was propositioned by two women. (The high point of my day.) But for the first time the editor will have to bail me out. What a disappointment.

August 3
Shot the scene at the Porsche dealership today. It was fun. I feel a lot better today than I did yesterday. (Producer) Jim O'Fallon was very complimentary about my work today—mine and Bronson's especially. I felt encouraged. What the hell is going to happen? Jennifer Brickman (director Paul Brickman's wife) also said I was at the beginning of a brilliant career. Was she just being nice or does she know something I don't know? Is there anything I do know?

I know when the director smiles into his shirt, I'm doing all right.

I know when the producer insults me I'm on the right track.

I know when I get winks and phone numbers hastily scribbled I'm attractive to a woman or two.

I know when I talk with my wife late at night that I want a home.

I know when I talk to old friends that nothing has changed and everything has changed.

I know smoking and drinking is bad for my health.

I know I'm guilty.

I know I get on well with people.

I know that's good for me.
I know I'd rather be in New York.
I know I could be a movie star.
I know I write well when I'm drunk.
I know that's bad for me and I don't care.
And I know knowing that is better than knowing nothing.

This entry makes me smile. I remember Paul's habit of pulling up his shirt collar over his mouth when I made him laugh during a scene. But it amazes me how much of this self-indulgent dreck remains essentially true, even thirty years on. When I talk at night to my wife from a location somewhere, I still know I want a home, and this isn't even the same wife I was talking to in 1982. I'm still guilty.

There are obvious differences, too: I haven't smoked in decades. I don't get drunk anymore. I now know I didn't really write well when I was drunk. I just thought I did. I know the difference between a successful working actor and a "movie star" and I know I will never be the latter. I know a lot more now than I did then. One I would append to my list above:

I know being 28 makes me feel really mature. 28 is far from mature.

August 4
(Director of photography) Peter Sova quit today. This is hot off the presses. I was over at the production office and Peter took me aside to tell me. I was the first actor to be told. I'm

to say nothing to the others because he wants to tell them
personally. That's all for now.

Except it wasn't, really. For one thing, he had been fired. I had been aware of the tensions before this. Peter made no bones about the fact that he thought the way Paul wanted the film to look was "ridiculous." Peter had actually been briefly hospitalized at one point during the shoot. High blood pressure, some said. An ulcer, according to others.

"You know," he had told me one day, "it's a fucking teenage sex comedy. He's shooting it like it's an art film. Bullshit."

"Good luck," he told me the day he left. "You're really good in the film, but he's going to screw it up. You all deserve better."

What we got was Rey Villalobos. Then it turned out he had a scheduling conflict, and he was replaced by Bruce Surtees. So, all told, three D.P.'s on the film. To give an example of how this played out, let's take the sequence that begins inside the Drake Hotel, continues out on the street with Miles, Joel and Lana and the arrival of Guido and goes all the way through the car chase, ending with "Porsche. There is no substitute." The Drake interior was shot by Sova. The scene on the street by Villalobos. The chase itself by Villalobos and Surtees on different nights. And the final Porsche exchange by Sova.

It says something about Paul Brickman's relentless vision that *Risky Business* looks as gorgeous—and consistent—as it does. No movie of its type during the 1980s looked anything like it. Unique. Funny, erotic, dramatic, imaginatively scored, well cast and framed and shot beautifully.

Just like an art film.

August 5
It's been a long road. Today it came to me that I have a week
or two left here and then I'll be gone and all of this will be
history. Oddly, this depresses me. As miserable as I've been—
the loneliness, the late night drunks alone, the pressure, the
tensions, the politics—I don't want it to end now.

Everyone's been swell. I know I've bitched a bit about
Tom and all that, but in the long run he was great to work
with. I spoke to Avnet about seeing some of the dailies before I
leave and to my surprise he's willing to show them to me
now. Not a chance, I told him. When I'm done and there's
nothing for it, fine. Not a second before. What a learning
experience.

And the biggest lesson I've learned is I don't want to make
movies for a living—ever.

We shot the wrestling scene tonight. As at the Drake
(which I heard came out well, despite my reservations) some of
it was improvised. An interesting side note: As soon as we
started rehearsing the scene, Tom became incredibly competitive
with me in a way he never has before. And it was because
we were doing something physical. He was a wrestler in
high school and wanted to look better. Paul had to keep him
on a tight rein.

August 8
Tom and Rebecca are having it off in a grand style. In my
naiveté I thought it wasn't all that serious, but last night
Shera and I interrupted them and threw ice all over the
bed.

We had, the four of us, a party in the bar tonight, during which we danced and stripped. It was the best floorshow in that bar since I've been there . . .

August 9
An all-nighter at the Drake. Wound up at dawn with two shots not complete, which means I'll be here longer than I thought. Tonight we'll shoot the rest of the interior Porsche scenes during the chase. I hope to God we finish those. Today was also our first day with Rey (Villalobos) behind the camera.

Everything was very tense but Tom, Joe (Pantoliano), Rebecca and I rose above it. I felt the scene went well.

I got the word today that I will be here pretty much for the duration of the filming. I'm going to insist that I be allowed to go back to New York to meet with Forman. I've been assured that won't be a problem.

Note: Milos Forman pops up in the story again at this point. Before I had left New York to do *Risky Business* I had read for the role of Mozart in Forman's upcoming film version of Peter Shaffer's play *Amadeus*. I had read for Shaffer before for the Broadway production and had not gotten the part. I considered the film even a longer shot. But I had been told that Forman had liked the audition and wanted to read me himself, in his apartment on Central Park South. I did get back for it and it was a thrill. Just the two of us, back and forth, him reading all the other parts. An unforgettable experience. Later I was brought in to screen-test with Christine Ebersole and others. Tom Hulce, of course, was eventually cast in the role.

*We shot some of the Porsche interiors tonight—the start of
the chase scene. Joel and Lana's singles first, with Rey
(Villalobos) and me squeezed in the back and (camera
operators) Peter and George riding outside the car wearing
crash helmets. Then, just as dawn broke, the front seat was
pulled and replaced with George and the camera. Paul
Brickman donned Tom's jacket and sat in the driver's seat,
holding the script and reading Tom's and Rebecca's lines.
So for my close-ups in the scene, the two other actors were
back in the honey-wagon.*

*As it happens, because of the daylight and the Porsche's
rapidly deteriorating shocks, the whole thing will probably
have to be re-shot anyway. The tension on the set is
terrific. Brickman and Villalobos talk between clenched
teeth.*

August 12
*My first day off in a week of night shoots. I'm pooped and
lethargic. Can't get anything done at all. Just slept till three,
ate in my room and watched television. Was still so wound
up, didn't get to sleep until four. Last night shot more
Porsche chase scenes and the bank vault scene in Ravinia.
That leaves one last shot for me. Unfortunately, it's an
exterior (outside the Drake) and the current schedule is to
shoot on the stage for the next 9 days. They are apparently
trying to catch up a bit, since the stage shoots seem to move
faster than the locations. But from what I've seen, the new
crew is just as slow inside as they are out. With Sova, the
set-ups may have taken five hours, but once they were set,*

they were set. Now they take five hours and then adjust for another hour. Sometimes, dare I say it, their lassitude seems almost deliberate. This may just be paranoia setting in. Kind of like the feeling that Rey Villalobos hates us.

August 13

Spent my last day on the set today (as it turned out, it was not). We shot Joel's side of the phone conversation about Jackie. Tom wanted me to be there to read my lines for him, a fact that seemed to irritate Jon Avnet quite a bit. ("An actor talks into a phone! Easiest thing in the world! What if we told Tom that Curtis is dead and can't do the scene . . ."). I wore a headset and dashed around in front or behind the Steadicam. It helped Tom a lot as he seemed to be having some trouble and he was so gracious and appreciative afterward, I couldn't believe it.

August 26

Today they shot the first sex scenes. They threw everyone off the set, save George (Kohut, camera operator) and Paul. I spoke to Rebecca at lunch and she said she wasn't uncomfortable about it at all. The thing is, someone had set up a ladder on the outside of the set and from that vantage point, we could watch the action quite clearly. Bronson and Shera took advantage of this and watched the whole thing, for the better part of two hours. Jerry Grandy caught them though and threw them out, much to Bronson's shame. Shera, bless her, didn't give a shit.

August 27
Paul Brickman has invited Bronson, Shera and me to his
house for drinks tonight. We'll be leaving soon and the
evening will be fraught with interest. Bronson is afraid that
Tom and Rebecca found out about his and Shera's surveillance
mission of the set yesterday because T and R have been even
ruder to Bronson today than they usually are.

And on that note, the journal ends. No description of my last day on set, whether there was a party or how I bid farewell to my coworkers. Whatever day it was that I finished shooting, I was on the plane the following day back to New York and into the long, long period of waiting.

Paul had had a lot of support from David Geffen in the making and shooting of *Risky Business*. He had gotten some notes from Warner Bros. about how he needed to include more sex. They were particularly adamant that the party scene needed a lot more sex. Here was this long sequence, packed with hookers and horny high school boys, and not a single bare breast was revealed. Brickman ignored them. Just like he ignored the executive at Geffen's company who insisted that Paul fire Joe Pantoliano, whose performance as Guido the Killer Pimp is one of the standouts in the film. In general, though, by the time the movie was wrapped, everyone was feeling that they had accomplished what they'd set out to do. There was still cutting and scoring to do, but Paul felt pleased and vindicated.

"You can call off your dogs," Paul joked to studio executives after a highly successful test screening.

They intended to do no such thing. Brickman was completely blindsided by the request, which quickly became a demand, that he scrap the end of the film and reshoot scenes that would make it less of a "downer." Make it more upbeat. More "teen movie." The original ending—subsequently issued as an extra on the Blu-ray DVD release—was darker, but truer to Brickman's concept from the beginning: Greed has consequences. People can be hurt.

"Warner's never really knew what to make of it, through the whole process," Brickman told me. "I don't think anyone could have understood what I was trying to do. I wouldn't, if I were sitting there. How could they intuit off the page what I had in mind? Then they saw the finished film and they still didn't get it. And their marketing campaign looked like they were trying to sell *Porky's*! That was another fight, one fight after the next. They had a cartoon character of Tom, winking, in bed with girls in bikinis all around him and money raining down. That was the poster the studio wanted to use. That was my big fight. I was, like, throwing posters across the room. Not to mention the ending. Geffen was going to fire me if I didn't reshoot the ending. They were talking to some television director about doing it. I had refused to do it, but finally, in order to protect 90 percent I had to sacrifice 10 percent. Which was really hard for me."

Paul brought Tom and Rebecca back after months of bitter dispute and reshot the ending. He completed the mix for Tangerine Dream's haunting score, delivered the finished film and didn't watch it again for thirty years. The battle over the ending didn't end with the release of the film. Warner's and Geffen canceled the cast and crew screening out of sheer vindictiveness and there was no premiere. To this day, Geffen has refused to release a director's cut DVD.

Meanwhile, as the *Risky Business* post-production wars raged on, Bronson and I were wandering around New York, jobless but undaunted, taking turns convincing each other that we were on the verge of great things. A letter I received from him during that period sums it up as only a real nerd could, and Bronnie was nothing if not a real nerd:

"You know," he wrote, "how Tolkien refers (in his ages-long chronology of Middle Earth) to the period of his trilogy as the "great years"? Well, I think we're on the brink of one of our great years. Now I know how incredibly pious people feel, preparing themselves for the Kingdom—because I can only keep my sanity by preparing myself for the opening of *Risky Business*, by keeping myself pure and so on. . . . But then again it might open and disappear again without anything happening, and I'll transfer my Godot to some other event. I'm not particular."

Then one day *Superman 3* opened and we heard that there was a trailer for *Risky Business* showing before the movie *and*—we were both in the trailer! We were both thrilled at the prospect of seeing ourselves, even briefly, on the big screen, but we also didn't feel we should pay to see *Superman 3* when we were just going to stay in the theater long enough to see our trailer. I suggested Bronson call the manager of the theater and explain our situation and see if we could get a couple of passes.

This magical man arranged for passes for us and Bronson and I finally saw ourselves on the big screen.

Bronson, who was raised right, wrote a thank-you note to

the manager, a copy of which I have before me. There's no way I could not include it.

July 1st, 1983
To The Manager
Dear Sir,

Sorry I don't know your name, I forgot to ask when I spoke to you a few days ago. But thank you very much for leaving the two passes to see the preview for "Risky Business." My friend Curtis gave me the idea to call you. It was our first film. We made it last summer and we've been waiting around for another job ever since. He's the one with the gravelly voice and the long black hair that you see at the beginning of the preview, and I'm the one with the big nose and the big bald forehead that you see in the middle, opening the door for the ladies. They used real playboy bunnies to play those girls. They walked around in lingerie the whole time we were shooting and sat behind a big velvet curtain and took coke. I never saw them in street clothes.

Thank you again, and if I can ever return the favor, let me know.

Yours truly,
Bronson Pinchot

When the movie finally opened the following summer, Bronson and I went to see the very first screening—a 1:00 p.m. matinee at a Times Square theater where people were screaming back at the screen and a guy walked up and down the aisle with a flashlight to dissuade the old guys from whacking off during the movie.

Shortly before the film's opening Tom and Rebecca came through New York and invited Bronson and me to dinner with them at their suite at the Sherry-Netherland Hotel. I recall it as a strangely formal occasion; we dined on starched white tablecloths and talked about the vagaries of show business, and there was certainly no drunken striptease at 2:00 a.m. to top it off. The Sherry-Netherland felt a long way from the Lincolnwood Hyatt, that's for sure. That was the last time I saw or spoke to Tom. The next time I saw Rebecca, we were seated together at Bruce Willis's and Demi Moore's wedding, when *Risky Business* seemed like something that had happened a lifetime ago.

The gap between filming *Risky Business* and my next film job seemed to stretch out before me like a trackless desert. But by the time it opened in the summer of 1983, I had been back at work onstage. There had been an extraordinary production of Bertolt Brecht's *Life of Galileo* at the Pittsburgh Public Theatre; and in town I'd done Romulus Linney's *El Hermano* at Curt Dempster's Ensemble Studio Theatre. Then I returned to Roadside Attractions, now moved to downtown Detroit from Ann Arbor and renamed the Attic Theatre, to do Amlin Gray's great two-hander *How I Got That Story*. This production happened to coincide with the release of *Risky Business* that August. It was like a dream: returning to my hometown to appear at a theater I had cofounded, while my first film was opening.

But by the winter of 1983–84, the theater work had dried up

and I seemed to be stuck in limbo. I had some film auditions after *Risky Business* opened but none of them panned out. Just when it began to feel like *Risky Business* really had been a fluke, another picture finally came along and it turned out to have been worth the wait. It was *Revenge of the Nerds*.

REVENGE OF THE NERDS

TUCSON, 1984

But before I talk about *Revenge of the Nerds*, I'd like to say a few words about the man who made all this possible. He's the one to whom I owe most of my career in film. This is the Man, the Founder of the Feast. The nerd everyone loves but no one wants to shake hands with. I'm talking about Dudley "Booger" Dawson.

Now, Booger looms large in my legend so I want to get something clear before we go any further:

I hated him on sight.

Actually, that's not true, because the first time I read the script for *Revenge of the Nerds*, I understood that I was reading for the role of Gilbert Lowe, the lovely lead role eventually played with great sensitivity and humor by Anthony Edwards. So, strictly speaking, I paid scant attention to the insignificant, unattractive role of Booger, except to think how lucky I was that I'd never be associated with a character like that.

The truth is the role of Booger was so small that there was nothing to audition *with*, which is why Susan Arnold, the casting director, had me read the altogether meatier role of Gilbert.

Even so, when the script for *Nerds* arrived I was unimpressed. *Revenge of the Nerds* would never have been my first choice as a follow-up to *Risky Business*. Which goes to show how an experience like *Risky Business* can change a person. I had to be dragged kicking and screaming to do that movie because movies "weren't theater" and now I was complaining about *Revenge of the Nerds* because it wasn't a worthy follow-up!

My friend Bronson Pinchot also auditioned for *Revenge of the Nerds*. At the time we first read for it, we talked regularly about the film, particularly about how unenthusiastic we both were about doing it at all.

Then came the callbacks and Bronson was told he was out of the running.

I could barely contain my outrage. "How can they not call you back? What's the matter with these people?! Well, you know what? You are well out of it! It's a stupid movie anyway!" I yelled.

Then I got my call.

It was during this phone call from my agent that I discovered that I was not being considered for Gilbert. The two leads had already been cast: Robert Carradine as Lewis and Anthony Edwards as Gilbert. "That," said my agent, "is the bad news. The good news is they really love you and they really want you in the picture!"

"Okay," I said, warily.

"They want to offer you a different role! I'll tell them you're interested and they'll come back with the offer!"

"But what's the role?"

There was a fraction of a second's hesitation.

"You'd definitely be playing another nerd," my agent said reassuringly. "They told me it is definitely a nerd. Just not that particular nerd."

I sat there for a moment, reflecting. As she said, the good news was I had a job. But now that I came to think about it, which of the other nerds could they possibly be talking about? Obviously it's not Lamar. It couldn't be Takashi. I'm too old for Wormser. That leaves Poindexter . . . or Booger.

"Okay," I said, "here's the deal. If they offer me Poindexter, I'll do it. But if they offer me Booger, forget it."

"Really? You sure?"

"Yes, I'm sure," I snapped. "Forget it! It's a terrible part! There is nothing there! NOTHING!! I mean, you've read this script!!" (I was still new enough to the business to think agents actually read scripts.) "All the guy does is pick his nose and belch. No! I won't do it! Poindexter yes, Booger NO!"

No sooner had the agent rung off than I was back on the phone to Bronson. Now it was his turn to be outraged. He had just lost a part. I had lost a part and it was now possible that I was going to be offered something disgusting as a consolation prize.

"Curtie," Bronson screamed, "it's inhuman! It's humiliating!! They can't offer you that!! You're a cultured individual!!"

"Bronnie," I said, and my voice was even and strangely calm, "if they offer me that part, I'm going to say no."

"Really?" gasped Bronson. It would never have occurred to him to turn down anything. Actually, it hadn't occurred to me until now.

"I'm not kidding! Not after *Risky Business*, not this!! I don't care what my agent says. I don't care what anybody says! They can't offer me enough money to embarrass myself this way. I'm a classically trained actor! I'm not going to pick my nose in front of millions of people. It's NO!"

Moments later, my agent called back.

"Well, they offered you Booger. What should I tell them?"

"Okay. I'll take it."

Actors.

For those who love *Revenge of the Nerds* and take for granted the impact it had on popular culture today, it's important to remember how close this film came to never being made at all.

In the early 1980s, 20th Century Fox—the studio producing the film—was in virtual shambles. It was not the first time that a combination of gross mismanagement, oversized egos and a general sense of complacency (after spending years living off *Star Wars* fat) had led to a studio's near-implosion and it wouldn't be the last.

But in 1984, all hell was breaking loose and *Revenge of the Nerds*, a modestly budgeted little teen sex comedy, was caught in the crossfire.

After hemorrhaging profits, the studio was acquired by mega-investors Marvin Davis and Marc Rich. The studio president, Sherry Lansing, under whose administration *Nerds* had been green-lit, bolted soon after. Having suffered a string of flops,

20th was in need of a hit . . . and the new regime was pretty certain *Nerds* wasn't it. Assigned a budget of $8 million, it was clear they weren't expecting much. As the studio's new head of production, Joe Wizan was in charge of upcoming productions and was working with *Nerds* executive producers Ted Field, Peter Samuelson and David Obst to find a director. And Wizan knew just the right guy.

Enter Jeff Kanew.

Kanew had been involved in the movie business since the sixties, when he had begun his career shooting soft porn and low-budget features. He had gradually moved into cutting trailers and became highly successful at it: trailers for *One Flew Over the Cuckoo's Nest*, *Rocky*, *Annie Hall*, *Jeremiah Johnson* and many others were cut by him. Eventually he moved into editing, which included cutting Robert Redford's Academy Award–winning film *Ordinary People*.

Kanew had directed two features with Joe Wizan producing: *Unnatural Enemies* and *Eddie Macon's Run*. Both films were serious dramas, and neither well received. Kanew was feeling that his directing days were over when Wizan contacted him with news. Wizan was now in a position to throw something Jeff's way. He offered him three scripts to choose from: *Bachelor Party*, *Gimme an "F"* (which took place at cheerleader camp) and *Revenge of the Nerds*.

Any of these films would be a step down after *Ordinary People*—especially a movie about nerds. But a step up from porn—or so he thought. He was surprised to find that as silly as it was, there was something in the script that spoke to him.

"I related to it," he told me in a retrospective interview in 2015. "These guys going to college, being put down, picked on . . . that was me."

He told Wizan that he wanted to direct *Revenge of the Nerds*, but there was a problem.

The executive producers had seen *Eddie Macon's Run* and hated it. They didn't even want to take a meeting with Kanew, but Wizan forced them.

"So how'd it go?" Wizan asked, calling Kanew after the meeting.

"Okay, I guess," said Kanew. "Meeting went on a long time."

"Yeah, but you screwed up. You told them *Risky Business* was a better movie than *Animal House*."

"*Risky Business is* a better movie than *Animal House*," Kanew said.

"Yeah, maybe, but *Animal House* was a big hit . . . so, look, what kind of a movie do you want to make from this script?"

"Well," Kanew said, "I want to make the very best movie I can."

"Yeah," said Wizan, pointedly, "and what kind of a movie are you going to make of this script?"

"Look, Joe, what are you trying to get me to say, here? '*Animal House*, sir!'?"

Wizan said, "That'd be good."

"Here's the thing," said Kanew. "What made *Risky Business* a great movie is that it was real. It was funny, it was serious and it wasn't a cartoon. The trouble with this *Nerds* thing is it could turn into a cartoon. And I don't want to make a cartoon."

"Jeff? What kind of a movie are you going to make out of *Revenge of the Nerds?*"

"Okay, Joe," said Kanew. "Tell you what. How about I say I'll make a movie I'd be ashamed to put my name on?"

"You got the job!"

By the time we all descended on Tucson, Arizona, Jeff had done his job well. Pre-production had gone easily and all the key positions on the crew were filled with talented and sympathetic people, including cinematographer King Baggot and casting director Susan Arnold. Kanew and Arnold had cast the nerds, Alpha Betas and all the other supporting roles flawlessly. Things were flowing. He had hired writers Jeff Buhai and Steve Zacharias to reshape the original script by Tim Metcalfe and Miguel Tejada-Flores with generous input from the actors.

This process turned out to be unique in my experience. At the time, I had little to compare it to. On *Risky Business* we had a week or so before filming to do read-throughs, play a lot of poker and basically get everyone comfortable. *Revenge of the Nerds* was a different matter entirely. Kanew made it clear from the very beginning that he welcomed—expected even—the actors to be part of the process. This didn't mean just showing up on the day with our lines learned. In many respects, it meant tearing the whole script up and starting over again.

Our work began with understanding who our characters were from the ground up. In the case of Tim Busfield, Brian

Tochi and me, this proved a little more difficult because in the beginning there was so little of our characters in the script. We worked closely with Eddie Marks, our costume designer (he had a great vision about how the nerds would look), but to get deeper into who the characters were, beyond the cartoon depictions on the page, we had to make stuff up.

For a week, we sat around the pool, talking and going through the script, trying to find character motives and relationships where, in many cases, none existed. Periodically, one of us would be called into a room with the writers, producers and Kanew. Everyone would start throwing out thoughts, character traits, comic bits, discussing, sometimes arguing, gradually coming up with a kind of actual arc for these characters, which I never would've believed possible. The actor would leave, return to the pool and another actor would go in and the procedure would start again.

Tim Busfield recalled in 2016: "I remember us coagulating as a group. There are so many difficulties that can occur when you're forming an ensemble and I remember at that time the ensemble just came together really quickly. There was no 'NO' on anything, there was no sense of, 'Well, you can't do that . . .' Everybody just slouched into these characters that Kanew had cast. We didn't have any idea what we'd be like together but he did. He chose us rhythmically right. It was just a really great professional environment in the rehearsal spaces in Tucson."

I had started my character work by going through the script marking scenes in which Booger appeared and then, basically, asking that he be taken out. I was ruthless, and according to the notebook I kept at the time, I seemed determined to make this character as invisible as possible. My loathing at having to follow the classy *Risky Business* with this low-rent nonsense was such that I seemed to be trying to eliminate the character entirely.

Among my notes for the writers? "Cut my first line," I told them. "In the gym, taking roll-call, Dean Ulich calls out, 'Dawson, Dudley?' and then I say, 'Call me Booger?' Let's cut that line."

"But . . . why?" asked screenwriter Jeff Buhai. It was a fair question.

Here's what I was thinking: If I didn't self-identify as "Booger," all the other characters would just call me Dudley for the rest of the film. I clearly wanted to avoid nonsense like the following exchange: As Dudley reclines on his cot in the gymnasium, Takashi, in the cot next to him, says, "'Scuse prease, why do they call you Booger?"

"I don't know," Booger replies, digging around with his forefinger in his nose. You see? If nobody called me Booger, then all the nose-picking scenes could disappear, too. There was an insane logic to this. It may have been a pride thing: What would my teachers at the Academy think about me playing a character who answered to the name "Booger"? Whatever my prospects as a real actor may have been, I wouldn't be living up to them in a role like this. I was actually fighting to have a large chunk of my already microscopic role cut, because I didn't want to pick my nose, belch and pop a pimple on screen. (They ceded that one). But it's mind-boggling to me now that I actually tried to cut the line "Call me Booger."

Steve and Jeff tried to reassure me of Booger's value by explaining he was based on a real person they had known in college.

"Yeah?" I said, uncertainly. "So you're saying he's, like, a historical character?"

"Yeah!" the guys exclaimed.

"Like Winston Churchill?" I hazarded.

"Well, no," conceded Steve. "He was just a guy we knew in college. His name wasn't Booger, obviously, but everyone called him that."

"Because," Jeff interjected, "he would drive around in this pickup truck and under the front seat he kept this cardboard box. And inside the box he kept his collection of boogers!"

The room broke up. I was feeling a little queasy.

"A collection of boogers?" I said, when the laughter settled down. "Were these boogers his or other people's?"

Steve looked at me like I was crazy.

"Well, his, obviously!!" he said. "Who'd collect other people's boogers? Anyway, he'd just drive around in his truck picking his nose. He was, like, addicted to nose picking. Every time he'd pull one out, it went into the box."

"Uh huh . . ."

"Whenever we met new people we'd say, 'Hey, Booger, show 'em your collection.' He always would."

"Okay," I said, wanting to get this whole episode behind me as quickly as possible, "but this is not something we're doing in the movie, right? The box of boogers?"

No, no, everyone said. "Unless," said Steve, "you want to work it in . . . ?"

I assured him I was fine without it and we moved on with more attempts at deconstruction on my part.

I had waded into that script, red pen in hand, with a kind of suicidal abandon. Next, I wanted to cut the belching contest with Ogre (Don Gibb): one of the most famous scenes in the movie. Alan Arkin, one of the best actors on the planet, told me a couple of years later it was his *favorite* scene in the movie. But it wasn't mine. I wanted it cut.

Thankfully, despite my best efforts, I lost most of these battles. And Booger, miraculously and mercifully, came to life.

Contributing to Booger's development, and a more productive part of my preparation, was my character biography.

This was something that was a basic part of our training at the Academy. Our instructors had a strong belief that actors should write their own personal biography of every character they played, no matter how small. In fact, the theory went, the smaller the role, the more important the biography was. For the actor, the biography would fill in all the background of your character that the playwright hadn't thought worth putting in. The audience would never know, for example, that Rodey, a lineless part in Chekov's *Three Sisters* that I had played at the Academy, was a young man struggling to conceal his progressive tuberculosis. Or that he had taken an axe handle to his violently abusive father for beating his mother in the barn back in St. Petersburg. The important thing, our teachers told us, was that *we* knew it. It would inform and deepen our performance, even if we had no lines at all.

So, according to my journal during that first week of rehearsal, this was my take on the psychology of Dudley Dawson:

Dudley Dawson comes from a good, middle-class home. But from the sixth grade has been persecuted because of his height and the fact that he looked like a girl. The hurt and anger have built up through high school till he has taken refuge in cynicism, sloppy dress and obnoxious behavior. The sexual slurs come from the fact that he is frustrated and beautiful girls are never attracted to him. He's horny but never shows or admits it. He's quick, well-read and educated but he doesn't show that either, because to be bookish is to be nerd-like and he doesn't consider himself a nerd, though books have been his other refuge.

He is with the nerds because they never question him or make demands of him. They accept him. Never do they tell him to clean his room or bathe or comb his hair. His sloppy dress, manners and unshaven face are attempts to show he is male. He maintains his fuck-all attitude till the end. But as the nerds are attacked, he cares deeply. Much of his attitude can be dropped then.

At the time, this thoughtful reflection on the personal history and motivations of a misogynistic nose-picker pleased me, I think. As grounding for a portrayal that will follow me to the grave, it would be hard to improve upon it. What I didn't realize until I rediscovered the journal some thirty years later was that this was not Booger's biography, but Curtis's autobiography. I didn't know it as I was doing it, but Booger—my creation, this nerd monster who didn't even know he was a nerd—was I.

One of the things that made this film special was that *Nerds* was a sincerely collaborative process. Once we realized we were all participants responsible for its creation, everything changed. From that point onward, any reluctance we may have felt about offering suggestions vanished like breath off a razor. All of the Takashi/Booger scenes were built upon a poker-playing improv, done just minutes before the first take and Larry B. Scott's nerd rap at the talent show was partially written and choreographed by him. Busfield became a constant font of comic inventive suggestions, for both his character and everyone else's. Edwards's and Michelle Meyrink's gorgeous scene at the Tri Lamb party when they realize they share the same eyeglass prescription, Booger's odd encounter with the man in the mail slot (actually producer Peter Macgregor-Scott) and even the final speeches of Lewis and Gilbert at the pep rally were either created entirely by the actors or improved beyond measure from the scripted versions.

The core and emotional center of the film were the characters played by Robert Carradine and Anthony Edwards, as Lewis and Gilbert. Anthony was a relative newcomer to the business but Robert had over a decade's worth of moviemaking behind him. This proved to be something of a double-edged sword.

Robert Carradine carried the weight of the Carradine dynasty on his shoulders and, in some ways, still does to this day. His father, John Carradine, had been a legendary film actor going back decades to the early days of talkies. He was a classically trained stage actor who brought much of the power and charisma of the stage onto the silver screen. By the forties, John Carradine had become best known for his work in Universal's second horror film cycle, playing Dracula several times in the studio's programmers, but he still made his mark in A pictures like *Captains Courageous* (Bobby's favorite) and *Grapes of Wrath* (mine). He had continued to work in horror films, of sadly diminishing quality, into the fifties and sixties, while touring his Shakespeare one-man show, which was his true love. Even into the seventies he was still working, memorably in Woody Allen's *Everything You Always Wanted to Know About Sex (but were afraid to ask)*.

Bobby had two older brothers who had followed John into the family business, David and Keith. Robert was the baby, but by 1969 he had made his film debut as one of the title characters in *The Cowboys*, starring John Wayne. As David's and Keith's careers started to take off in the seventies and eighties, so did Bobby's, but in supporting roles: memorably in *Coming Home*, *The Big Red One* and, with his brothers, in *The Long Riders*.

Still, as I told him in a conversation in 2016, he was a part of the Carradine dynasty.

"Yeah," Bobby replied, quietly. "Whether I liked it or not."

"In 1980," Bobby told me, "I had three or four motorcycles, half a dozen guitars. I was in two of the four American entries at the Cannes Film Festival that year. I was on the cover of Italian *Vogue*. I was hotter than shit. I was Bobby Carradine. One of the Princes of Hollywood, as far as I was concerned. So I got the script of *Revenge of the Nerds* and just the title was a turnoff: 'I'm not a fucking nerd! I hate nerds!' But my agent said, 'Look, it is a major studio movie. You should go.' So I met Jeff Kanew. He wanted me to read for it but I refused. The meeting was very stilted, I couldn't wait to get out of there and he couldn't wait to get me out of there.

"But they wanted me to come back. I figured, fuck it, I'll go for it. I had long hair at the time, so I went to a barbershop in North Hollywood and got a regular boy's haircut. Then I go to an eyeglass place and I'm looking around at all these frames on the shelves, it was insane, they were all, like, fifteen-hundred-dollar frames. The guy comes up to me and asks what I'd like.

"'Well, not this,'" I told him. I said I was trying out for a movie and the part I was doing was—and I kind of looked around and lowered my voice—'a nerd.'

"'Oh,' he says, 'I got just what you're looking for.' He goes into the back and brings out a shoebox, blew the dust off the top, literally, reaches into the box and takes out the glasses I wore in the movie.

"So, I go to meet Jeff. And I'm kind of regaling him with stories about my father, it's going great. Then they want me to read and I *really* didn't want to read. The reading was subpar. But I got the part anyway, because I looked like that. I looked like Lewis."

But with all his apparent confidence and swagger, one thing Robert Carradine had never done was open a film. Now he was going to and he wasn't sure he could carry it off. Bobby Carradine was suffering from a serious bout of insecurity.

"I was sweating bullets," Bobby told me. "I knew the whole thing was resting on my shoulders. I couldn't figure out why they didn't want Eddie Desey."

Eddie Desey was the classic nerd character actor of the day, and indeed had been Jeff Kanew's first choice for the part of Lewis. Bobby's inability to read for the part had worried Kanew, but the studio had been insisting on Carradine. Knowing under the circumstances he needed to pick his fights, Kanew agreed.

But during the first couple days of shooting, wracked with an almost crippling self-doubt, Bobby had convinced himself he was going to be fired and be replaced by Eddie Desey. He exiled himself from viewing the dailies.

Unlike the dailies screenings for *Risky Business*, everyone was welcome at these viewings and everyone jumped at the opportunity, except Bobby. After the second night's dailies, Jeff Kanew had left the screening room at the motel and was headed back to his room, when Carradine jumped out of the bushes.

"Jesus Christ!" Jeff exclaimed. "Bobby, what's the matter with you, man, you scared the shit out of me!"

Bobby was trembling. "Am I okay?" he asked. "Am I doing okay?"

"Of course," Jeff reassured him and not for the first time.

"They're not going to fire me?" Bobby said.

Jeff almost laughed. "They're not going to fire you. You're doing great. Just come to the dailies, believe me, you'll feel a lot better."

Kanew's constant reassurance and a few days of Bobby watching his dailies solved the problem. He had owned this role from the first frame. He had only to believe it.

Gradually, the film took shape and as it did, everyone's confidence rose. The atmosphere in dailies felt almost celebratory. All of us began to look at *Revenge of the Nerds* a little differently. We had come to Tucson prepared to do a stupid sex comedy. Well, it might still be a stupid sex comedy, but now it was *our* stupid sex comedy. *Revenge of the Nerds* wound up becoming a testament to what happens when the hard work, talent and determination of actors, writers, producers, director and crew are brought to bear on a project that, on the face of it, didn't really seem worth the bother. Everyone involved with this picture just seemed determined to make it a better film than it had any right to be. Somehow, it became worthy.

The first day of filming, technically a "pre-production" day, was the first sequence in the film—the introduction of Lewis and Gilbert and the car ride with Lewis's father (James Cromwell) to Adams College. That continued into the second day, but the third day of shooting, January 31, 1984, was the first day with the whole cast, as the nerds were thrown out of their freshman dorms. For the next six weeks, we worked on a film that would wind up being a kind of Urtext of modern nerd culture. It would've been inconceivable to imagine that, for at least Robert and me, this would be a life-altering event.

Our professional bond of this now shared investment manifested itself into a brotherhood. We became a community that worked together, so it was only natural for us to play together as well. Or maybe I'm giving us too much credit or reason, because we didn't need to love each other to want to get high together. It was just a perk.

Movie locations in the 1980s were notoriously rife with sex, drugs and overindulgence in general, and *Revenge of the Nerds* was no different. Tim Busfield told me, "We were still part of the old school, that golden era, that 'Animal House' period. You know, even Paul Newman would be drinking a case of beer a day; the spirit was just conducive to that, it was no big deal. You partied and everybody turned the other way."

It was, in fact, the most gleefully debauched set I've ever been on. It actually seems incredible that any work got done at all. From the moment wrap was called, everyone would descend on Scordato's, Greasy Tony's or one of our other watering holes. Then, after an hour or four, in an overheated swarm, back we went to the hotel: a mob of horny, inebriated animals trying to fit as much misbehavior in as possible before set call the next morning.

As Tim recalled: "We were in our twenties and we liked to party. When we were finished with work, we got to it. Somehow we were going to make our way to one of about three hotel rooms. Even before we started shooting we'd established where the pot room was, where the coke room was . . ."

In 2015, I asked Brian Tochi, a veteran of many similar unhinged productions during that decade, where he thought *Nerds* stood in the rankings of movie set excess.

"Actually," he said, "pretty near the top."

For the men on that crew, Tucson that summer was like Tahiti had been for the crew of the H.M.S. *Bounty*, with regular shuttles of eager young women from the University of Arizona going to and from the camera crew's rooms. An apparently endless flow of weed and cocaine arrived daily, care of one of the well-connected fraternities on campus. (There was a delicious irony in the fact that a fraternal organization that would never have accepted any of us as members was happy to supply us with drugs.) Whether it was the heat, the unstable chemistry of so many young men and women in heady proximity for so long, or whether a residual whiff of the lawless Old West still pervaded the place, the memory of that summer in Tucson remains suffused with danger, yearning and nostalgia. It does for me anyway.

If there was an epicenter of the madness, at least in those early days, it was in actor John Goodman's room. Though sober now for many years, in those days he was the Lord of Misrule. Even in his days as a young actor in New York, his reputation as a man of appetites preceded him. He arrived in Tucson like a modern-day buck of the Regency, exuding an aura of intemperance and raffish bonhomie. His consumption of alcohol, while remaining upright and articulate, had to be seen to be believed. By the time the rest of us were ready to indulge John had already started, often accompanied by Treat Williams (who was also staying at our the hotel while shooting an action picture called *Flashpoint* with Kris Kristofferson). Treat had no one to party with on his film—or at least no one who could keep up with him—so he usually wound up with us. But we were all pikers compared to Goodman. No one ever saw him go to bed.

One morning, when I had an early call and John, thankfully, didn't, I emerged into the courtyard of the hotel to find Goodman's furniture in the swimming pool. The details of that particular blowout remain shrouded in gaudy speculation and rumor but there was one memorable gathering I attended that became the stuff of legend.

A group of the usual suspects were gathered in John's room: Williams, Busfield, Tochi, Larry B. and me. There were also various other young fellows present, locals, who were unknown to me but thanks to whose largess, joints were being passed and there was even a bit of "rocket fuel" for anyone who fancied some. Goodman, who was about three-quarters of the way through a bottle of vodka, looked on the rest of us junior imbibers with a sleepy benignity. One of our nameless visitors had availed himself of a guitar and was wailing on it, tunelessly but with terrific enthusiasm, trying to get everyone to join him in a sing along to the Stones' *You Can't Always Get What You Want*. His friend, meanwhile, got his blow and razor out, but was looking around helplessly. The room was a complete shambles and there was no clean surface to cut lines.

Laughing, he said, "Jesus, what do we cut it on?"

"I'll get you something to cut it on," rumbled Goodman.

He leapt up onto his bed and grabbed hold of the painting hanging above it with both hands. It was one of those dreadful things you see in all hotels, of stallions splashing through a river, or something. John yanked at the picture. It didn't budge. John pulled harder. It was just a lousy, cheaply framed piece of crap, but clearly the Hilton management thought highly of it. It was clamped to the wall with hoops of steel.

"Um, John . . ." I said. "I think that's bolted to the wall."

"Fuck that shit," John snapped. Face reddening, muscles bulging, John pulled at the picture and pulled and pulled, emitting a growl that became a howl of frustration. I realize now I was getting my first glimpse of Walter Sobchak.

Suddenly, with an explosion, the painting burst loose from the wall in a shower of plaster dust and cement. Goodman flew backward off the bed onto the floor, the painting still clenched in his hands. He crashed on his back, cursing, but scrambled back on his feet and triumphantly tossed the picture face up on his bed.

"Now you've got something to cut it on!" he boomed.

We learned later that two of our mysterious party guests, whom everyone thought were friends of someone else, turned out to be criminals, who had robbed a party store down the street from the hotel that very evening. Armed and pursued by police, they had taken refuge in John Goodman's hotel room, where they were the life of the party until the moment they decided the coast was clear, and vanished as mysteriously as they had arrived.

Some of our after-work bacchanals did occasionally produce something worthwhile. Well, one did, anyway. That was the night Ted McGinley came in from the cold.

From the beginning that summer, there had been slight but noticeable divisions when it came to after-hours shenanigans. As a general rule of thumb, the nerds tended to party together, though Robert seldom if ever made an appearance. We also had Julie Montgomery and Goodman. The Alpha Betas seemed to party together too, though their formation was a little looser. Ted (Stan Gable), Don Gibb (Ogre) and Matt Salinger were the core of that group, which also included Michelle Meyrink, who acted nerd but partied Alpha Beta. As with Julie and me, Michelle and Matt spent a lot of time together apart from the group and Don often would disappear for days on motorcycles with some of the tougher locals, doing God knows what for entertainment.

But Ted McGinley, the King of the Alpha Betas on-screen, secretly yearned to get to know the nerds a little better off-camera. It should be said that Ted was the straightest of straight arrows: conservative (politically and personally), charming and a very good actor. Ted started the shoot by handing out homemade buttons with his face on them, as if he were running for student body president. It was a brilliant little piece of character work because you could imagine Stan Gable doing exactly the same thing.

But it was understood that there was no sex or drugs for Ted on this set. Until the night he appeared unexpectedly at John Goodman's door looking for company. We almost never saw Ted after sunset and he was hailed enthusiastically. John's tape deck blasted as we sat around drinking beer and, finally, started passing around a large joint.

But as it reached Ted, not unexpectedly, he declined.

"Ah, no thanks," he murmured, politely passing it to the next person.

"You don't smoke?" asked Busfield, probably as unsurprised as anyone.

"Nope," said Ted, virtuously. "Not even cigarettes. Have a beer, though!"

"But wait," Tim went on. "Seriously, you've never smoked? Ever?"

"Naw," said Ted, "I just don't think it's for me. Drugs are just . . . not my thing, you know?"

"How do you know if you don't try," I encouraged him, and soon the whole room was earnestly encouraging him to try a hit. Just one hit . . .

Finally, the peer pressure overwhelmed him and he took a hit off his first joint. We all felt like proud parents. He then sat there, staring at the joint. We all stared at him, expectantly.

After a moment, puzzled, he said, "Umm. Is that it? What's supposed to happen?"

"You don't feel anything?" Tim asked.

He shook his head. "Nope, nothing," Ted said. "Maybe it just doesn't affect me."

"Try another one," Tim urged. Ted tried another hit.

"Still nothing?" I asked

"Nothing," Ted said, firmly. "I dunno, maybe it's defective or something."

He passed the joint on and, disappointed, the rest of us went back to our various conversations. After a few moments, we heard a throaty giggle coming from deep in the interior of Ted McGinley. We all stared. The giggle got louder and finally Ted broke into a full, loud laugh. It got even louder as he doubled over in hysterics. After a moment he tipped forward helplessly on Goodman's floor, by now *screaming* with laughter.

It must've gone on for ten minutes. Every time he seemed to recover, he would take one look at us and go off again. By the end, we were all weeping with laughter.

Ted's first tentative experiment with weed was something none of us ever forgot, but Tim Busfield brilliantly made practical use of it. A few days later when we were shooting the

Tri Lamb / Omega Mu party scene—during which Booger produces his wonder-joints—Tim improvised a scene where Poindexter is given his first taste of weed by his Mu date. Compressed into those few seconds of film is Tim's spot-on imitation of Ted McGinley, for the first and probably only time, high on marijuana. Brian Tochi and I used it, too, during an improvised scene where Booger gets Takashi high while they're fixing up the nerd house.

With our Arizona local fraternity suppliers appearing like elves with magic pies, bearing illicit substances of all descriptions (mushrooms were also on the menu for those of us who fancied long, Don Juan–like strolls in the desert in search of higher truths), it never occurred to us where our task masters—the people farther up the Hollywood food chain—were getting theirs.

It turned out, they were getting theirs shipped in cut-out telephone books straight from Los Angeles. This convenient and ultimately foolhardy arrangement came close to shutting *Revenge of the Nerds* down right and proper.

All movie sets have police present for security purposes. Most of these guys welcome the down time, free food and a chance to flirt with the actresses and women on the crew. The more laid-back actually become friends of some of us and at the conclusion of filming, everyone parts with expressions of mutual regret. If crews later return to that city for another film, and find their pet cop still in residence, the reunion is almost touching, like Odysseus on his return home being greeted by his dog.

This was not one of those cases.

Our cop was not friendly. He didn't chat, didn't flirt, didn't

A very quiet birthday party. Only this pony showed up. Our house in Detroit, Michigan. Probably 1954. *(Courtesy of the Author)*

A ski weekend, mid-sixties. Switzerland. Possibly Diablerets. "Go that way! Really fast. If something gets in your way, turn!" *(Courtesy of the Author)*

1971. An early attempt at cosplay, thanks to an unhealthy obsession with *A Clockwork Orange*. *(Courtesy of Elliott Milstein)*

Meadow Brook Theatre. *A Midsummer Night's Dream*, my first professional job. With Suzanne Peters and Eric Tavares. Director Terence Kilburn. Rochester, Michigan, 1975 *(Courtesy of Kresge Library Archives, Oakland University)*

Auditioning for *Risky Business*, my first film. From left, Raphael Sbarge, Bronson Pinchot, Brian Backer, and self. Backer, a fine actor, was later replaced by Tom Cruise. New York, 1982. *(Courtesy of Paul Brickman)*

Camera rolls for the first scene in *Risky Business*. From left, Kevin Anderson, Raphael Sbarge, self, Tom Cruise, and Bronson Pinchot. July 7, 1982. *(Courtesy of Warner Bros.)*

Revenge of the Nerds, Tuscon, Arizona, 1984. Director Jeff Kanew. *(Courtesy of Interscope/20th Century Fox)*

Revenge of the Nerds. An on-set snap with Tim Busfield (Poindexter). *(Courtesy of the Author)*

(Right) Clan of the Cave Bear, 1984, Director Michael Chapman, British Columbia. Some days, in the helicopter on the way back to base camp, I just couldn't wait to get my makeup off. *(Courtesy of the Author)*

(Below) Better off Dead, 1984. Director Savage Steve Holland. Snowbird, Utah. Wrap party on the last day of shooting. Alcohol was suspected. From left: Diane Franklin, John Cusack, self, Savage Steve Holland, Dan Schneider, Amanda Wyss, and Aaron Dozier. *(Courtesy of the Author)*

Bad Medicine, 1985. On location in a pueblo in the South of Spain. From left, Alan Corduner, Gilbert Gottfried, and me singing, if memory serves, "If I Were A Rich Man." Steve Gutenberg (background) does not join in. *(Courtesy of the Author)*

One Crazy Summer, 1985. Director Savage Steve Holland. Cape Cod, Massachusetts. With John Cusack. Neither of us appear old enough to drink. I was 32. *(Courtesy of the Author)*

Moonlighting, 1986. "Atomic Shakespeare." Director Will MacKenzie. Los Angeles. At Universal Studios' Court of Miracles with Allyce Beasley. *(Picturemaker Productions/ABC Television)*

Moonlighting. Curtis Armstrong Day, 1989. Stage 20. From left, Jon Ames and Bruce Willis hoist me into the lead car (with Miss Pacoima, partially obscured) for the parade around 20th Century Fox Studios. *(Courtesy of the Author)*

Revenge of the Nerds 2: Nerds in Paradise, 1987. Director Joe Roth. Fort Lauderdale, Florida. From a photo shoot which accompanied a feature article in *US* magazine. *(Courtesy of the Author)*

(Top) Ray, 2004. Director Taylor Hackford. New Orleans. As Ahmet Ertegun, with Jamie Foxx as Ray Charles. The role garnered me some of the best reviews of my career, even though many mistook me for Clint Howard. Hair matters. *(Courtesy of the Author)*

(Left) King of the Nerds, 2012. Craig Armstrong and Rick Ringbaak Executive Producers. Los Angeles. With Robert Carradine, in one of many incarnations over three seasons. Costumes by Robin Gurney. Makeup by the late and deeply lamented Branwyne Smith. *(Courtesy of the Author)*

Supernatural, 2015. "Book of the Damned." Director P. J. Pesce. Vancouver, British Columbia. Metatron, The Scribe of God, and everyone's least favorite character on the show (at this point, anyway) on a memorable road trip with the Angel Castiel, Misha Collins. *(Courtesy of Misha Collins)*

Supernatural, 2015. "All in the Family." Director Thomas G. Wright. Exit Metatron. My last scene with Jensen Ackles and Jared Padalecki. *(Courtesy of the Author)*

All for one... *(Courtesy of the Author)*

talk shop with the drivers and stunt guys. You got the feeling that he thought these people from Hollywood were all a bunch of Sodomites, and probably left-leaning Sodomites at that. His skin was tanned a high-desert brown and so tough you could make a pair of leather chaps out of it. He seldom spoke, smiled mysteriously and wore mirrored shades, just like The Man With No Eyes in *Cool Hand Luke*. He didn't enjoy down time, and he did something about it.

This cop suspected that there may have been some drug use by certain individuals on set. One day after everyone had left, he had the dressing rooms tested and found drug residue in virtually all of them. The trick was finding out where the drugs came from, and who was receiving and distributing. But this cop was going to do it right. He lay low, smiled secretly and waited.

We had reached a point in the schedule where we had switched to night shoots. At some point, I had been called for work but had been released from the set temporarily. I went back to my dressing room and, after a while, dozed off.

When I awoke, hours later, it was 3:00 a.m. I sat up, muzzy-headed and confused. It had been hours since I'd worked. What the hell? For a moment I thought they'd wrapped and forgotten I was there. There was a sort of hushed stillness as I left the honey-wagon, but over in the shadows, next to the production van, I saw one of our production assistants. He was standing still and ramrod straight, staring with a kind of rictus-like expression into the middle distance.

"Hey, what's happening?" I said, in a slightly aggrieved tone. "Am I released?"

He didn't respond. It was as if I had not spoken. I gave him a moment and then, irritably, walked away, leaving him there looking like a cigar store Indian, staring. It was only later that I heard what had happened.

Our cop on his rounds that night had wandered a little off the beaten track, up a slight incline behind the production trailer. From this vantage point, he was able to easily look inside and see someone cutting and dividing the most recent shipment from the West Coast. To alert his pals on the force, secure the set and take possession of the evidence was, for him, the work of an instant.

And I had slept through the whole thing.

The word spread quickly, though, and panic set in, sending at least one actress running into the nearby woods to bury her mirror and anything else that might have fingerprints or DNA on it. An amazing number of people on the set were on edge for weeks. It's hard to imagine how much contraband was dumped into toilets that night. Two lower-level members of the crew disappeared, and one of them was told that if he kept his mouth shut and took the fall, there would be a plum job awaiting him in Los Angeles when he got out. And today that man is a producer in Hollywood.

There's a lesson there, but I can't put my finger on it.

It had gotten around that Julie and I, who had bonded pretty much from the start, had become intimate, or, as Larry B. Scott put it, "We couldn't believe that book-reading motherfucker got that shit!" We thought the rumors were funny, because at first we were actually listening to music in her room, while occasionally sampling some of Arizona's finest locally produced intoxicants. Later, when people started suggesting that we weren't sleeping with each other but were getting high, we quickly assured them that they were right the first time and we were just sleeping together. It's hard to say what bothered me the most about this situation: that I was getting wrecked or that I was having an affair, or that I was lying about everything. There was undoubtedly a curious alternative reality that existed on film sets then and probably still does today: that unspoken rule that the old sailors had, that once they passed Portugal, all the rules went by the board. Why Portugal? Why Tucson, for that matter? I had always believed myself above these things but that was the summer I realized how human I was. Julie and I started as friends, and wherever our relationship took us we stayed friends. There were times when things got a little near the knuckle, but not with us.

Throughout the shoot, Bobby had remained the good-natured, laconic, totally-in-charge scion of a legendary Hollywood acting dynasty. Nothing seemed to faze him and once he became comfortable in Lewis's skin, his work was faultless. But gradually, cracks in the veneer were starting to show. It could have been the extended presence of both his girlfriend (who memorably introduced herself to me by saying, "Hi. I'm Bobby's girl"), and Ever, his adorable young daughter from a previous relationship. While everyone else on the set appeared to be partying all night and getting regular sex with strings of coeds, Bobby, the star of the picture, was being the doting father and boyfriend. Like many of his peers in Hollywood, Bobby felt an ingrained sense of entitlement when it came to women. In this case, for example, if Lewis got to have sex with the most desirable girl on campus, it stood to reason that Bobby should have the same freedom with the most gorgeous woman on the picture, and that was Julie Montgomery. It was Hollywood's version of *droit de seigneur.*

We had reached the point in the schedule where we were to shoot the infamous "moon bounce" scene, in which Lewis, disguised in Stan Gable's Darth Vader suit, follows a troubled Betty into the fun house and goes down on her. Julie had told me she was feeling anxious about the scene and asked if I would come to the set for support. But as I made my way toward the fun house set, I was stopped by a visibly uncomfortable A.D.

"Sorry, Curtis," he said. "They're asking that you not come to the set."

"Not come to the set? Why?"

"Umm, dunno."

I felt a brief stab of paranoid irritation. "Well, can you find out?"

The A.D. muttered into his walkie and after a moment said, "Not sure. Something to do with Bobby."

Julie and I had unwittingly fed the fire that night. She had showed up on the set wearing my *Risky Business* crew jacket, with the neatly embossed "Curtis" on the front, which she had borrowed from me to wear over her costume because she was cold. When Bobby saw it, he went nuts, instantly ordering that I be banished from the set whenever he was doing scenes with

Julie. In a furious aside with director Jeff Kanew, Bobby added he never wanted to see that jacket again, because, as Jeff told me later, "It was fucking with his process."

Despite everything, by the time we finished filming that spring we felt like we'd accomplished something. But 20th Century Fox, now under a new regime far less accommodating to movies like *Revenge of the Nerds*, begged to disagree and did everything it could to bury the picture. Ultimately, it became a case of life imitating art, as the jocks at the studio tried to destroy the little underdog nerd movie and failed completely. It made money. Quite a lot of money. They instituted a studio-wide embargo against any sequels at 20th Century Fox, which was lifted under a different administration three years later. The first sequel to be green-lighted at that point was *Revenge of the Nerds II: Nerds in Paradise.*

Revenge of the Nerds might not be a film that would make any critic's Top 10 list—or top 100 list for that matter—but it was a solid piece of work by everyone involved. It made us laugh.

It also made some points that a lot of us felt were worth making. The prescient analogy between frat-house bullying and racist and anti-Semitic behavior is sometimes overlooked in a movie that's better remembered for belching contests and panty raids. Like many comedies of the period the misogyny, both on the screen and behind the scenes, was off the charts. In the case of *Revenge of the Nerds* it seems a little more extreme because the rest of the film makes such a point of its progressive message. Its treatment of blacks, women and gays certainly doesn't stand up to scrutiny by today's standards, assuming today's standards are that much of an improvement over those of 1984.

Still, the film does have a positive message at the end, with nerds, African Americans, women, children and gays all joining together as Queen's "We Are the Champions" swells on the soundtrack—standing as one against the fascist bully boys of the football team and their dictator coach. There is something moving about that last moment where the persecuted and downtrodden claim the epithet so often used against them— "nerd"—as a badge of honor, chanting it in victory over Stan, Ogre and their friends, who chanted it at them in the beginning of the film. In spite of its faults, which are many, *Revenge of the Nerds* remains a triumphant success because it shows how an ultimately lovable group of ostracized brainiacs and misfits embrace each other, and each other's differences, and come out on top in the end.

That message of tolerance and inclusion, along with characters that spoke to people and comedy that stands the test of time, makes *Revenge of the Nerds* remain after all these years a movie I was proud to put my name on.

Revenge of the Nerds had a quiet sneak preview in Westwood the week before it opened. There was no publicity, but the line for tickets went around the block. Robert Carradine wanted to share his first starring role in a feature film with his legendary father, John Carradine, and brought him along.

"So I got a couple seats fifth row center," Bobby told me. "He's looking straight up, you know, his head is stretched back, like he's getting a shave. So we watch the movie. After it was over, I said, 'So, what did you think, Dad?'"

"Well, son," said his father, "it isn't Shakespeare."

No, it wasn't. And Booger wasn't Hamlet. But it was the role that put me forever on the map as a character actor in Hollywood. Foolishly, there were times when I'd wished I'd never done it. It was some time before I could understand what anyone saw in the guy. It would be even longer before I could get enough distance to realize that my performance as Booger is one of probably the top three in my entire career. And it was only in the last twenty years or so that I could admit to a sneaking fondness for him. In the early nineties I attended the twentieth anniversary of our graduating class at the Academy. All but one or two of the students were there, as was most of the faculty. At one point I found myself in a conversation with Alex Grey, my beloved acting teacher, who had once commented on my "glibness" as an actor.

I was babbling, basically apologizing for the direction my career had taken, regretting I hadn't stayed true to my roots as a theater actor, denigrating the roles I'd become famous for, when Alex interrupted me.

"Curtis, what on earth are you complaining about?" he asked, mildly. "You're making a living as an actor. That was the idea, wasn't it? That's what we trained you to do." He gave me a warm smile. "For heaven's sake, congratulations!"

CLAN OF THE CAVE BEAR

VANCOUVER, BRITISH COLUMBIA, 1984

It was 1984 and we were in our third grueling month of production of Jean Auel's *Clan of the Cave Bear*, a film so complex and challenging it took five months to shoot, and so bad it destroyed Auel's epic Neanderthal franchise at a single stroke. The book was an immense, exhaustively researched novel, following the adventures of a Cro-Magnon orphan, Ayla (played as an adult by Daryl Hannah), who is taken in by a clan of the fading Neanderthals and raised as one of their own.

Aside from Hannah, the film starred Pamela Reed, James Remar, John Doolittle, Thomas G. Waites and a supporting cast of fifteen others chosen because of a general similarity in body type and coloring.

My audition for *Clan* happened immediately after returning to Los Angeles following *Revenge of the Nerds*. As in the case of *Nerds*, the nature of this picture pretty much precluded a traditional reading: screenwriter John Sayles had written the script in colloquial English (his script was dropped before we started filming), but there weren't enough lines for most of the characters to attempt that kind of audition.

So I went to the Producer Sales Organization building on Little Santa Monica Boulevard one day to have a meeting with director Michael Chapman. Chapman had never directed before but he was already a legendary cinematographer for his work on films with Martin Scorsese and Francis Ford Coppola.

I was shown into a completely empty office and found Chapman sitting on the floor in the corner. He asked me to sit down so I sat down in the corner with him. He picked up my picture and resume from a pile in front of him.

"Hmm," he said, after studying it for a while. "You've done a lot of theater."

I assured him that I had, indeed, done a lot of theater. I pointed out, though, that I had done a couple of movies as well.

"Yeah, *Risky Business*!" he said. "Who directed that?"

"Paul Brickman," I said. "He also did the screenplay . . ."

"Must've missed that one."

There was a brief pause. Looking again at the resume, he suddenly brightened.

"*Revenge of the Nerds*! Is that out?"

"No, not yet . . ."

"I love that title!!" Chapman enthused. "So what is it, like kind of a Mark David Chapman thing?"

I thought I couldn't possibly have heard him correctly.

"Mark David . . . ?"

"Yeah!" he said, excitedly. "The guy who shot Lennon. That kind of thing?"

"Ahhh, no," I said. "No, nothing like that. It's more like . . . a comedy, really. About nerds."

Chapman's face fell.

"Oh, I was hoping it was about that. You know, nerdy guy killing someone famous for revenge."

"No, no. Just about regular nerds."

"Chapman was kind of a nerd," Chapman said, sulkily. "Well, that's too bad. It should've been about that."

A silence fell on the room as the two of us sat there on the floor, reflecting: Chapman, I assume, about the tragedy of squandered opportunities, I about how weird it was that I was having this conversation about Mark David Chapman with a guy named Michael Chapman. The meeting never really recovered from Chapman's disappointment that *Revenge of the Nerds* wasn't somehow related to his psychotic namesake.

Still, I got the job, but only because he thought that beneath Michael Westmore's prosthetic makeup, I'd make a believable-enough second-tier Neanderthal. The character's name was Goov and I figured he was at least one evolutionary step above Booger, which was something.

Michael Chapman had a vision, you could say that for him. The movie was to be about a clan and as actors, we were expected to be a clan. There would be weeks of rehearsal, classes, yoga, high-protein diets and training to prepare ourselves for what he envisioned as a kind of immersive journey into prehistory, by way of Breugel paintings. There were to be no fake fangs stuck on tigers, or shaggy coats attached to elephants. His goal, he said repeatedly, was to have a statement at the end of the credits from the National Geographic Society saying, in essence, "We can't be positive, but this is probably just what it was like back then."

The film was to be shot in Canada, but the American actors began our training in Los Angeles. For a couple of weeks, we went daily to the sports medicine clinic of Dr. LeRoy Perry, in Santa Monica. He started us on our diet—essentially what would later be known as a paleo diet—and our physical regimen. We had our first yoga sessions, with Siri Dharma, whose impossibly lush physique and exotic beauty provided months of almost painful distraction from the work at hand, even after I discovered she was Italian, not Indian.

"Can you imagine," Jean Auel later beamed to a local reporter during her brief visit to our location in Penticton, British Columbia, "a better vacation than being able to drop into a movie set that's based on a book you've written?"

If she actually believed that at the time, she would be disabused of the notion in short order. But *Clan of the Cave Bear* was creating quite a stir among those in the feminist fiction/prehistoric nerd fantasy/romance novel crowd, which was a market no one else had even considered cracking before.

Her second book in her Children of the Earth series, *Valley of the Horses*, had already been published. The sequel was surprisingly heavy on explicit sex scenes, which led to an awkward incident as the U.S. actors were flying up to Vancouver to start filming.

We were all in first class, and James Remar had brought along his copy of *Valley of the Horses*. The sex scenes both tickled and outraged him. At first, we just listened to his hoarse bray of laughter from time to time, until he could take it no longer. He stood in the aisle, laughing, holding the book.

"Oh my God," he bellowed, loud enough to be heard at the back of the plane. "You guys are not going to believe this shit! Who the fuck is this woman? Listen . . ."

At which point he started, at the top of his brassy, smoke-roughened voice, to read out the sex scenes, in all their tawdry, purple glory. The rest of us started by laughing along, hoping this would be over quickly, but no: Remar had marked all the soft-core passages, and was planning on reading every single one of them.

"That's great, Jamey," I chuckled, weakly, "but maybe you should . . ." I gestured pointedly to the passengers behind us. One mother was trying to cover both of her children's ears with only two hands. People were getting angry and uncomfortable. A man who could scream out stuff like this on an airplane, people seemed to think, was capable of anything.

The flight attendants tried to intervene, but Jamey ignored them, continuing to bellow out overripe descriptions of Cro-Magnon orgasms. His voice was taking on an angry edge, made worse when people were trying to shut him up. Some of us were on our feet, begging him to sit down before he got in trouble. Finally, strangely, he suddenly blushed and looked embarrassed.

"Okay, okay," he said, laughing, and returned to his seat. "Jeez."

Once we arrived in Vancouver, the training continued, for weeks. Dr. Deborah Kramer, a professor of anthropology, gave lectures and showed films on different aspects of Neanderthal and Cro-Magnon life. A highly complex Clan sign language had been created for the film by Lou Fant, a prominent sign-language instructor. To this he added a very small spoken language, key words, to be added to the dialogue, now that John Sayles's contemporary English-language dialogue had been rejected. We had classes every day in this discipline, and after a while, for tests, had to create stories, which we would then tell to the whole class, using only Clan sign. If they could follow the story, we'd get an A. This actually came in handy. Later during our twice-daily ear-shattering helicopter trips to the set, we could continue whole conversations using Clan sign language.

Jim Riggs, a primitive-skills instructor, arrived one morning like something out of James Fenimore Cooper. Tall, rail-thin, with long, black hair shot through with silver, we found him one morning leaning against the cast van, dressed from cap to moccasins entirely in animal skins. Skins he had tanned, treated and sewn together from animals, we discovered later, he had killed himself. With a bow and arrows he had made. When we first saw him that day, he was whittling a stick with a knife with an obsidian blade that he had—yes—made himself. He had used that very blade, he told us, to cut his baby's umbilical cord.

Among the skills that Riggs taught us were the making of tools and blades out of stone; the identification, preparation and eating of indigenous plants; the making of cord out of plant fiber; the making of fire using sticks or flints; and—most memorably—the disemboweling and skinning of an entire cow, which one morning had been dragged up and dumped outside our studio. Our job that day was to completely remove all the cow's innards, including the stomach, which we had to then fill with water, plants and vegetables picked by hand, and then stretch over a fire—which we had, of course, started ourselves—and make soup. It actually turns my stomach just to think of it, thirty years later, up to my elbows in viscera, waving off clouds of bluebottles, bathed in the stink of congealing blood and spoiling intestines.

"Two years at the Academy," I remember muttering, through clenched teeth, "for this?"

While half of us were engaged in that, the other half were skinning and scraping the carcass, and preparing it for tanning.

Riggs then suddenly, like a kind of wilderness magician, pulled a dead hare out from nowhere and threw it on the ground in front of us. Our blood, apparently, was up. Without a word spoken, three of us pounced on the thing with our knives and started hacking away at it like we hadn't eaten for days. Somehow, this was even worse than the cow for Daryl and a few others. Several of them turned away, moaning objections.

In almost no time, we had pulled off the skin, cut up the edible bits and thrown them into the cow's stomach. The soup, oddly enough, was starting to actually smell good. At that point it had been hours since breakfast and I was surprised to discover I had worked up an appetite. Several of us stood around, gazing into the murky mess in the cow's stomach and exchanging uncertain glances.

Finally, the only one who had the nerve to actually taste the stuff was James Remar, who had long enjoyed a reputation as someone who would try anything. He retched a little, but got it down.

"Hm," he grunted, shrugging. "Could use some salt."

The shoot was a blur. Time ceased to have any meaning at all. We were up before dawn to put on makeup, flown to distant locations, filmed until the light went, then taken back to begin the long process of removing makeup, wigs, prosthetics and body makeup. By the time we were done there was barely enough time to drink before collapsing in a kind of coma until the next day. Apart from the five lead roles there wasn't a lot of opportunity to act, and the animal skins, from the day cameras first rolled to the bitter end, remained unwashed.

By that time we had long since ceased feeling remotely civilized. By month two, only the most fastidious among us could be bothered to bathe more than once or twice a week. My body makeup was basically touched up every few days because I couldn't be bothered to remove it. All the men grew impressive beards. We looked like a bunch of snowbound settlers on the verge of eating each other. Endless days in blazing summer heat when we were on our mountaintop location in Penticton to bitterly cold snowy days on a glacier in an isolated area near Tungsten, accessible only by helicopter, had left us ragged and exhausted. The four-hour makeup sessions in the morning began at 3:00 a.m. and went in shifts. Simultaneously, there was the shuttling of the *entire production* from base camp to the mountaintop by helicopter every day. By the time the last helicopter had deposited the last crew member on set, it was noon, so we'd break for lunch. So accustomed were the cast at that point to seeing each other without clothes, we stopped worrying about it and many of us just wandered about naked.

In our tent encampment in the mountains, with an ice-cold river running through it, cast and crew members paired off, humping the long nights away in sleeping bags for warmth and comfort. Within days, they would change partners and start the whole process over. Two sets of couples, recognizing a good thing when they saw it, wound up moving in together for the remainder of the shoot once we returned to Vancouver. In a desperate bid to hold onto his humanity, John Doolittle read and reread Flaubert's *Madame Bovary*, while I penned a retelling of *Clan of the Cave Bear*, meticulously written in the style of P. G. Wodehouse. Meanwhile, guards walked the perimeter of the camp all night with guns as bears were drawn to us by the scent of food. The women of the cast realized all their menstrual cycles had started occurring at the same time and all of them had to leave whenever Bart the Bear, our massive, titular cave bear, was on the set. At one point, Daryl and I realized we were having the same dreams. Not similar dreams. The same dreams. On the same *nights*.

On first viewing the film, even friends and spouses couldn't tell the Clan apart. And no one could bear seeing the movie more than once, so they were left wondering why we had abandoned our lives and careers for that length of time. It was, by September, a question we had asked ourselves repeatedly.

On paper, *Clan of the Cave Bear* looked like a winner. It seemed to me to be a definite step up from my first two films. Which just goes to show that in this line of work, you never know.

BETTER OFF DEAD

LOS ANGELES AND UTAH, 1984

Better Off Dead, starring a young John Cusack in his breakout role, is, next to *Revenge of the Nerds*, the most fondly regarded movie of any on my resume. It is, as they say, a fan favorite. Two generations of enthusiasts know the film by heart and will recite chunks of dialogue at the drop of a top hat. It isn't, though, the most *critically* regarded of my movies. Like *Revenge of the Nerds*, *Better Off Dead* is one of those films that went straight into the hearts of millions of people—both nerd and non-nerd alike—while somehow bypassing the collective heart of the reviewing fraternity entirely, assuming they had one. After five years of a deluge of "teen sex comedies" of varying degrees of awfulness, the ink-stained wretches of the Fourth Estate's Arts and Leisure sections had had enough. Almost to a person, they inveighed against these films in general—and this one, it seemed, in particular—with a bloody-minded ferocity.

And the critics were not alone. Studio executives, as well as other genre directors, producers and cineastes in general, received the film, at best, ambivalently. Others actively hated it. It was considered badly constructed, embarrassingly juvenile, unfunny, artless, in poor taste (whatever that is), derivative, badly acted, execrably scored and reactionary. And that was just John Cusack's opinion.

Yes, high on *Better Off Dead*'s long list of detractors was its young star himself. But more about that in its place. The first I heard about *Better Off Dead* was when I was huddled down in the main tent of our location village somewhere in the Canadian Yukon, shouting over a static-y radiophone, which was our only connection to the outside world during the filming of *Clan of the Cave Bear*. My agent was informing me that after my return to Los Angeles in the autumn, I had a job awaiting me, playing a supporting role in a feature called *Better Off Dead*, which was written and directed by Savage Steve Holland.

"This reception is terrible," I shouted into the receiver. "It sounded like you said 'Savage Steve Holland.'"

"That's right!" she chirped. "Don't ask me, but that's what he calls himself."

"Well, has he done anything?"

"Just a short. Called *Buster's First Date* or something. I never saw it. Leonard Maltin was in it," she added optimistically.

"Is it a horror film?" I yelled.

"*Buster's First Date?*"

"No," I shrieked, "*Better Off Dead*! Is it a horror film?"

"No, not really," she said. "More like a comedy. Kinda. I don't know, it's weird."

She was being evasive. "There's animation. It's not really my thing at all. But he's really eager for you to do it. He insisted that your role be cast before anyone else's. He says he wrote it for you. But I have to say the money's not very good. And the billing is not so hot either."

"Well, wait," I said. "If he wants me so much, maybe you could get better money."

"Mmmm, I don't think so. Very little money."

"But he wants me," I bellowed. "That should be good for at least better billing, don't you think?"

"Well," she said, doubtfully, "I guess I can try. But don't get your hopes up."

I remember this conversation so vividly for a couple of reasons. One, it was the last time this agent ever negotiated a deal for me. Neophyte though I was to Hollywood and its ways, I felt there was something wrong about me pleading with my representative to try to get better billing for a part that had been created for me. I signed with another agent on my return to town, who turned out to be the very one who had once referred to me as the new Michael J. Pollard. The fact that I considered this at least a lateral move gives you an idea of my sense of self-worth at the time.

Another reason I recall the conversation is that it presaged the general reception *Better Off Dead* received from the public as a whole. It wasn't just dismissal on artistic grounds. It was what seemed almost an obstinate inability of people to grasp what it was, or why it was unique; or to value it for what it represented, or to appreciate it for all its good qualities, which were legion. At the time, no one would have imagined that the film would be granted twenty-fifth- and thirtieth-anniversary screenings, that it would not only be embraced and celebrated by millions, but would actually influence a generation of other writers and directors and actors who were just children when it was released.

Our crew had returned to Vancouver some days later and I found the script of *Better Off Dead* awaiting me. I read it on the set in my caveman makeup and wardrobe, baffled, delighted and laughing out loud. It was funny and odd and endearing and smart and everything my agent had not led me to expect. Nothing that happened during the filming or immediately following shook my belief that *Better Off Dead* would not only be a huge hit, but that it would be the start of a stellar feature film career for Savage Steve Holland and might even change the nature of film comedy as we knew it. It turned out, of course, none of those things happened.

On its release even *Buster's First Date* costar Leonard Maltin gave *Better Off Dead* only two and a half stars.

For a film that touched as many people and that was so important to me professionally as *Better Off Dead* was, I have surprisingly few memories of it. My first day was the cast read-through of the script, which took place in Burbank and was attended, to the best of my recollection, by nearly everyone in the cast. John Cusack I liked instantly. He was funny, outgoing and politically astute, with a face that seemed to belong to a silent film comedian. David Ogden Stiers, then riding high as Major Winchester on the deathless series *M*A*S*H*, was there, genial, charming and avuncular. Kim Darby, quiet and haunted-looking, revealed none of the supreme goofiness she brought to Lane Meyer's mother. Vincent Schiavelli, the odd, angular, pipe-smoking intellectual held forth on Italy at one end of the table, while Dan Schneider, as Ricky, Lane's nightmarish neighbor, pink-cheeked and nearly cylindrical, cracked wise with the incomparable Laura Waterbury, who played Ricky's mother. Amanda Wyss, so memorable as the doomed Tina in *Nightmare on Elm Street*, huddled with Diane Franklin, who was on her way to breaking the hearts of countless boys as Lane Meyer's perfect girlfriend, Monique. Aaron Dozier, as Stalin, the evil jock with Robert Wagner's voice, had yet to be cast.

Steve Holland was twenty-four when he made *Better Off Dead*; the same age Orson Welles was when he made *Citizen Kane*, though the comparisons end there. Tall, blond, blue-eyed, he was giddy with excitement the day we all first got together. When I first saw him I couldn't imagine he could be the director. The directors of films I had met and worked with at that point were fairly serious guys. Savage seemed like the funny, self-effacing *son* of a film director, one who spent most of his days at the beach and his evenings in a comedy club. No one on the set of *Better Off Dead* could keep up with his wit. The jokes flowed in an unstoppable stream. In retrospect I suppose this stemmed from his incredible nervousness and insecurity at having been given his first feature to write and direct, and being supported by producers and a studio who believed that he was the next hot thing. Not that I think Savage believed that for an instant. He was, and is, the most genuinely modest man I've ever met in Hollywood. He would tell you he has a lot to be modest about. I would disagree, for reasons I'll go into later.

For now, that day, he put everyone utterly at their ease. He was complimentary, generous and self-deprecating. (He still is.) His spirit was contagious. By the time we were finished everyone's excitement matched his. Diane, Amanda and I jumped into John's car, and he drove us to a restaurant near Universal Studios for dinner. The dinner I don't recall, but the ride was memorable because for the first time in my film career, I was in Hollywood—really in Hollywood!—riding in Cusack's rented convertible with three terribly attractive and charming young actors, everyone talking at once, the sun shining in the women's hair. I didn't talk much. I just took them, and everything around us, in. It's a nice memory of a happy afternoon that promised only good things to come.

Better Off Dead was the first film I shot in Los Angeles, which is probably why I have so few actual memories of making it. When you are on location, as I had been for all three of the films that preceded this, you are in an unfamiliar place with a lot of people who are also in an unfamiliar place and you've all been stuck together in a hotel there and are reliant upon each other for amusement, friendship and comfort. When you are shooting "in town," you return to your regular life at the end of the day and, most importantly, sleep in your own bed with the person you're supposed to be sleeping with.

For this film, we were shooting at various locations in the San Fernando Valley, which is, at its best, uninspiring. We had no pre-shoot rehearsal process at all, which was a new experience for me. It gave the filming experience itself a sense of being on a tightrope at all times. Savage appeared to be eager for us to improve upon his script. I would come to realize that this was his method, if you could call it that: hire funny people, make sure that they had a sense of what the scene was about and then let them do whatever they felt like. For the glib among us, like Dan Schneider, John Cusack and me, this was an exhilarating way to work that usually resulted in something worthwhile and occasionally something even funnier than Savage had written. In the years since, Savage has done himself no favors by overstating the contributions made by his cast. Some were significant, but much of his original script remained intact.

But it was a bit of an unhinged process. I requested my skiing outfit with the top hat at the last minute as a tribute to George Harrison during the skiing sequences in *Help!* Somehow, a top hat was produced, though I know of only one person, Bobcat Goldthwait, who ever made the connection. Most of my dialogue with John at the top of the K-12 was improvised; as was the laughing jag Charles De Mar launches on during the school dance. Dan Schneider came up with the wonderful gag in which Ricky runs after Monique, loses his balloon and makes a feeble attempt to retrieve it.

Some of these changes I find scribbled in my copy of the script, or in the notebook I kept during filming, which shows at least some of the ideas I came up with were conceived before filming. Some were incorporated, some not.

In 2015, much of the cast gathered at the Castro Theatre in San Francisco to do a live reading of the script as a thirtieth-anniversary celebration, with actor Jon Heder sitting in for John Cusack. I think the audience was surprised to realize how much dialogue that they fondly remember from the film was missing from the original script.

It's my belief that the loose, party-like environment he created for his cast and crew gave us the freedom to create, and if this sounds familiar, it's because Jeff Kanew created a similar space for *Revenge of the Nerds.* But because we were in town, instead of Chicago or Tucson or British Columbia, there was less a sense of mice playing while the cats were taking meetings thousands of miles away. The shadow cast by the studio bosses—in this case, CBS Theatrical Films—lay a little more heavily on us. There was also less of a concern about creating an ensemble compared to the other films. Savage cast *Better Off Dead* perfectly, but it was seldom that there were more than two or three principals in any given scene at the same time.

In 2016, I arranged to meet Savage for dinner at Musso and Frank Grill in Hollywood to talk about *Better Off Dead* and its sequel, *One Crazy Summer.* It turned out to be a propitious location. His first meeting with *Better Off Dead* producer Michael Jaffe had been at that very restaurant.

"I must have had two hundred meetings with various 'producers' about making *Better Off Dead,*" said Savage, "and they all had their plans on how to make the movie. You know, it was 'Oh, yeah, I'm gonna make this movie,' only it never goes anywhere. Just all the bullshit artists everyone hears about in Hollywood. Finally, I arrange to meet Michael Jaffe at Musso and Frank to talk about it. He picked Musso's 'cause he could smoke cigars in here at the time. I remember calling my mom back in Connecticut telling her I was going to this meeting, but this was it. If this didn't work out, I was going back to Connecticut. I couldn't do this anymore. I was just done.

"Michael's company was CBS Theatrical Films and they had just done *Grandview, U.S.A.* It was a regular movie, not a teen movie or anything, but it had cost twenty-five million dollars, which was a lot of money back then, and it was not successful. So Michael was trying to find something that would be the next *Fast Times*, or *Revenge of the Nerds* or something, and he brought me this crappy script, just some teen shit. He wanted me to direct it because he had read *Better Off Dead* and it made him laugh. So, I'm saying, 'So what d'you want me to direct *this* for?' and I start talking about doing *Better Off Dead* instead. I had been planning this for two years. I had brought the storyboards with me and I pulled out everything right then and showed him, 'This is how I'm shooting this, here are the jokes; if you like it, let's do *this*.'

"He said, well, let me think about it. I figured that was it and then he calls me the next day and says, 'Let's talk about making *Better Off Dead*.' It was kind of like a miracle. And then it's, 'Here's a parking space! Here's an office!' Unbelievable.

"Then I met Caro Jones, the casting lady. And I didn't realize I could ask for people. She said, 'Who do you want to see in the room?' I thought she was going to tell *me*. I didn't think I had a choice.

"It turned out I really had to fight for John [Cusack]. Up till then, he was mainly known for nerd parts, you know. He'd already done *The Sure Thing* but it hadn't been released yet. Henry Winkler, who produced it, had seen a short of mine, *My 11-Year-Old Birthday Party*, at a film festival and he had given me an office at Paramount for a while. Such a nice man. That's where I wrote *Better Off Dead*. He really liked my stuff. He didn't buy it, but he was guiding me. And it was he who introduced me to John Cusack. He helped arrange for a special screening of *The Sure Thing* to convince Michael and the CBS Films people that John could be a romantic lead.

"And then I said to the casting director, 'Well, for Charles De Mar, can I get anybody I want?'

"'Well,' she said, 'you can *ask . . .'*"

Savage had seen *Risky Business* and the movie had an enormous impact on him, as it had on Jeff Kanew before him. Fortunately for me, he also saw something else: "We could talk about John Cusack all night," Savage said, "but the most important thing to me, even before getting John, was getting you. When I saw you as Miles [in *Risky Business*], that was a game-changer," he told me. "I mean when you have a second banana, a supporting character, steal the movie from the star—and not even by saying that much, but just saying the most important things—it just guided that movie. When I saw it in Westwood, my mind was blown. Then at some point, I saw *Revenge of the Nerds* and it's the same guy! And I thought if I had that guy in my movie, that's all I would ever need!" Savage shook his head and smiled. "I mean, that's so *me*!

"I mean, seriously, I figured people must be paying you a million dollars, or something but I said, 'I want Mr. Armstrong!'

"And they said, 'Well, we can't find him.'

"'What do you mean you can't find him?'

"'Well, he's up in the mountains in Canada, or something. We can't reach him.'"

Savage laughed. "I said, 'I don't care. Get a snowmobile. Get a moose. Just find him, you know?' Once they told me I could *maybe* have you in my movie, I was saying we can't stop until we get an answer of some kind!

"I think you were the first person actually signed to *Better Off Dead*. And having you—in my usual I-can-use-his-genius-to-my-advantage way—suddenly I was so confident in my movie. Then I could say, 'I love Diane Franklin, let's get her.' Or 'I loved Amanda Wyss in *Nightmare on Elm Street*, let's get her.' It was a game-changer, getting you in my movie."

Like Booger, Charles De Mar was based on a real person, whose name actually was Charles De Mar. Savage told me: "Charles De Mar was a guy I grew up with. Really funny, very confident; a goofball. I really liked him. So I was going to make the character someone like that, but then when I saw *Risky Business*, I thought someone like Miles, in high school, giving advice to everybody, but he's totally clueless, would be really funny. So he was inspired by you, but then when I actually got you to play him, that was a dream."

Part of Savage's dream that didn't come true was the idea of shooting the film in Connecticut—where he had grown up—and then shooting the skiing scenes in Vermont, where he used to go to ski as a boy. Not surprisingly, Michael Jaffe and the company nixed that idea due to the expense. Instead, the ski scenes were shot in Utah, at the Snowbird Ski Resort. We were all flown up for five days or so and for the first time I actually began to feel, unequivocally, that I had *really* chosen the right career. This was the life. Housed in the swank ski lodge at Snowbird with excellent company, good food and copious drinks, easy shooting days: as far as I was concerned this part of *Better Off Dead* could've gone on indefinitely.

It was only when we were shooting the scenes at the top of the K-12 that I felt I was really earning my money. The cold was brutal and the wind sometimes threatened to sweep us off the mountain. Now and then, it would clear enough to actually shoot something. Only a skeleton crew was taken up—just Savage, Cusack and me with the script supervisor, producer and enough people to operate the camera and sound. By the end it's obvious in the film that John's and my faces were so cold we could barely get our lines out. Savage, buried under masses of winter gear and wrapped under scarves with just a slit for his eyes, would stand just off camera, shouting out unintelligible ideas for new lines.

Savage: Mrurrhefe?

Curtis and John: Whaaat??

Savage: Mruffhefe, afeemmanf, doynfan sarrrnalhois! Hueapirkj mabcveips, tjwosrjf, he bdue nfe?

Curtis and John: WHAAAAAT???

Savage: (Pointing at me) Gurrfuz!!?

Curtis: WHAT?

Savage (trying to act out his direction as shouts into the wind): Horurrruph alhepffhed jriessss fhot!! Lanedvue, mfhepaken yoshs oktmq! Urba? AAAG. . . . AFEN!!

And so the long day wore on.

The wrap party for *Better Off Dead* took place on the last day of filming at Snowbird and it was one of those booze-ups that mark epochs. Everyone felt euphoric, as if we'd been a part of something that was, if not important, at least a comedy that would be noticed. Warner Bros. noticed and picked up *Better Off Dead*. They started doing test screenings and could barely contain their glee—the movie was testing phenomenally well. So well that the studio, in an almost profligate gesture of confidence, sent the young director out on a college tour to screen the film and do a Q and A. These screenings, as well, were markedly successful. Savage had been signed to one of the top agencies in Hollywood and the word was out: there was a new kid in town. He *was* something new: an unprecedented mix of John Hughes and Luis Buñuel. *Better Off Dead* was turning out to be what CBS Films and Warner's had fervently hoped it would be—the next *Fast Times at Ridgemont High*. John Cusack, also widely regarded as the next big thing in young leading men, was signed to do Savage's next film, a quasi-sequel to *Better Off Dead* called *My Summer Vacation*, scheduled to shoot the following summer at various locations on Cape Cod. The success of *Better Off Dead* was so confidently anticipated that rumors were already circulating that the upcoming film was only the second in a possible *trilogy*. Savage started rounding up actors from the first film to join him on the Cape, including Diane Franklin (whose cameo was later cut), Laura Waterbury, Taylor Negron and me, as well as newcomers: the subversive comic Bobcat Goldthwait; Joel Murray, the youngest brother of Bill Murray and Brian Doyle-Murray, but new to film himself; Tom Villard, late of the hit television show *Bosom Buddies*; and Demi Moore, then the smoldering "bad girl" doyenne of John Hughes's stable of "brat pack" actors.

It seemed like everything was perfect and nothing could possibly go wrong. Which is when you have to start looking over your shoulder, as Savage was shortly to find out.

BAD MEDICINE AND ONE CRAZY SUMMER

SPAIN AND CAPE COD, MA. 1985

I came late to the *One Crazy Summer* shoot, and as a result missed the initial rupture between John Cusack and Savage, which I will address in its place.

In the meantime, I had spent several months in Spain working on my fifth film, an oddity called *Bad Medicine*. Some films, like *Revenge of the Nerds*, turn out to be better than they have any right to be. *Bad Medicine* is an example of the opposite: a film that had everything going for it but managed to miss the mark by several parasangs. It wasn't a bad film really. Just peculiar.

It boasted a deep bench of character talent of the time: Alan Arkin, Julie Hagerty, Steve Guttenberg, Julie Kavner, Bill Macy, Joe Grifasi, Alan Corduner, Taylor Negron, Robert Romanus, Candi Milo and Gilbert Gottfried. Based on the book by Steven Horowitz and Neil Offen, it tells the story of a group of misfit medical students who, rejected by all the top medical colleges in the U.S., attend a cut-rate and frankly suspect medical school in Central America run by petty dictator Dr. Ramón Medera (Arkin). We were to shoot somewhere in Central America, but the ferocious war being sponsored by the CIA at the time made that impossible so we went to Spain instead.

It had been one of the most exhilarating experiences yet, but ultimately enormously frustrating. On the one hand, we had a handful of some of the best farceurs in the business, working at the top of their game and doing it during a Spanish spring of unsurpassed beauty. During several weeks we were housed in one of Franco's old posadas, in a tiny village near Lorca in the south of Spain, which featured nothing but a small café and-whorehouse across the street. For the whorehouse, these months early in 1985 became a kind of golden age. How it survived before we arrived, I can't fathom, but while we were there it did booming business. It was a kind of club for the crew after hours, and even those who didn't actually pay for sex paid for strong, wildly overpriced drinks and dancing with the women. The potent Moroccan hashish was plentiful and cheap and the countryside was beautiful.

On the other hand, there was Harvey Miller.

Harvey was such a character that, years later, he realized he was sitting on a gold mine and wrote a one-man play starring himself called *A Cheap Date with Harvey Miller*. At this point in 1985 he had come off running the television adaptations of *The Odd Couple* and *Private Benjamin*. He was a well-known comic writer and producer of the old school. He was also a "doctor": someone brought in to punch-up pilots that needed the kind of hard jokes he was famous for. He once told me that he hated the series *M*A*S*H* because there were "not enough jokes." He was acidly witty, avuncular, irascible, prone to prolonged sulks when he wasn't getting his way and full of stories about his famous friends, who appeared to number in the thousands. He had a reputation for helping everybody. Actors, producers, other writers were all beneficiaries of his comic largess. He had thick glasses and long gray hair and looked like someone Woody Allen would play in somebody else's movie. He was truly one of the funniest people I've ever worked for, but he was one of those writers who had a hard time interacting with humans outside of a writer's room. Probably inside, too, for all I know.

After a career of joke writing and bailing friends and associates out of script difficulties, often behind the scenes, Harvey decided it was time to call in his chips. Hence, *Bad Medicine.*

During the course of filming, he became known by his partisans as "eccentric" and by everyone else as "impossible." His partisans became fewer in number as time went on. I had been one of them at the start, but he finally wore me down.

The examples are too many to list, but a few stood out. When we first arrived in Madrid, Harvey decided that there were too many men in the cast with dark hair. This struck me as kind of arbitrary, since we all had different faces, but Harvey stuck to his guns. Someone was going to have to dye his hair. Some, like Gottfried and Romanos, were supposed to appear Hispanic so they weren't in the running. Arkin, who had not arrived yet, was going to be wearing a wig, which he hated, but getting a new one in a different color would be prohibitively expensive, so Harvey decided it was down to Guttenberg and me.

Harvey said to us, "There's too much dark brown hair in this picture. People aren't going to be able to tell anyone apart. I think one of you guys need to dye your hair."

Guttenberg, who was after all one of the stars of the film, just laughed good-naturedly like Harvey had made a joke, and walked away.

"Okay," said Harvey to me. "You."

"But . . ." I started whining.

"Nah, it'll look great!" he assured me. "Hey, and guess what?" Almost like he knew my soft spot, he leaned in and said, "Guess who our hairdresser is?"

"I don't know. Who?"

"He's the guy who cut John Lennon's hair for *How I Won the War*!"

"Really?" I squeaked. John Lennon's haircut in Richard Lester's anti-war comedy had been international news at a time when actual international news just couldn't compete with things like John Lennon's haircut. And here was my opportunity to actually talk to the man who had cut it! The man personally responsible for the most famous shearing since Samson! I could get the inside scoop! Details! Gossip! Who knew what?

"Swear to God," said Harvey. "You should talk to him about it. He'll come to your room tonight and dye your hair. Ask him. Trust me. He's got some great stories!"

Sure enough, that night the hairdresser, a Spanish man, probably in his fifties, showed up in my room to make me light-haired.

When I started talking to him, I realized he didn't speak a word of English. I was making valiant but fumbling attempts at Spanish but was at that time unequal to the task of doing anything but order things in restaurants. As he was working his magic on my hair, I was able to determine that he had, in fact, been the hairdresser who had cut Lennon's hair, but beyond this we could not go. I knew, of course, that Harvey spoke not a word of Spanish so his dangling of unheard Beatle stories was just something to shut me up long enough to get my hair dyed.

The next morning, I went to the mirror and shrieked. My hair had gone from dark brown to something similar to the color of the bottom of a Revere Ware saucepan. "Copper" doesn't begin to describe this color. I was mortified. I couldn't imagine what Harvey would do when he saw it.

I stormed up to him on the set later that day.

"Harvey?" I revealed the disaster.

He stared at me blankly for a moment. Then:

"What?"

"My hair!?"

"Oh! They did it?" He squinted at it for a moment; then nodded. "Looks good."

"Harvey," I yelled. "I look like a lit match."

"Hey," he said, "at least it's not dark brown anymore."

More awkward was when Harvey shot an extensive sequence with Alan Arkin that went awry. In the dailies Harvey saw some massive problem that was significant enough that the whole sequence was going to have to be shot again. To make matters worse, it was something that Harvey should've seen, and hadn't. Now he was going to have to tell Arkin that he'd have to re-do the sequence because of his mistake. What to say?

Then, he came up with the perfect solution.

Harvey went to Arkin in his trailer and told him they were going to have to reshoot. Alan, unsurprisingly, asked why. Harvey had his answer all ready.

"It's Arlene and Alex," he said, shaking his head, referring to the film's executives in Los Angeles. "I don't know what the problem is, but they had this big issue with your performance . . ."

"What?" snapped Arkin.

"I'm really sorry, Alan," Harvey replied, with a sincere regret that became him nicely. "I thought you were great but they're just not having it. I defended you, but it looks like there's nothing to do but shoot the whole thing over again."

Of course, Harvey had forgotten that Arlene Sellers and Alex Winitsky were close friends of Alan's. So Alan immediately called them in L.A. to ask what the problem was with his performance . . .

What exactly Harvey was told in subsequent phone calls—first from Alan and then from Arlene and Alex—is shrouded in mystery, but for the next couple of days Alan Arkin boycotted the movie and Harvey Miller wandered around, speechless, hollow-eyed, jumping when people spoke to him and generally looking like someone who hadn't known it was loaded.

One morning we were all on the bus about to head out to the distant pueblo where we were shooting many of our exteriors. We were waiting for our makeup artist, who was unaccountably late. Finally, she came out of the posada with her assistant. The makeup artist was in tears, clinging to her friend and talking in Spanish a mile a minute. Meanwhile, the assistant was explaining the situation in Spanish to the first A.D. As she spoke, with the makeup artist sobbing next to her, the bus got very quiet, except for Harvey yelling, "What?! What is it?! What's going on?!" Finally, the A.D. turned to Harvey with a very serious expression.

"Harvey," he said, "her sister is a flight attendant on the Spanish national airline. One of the planes crashed this morning and she thinks perhaps her sister was on it."

"Oh my God," yelled Harvey. "Was any of our film on it?"

By our return to Madrid following weeks in the south, Harvey had antagonized everyone on the film. People were taking turns pulling one another back from physically assaulting him. Julie Hagerty came to my room one night after a particularly brutal day on the set to find me practically in tears, writing a hate note to Harvey. She actually had to take it away from me by force and tear it up to keep me from marching to his room—it was about one in the morning—and delivering it to him personally.

Finally, things had become so toxic between Harvey and the crew that serious measures had to be taken. Harvey's producer Jeff Ganz told him if he didn't take the whole crew out for a really expensive dinner at one of the really nice restaurants in Madrid, he, Jeff, wouldn't answer for the consequences. Harvey whined and argued and complained but he finally gave in.

They booked a private dining room at a four-star restaurant and then the invitations went out to all the crew people that

Harvey had brutalized one way or another over the last couple of months. Some had to be talked into attending, but this, they were told, was Harvey's olive branch to everyone. They all arrived to find Harvey awaiting them. The wine started flowing immediately. The dishes came, one course after another. Gradually, everyone started loosening up. Even Harvey was becoming, for him, the life of the party, which for Harvey meant not talking much and bolting his food like he didn't know where his next meal was coming from.

When it came to sheer rapidity of mastication and swallowing, no one could keep up with him. Then he sat, waiting for the next course, barely containing his impatience, tapping his fingers restlessly at the end of the table and muttering to himself. Then he got up and started pacing back and forth. Everyone was having such a good time no one even noticed when Harvey slipped quietly out of the restaurant and into the night.

Ever the mensch, he had paid for his dinner on the way out, leaving the producers to foot the bill for everyone else.

Needless to say, by the time I had returned to the States from *Bad Medicine* I was eagerly anticipating the laughter, joy and youthful high spirits of a Savage Steve Holland set.

I had only spoken with Savage once, over the phone, in the months that had passed since we wrapped *Better Off Dead*. He was excited but sounded stressed. At that point everything was still looking up, but he was under enormous pressure from the studio to have the script for *My Summer Vacation*—now re-titled

One Crazy Summer—ready for a summer shoot even before his first movie was ready to be released. He was feeling rushed and panicked but really looking forward to spending the summer making a movie on his beloved Cape Cod with his friends.

He talked at some length about Ack Ack Raymond, the character he had written for me. He wanted to do something a little different from the roles I'd been playing so far, so he was casting me against type as a young, sweet innocent; the only son, and disappointment, of a military father (played wonderfully by SCTV's Joe Flaherty), who named him for gunfire. Never was a child more inappropriately named.

Ack Ack was to be dressed in an odd combination of military fatigues and T-shirts emblazoned with characters from the classic *Rocky and Bullwinkle Show*. He was kind of awkward, pained at the fact that his father disapproved of him. He gives a sensitive little monologue over a discarded doll he finds on the beach. And his best friend was a crab.

In one of Savage's signature touches, he included a B story in which Ack Ack befriends a hermit crab. He has conversations with the crab, goes for long walks on a beach at sunset with the crab. The crab (I'm sorry, I've forgotten the crab's name) was a real crab but was kitted out with some kind of auto-animatronic system that allowed him (or her—I've forgotten the crab's gender, too) to move around for his (or her) scenes.

This was essential, because crabs aren't known as great walkers, and when it came to technical things like hitting their marks, they are hopeless. Plus, because it was an actual crab, we had to keep it in a tank until we were rolling and then resubmerge it immediately at the end of the scene. This meant me rehearsing and even doing my close-ups with a patently fake plastic crab who gave me nothing. In all fairness, the real crab didn't give me that much more than the plastic one, but in the years since I've worked with people like Gary Busey and Arnold Schwarzenegger, who gave me even less.

The crab scenes were all shot and eventually cut from the film, as the whole boy/crab thing was deemed just too weird, even for a Savage Steve Holland movie. The crab, as far as I know, never did another picture.

Many of the actors, producers and much of the crew of *Better Off Dead* were returning for *One Crazy Summer*, and it looked as if it was to be a lovely summer on Cape Cod. Which leads me to the cast and crew screening of *Better Off Dead*, which was to be held just a couple of days before my arrival.

And this was where everything started to go south.

There couldn't have been a more enthusiastic audience crowded into the theater for the screening. It was the Saturday before principal photography began the following Monday on Cape Cod. Under the circumstances, this was kind of like everyone watching home movies. All the cast was there, including John Cusack and Demi Moore, who had driven down together from Chicago to get acquainted. Also present, for his first film and on Cusack's recommendation, was his friend Jeremy Piven.

"We thought the screening would be fun," Savage told me. "It was kind of unusual that so many of the cast and crew were actually together for the second movie. So we started the screening on that Saturday night and I would say it was at the most fifteen minutes into the movie—maybe even ten minutes into the movie—John got up and left. I thought he'd gone to the bathroom or something but then . . . he never came back.

"And I got really paranoid about it. I mean, he hadn't even seen the movie yet, so how could he not like it? It was just weird. I didn't see him all day Sunday. Then on Monday I got word that he was really upset. Then when he showed up on the set, I asked him what was wrong.

"'I just want you to know,' John told me, 'that I don't trust you. You're the worst director I've ever worked with. I will never listen to anything you have to say to me ever again.' This was on the set, just outside the house we were using for your [Ack Ack's] house.

"I was crushed, but we had to keep going. I mean this was day one—*hour* one—of shooting this eight-million-dollar movie. There are Warner executives on the set. The last thing I need is to have them getting the sense that there's a problem on the first day.

"So I told John, 'Well, okay. Don't worry. Um, you can do whatever you want to do, I just need to have you here, talking to Joel about . . . whatever.' Joel [Murray] was a good sport about it. You know, I still had to *direct*. It was just super awkward. My leading man doesn't trust me, won't talk to me, I'm supposed to be directing him and he won't even look me in the eye and there are grown-ups on the set watching this, you know? It was scary.

"What I learned as the movie went on, you and Joel and Bobcat were still outstandingly funny and I think John eventually kind of wanted to get back in on that. He came up and tried, a little bit. But it was a bad way to start."

By the time I arrived a few days later, everything had settled into a hot, restless stew of uncertainty and resentment. I almost didn't recognize Savage when I saw him the first time. Far from the cheerful, positive, wisecracking ball of energy I was accustomed to, he had the bowed head and slightly glassy-eyed appearance of a whipped dog.

"John hates me," were the first three words out of him that morning.

Bewildered, I responded, "John who?"

"Cusack," Savage said flatly. I laughed.

"That's ridiculous," I said. "He doesn't hate you!"

The story came stuttering out. It seemed incredible that someone as easy-going and generous as Cusack would've had such a violent reaction to *Better Off Dead*. Of course, I hadn't seen the film yet, so I couldn't help but wonder whether John was right. There is also an old saw in the movie business: the more fun you have on the set, the less fun the finished film turns out to be, and we'd had a lot of fun on *Better Off Dead*. I reassured Savage to the best of my ability and waited until I could talk to Cusack and hear it all straight from him.

Only that didn't happen all at once. After his initial outburst, John seemed reluctant to discuss his feelings about *Better Off Dead*, at least with me. This was strange because we had really bonded during the movie. Perhaps he was concerned about throwing me off my game by denigrating the talent of the person we were working for. Maybe he just didn't care. I still discussed it with Savage from time to time, and still wondered whether this was all just insecurity on his part.

But it wasn't. John's attitude was undeniable once we were on the set. He was simply not among those present.

"There was a conversation," Savage recalled. "There was a discussion with Michael Jaffe about whether we were just going to have to find somebody else. If he wasn't going to play ball here, I mean, he's in a funny movie but he's totally mad, he's actually *playing* it mad. I'll never forget, it was the first scene we shot with you that it really stood out that John was just not in the moment. He just showed up for work and I'm saying, 'Okay, John, you stand here. Do what you want, but we just have to get through this scene.' It's the scene where he looks the most pissed off, as if he just doesn't want to be there. And that was when Jaffee said, 'We may have to talk to Warner Bros. about replacing him. We may have to just start over with someone else. This is bad.' And that's when I fucking panicked. Somehow, we pushed through it but there was a while there I thought they were going to stop the movie."

Then one day, something seemingly inconsequential occurred that brought everything out in the open for me.

We were watching Savage direct a scene in which Squid (Kristen Goelz), a silent, curious little girl with apparently supernatural powers, is seen walking down the street with her mangy-looking dog, Bosco, and her Ron and Nancy Reagan lunchbox. John and I both despised Reagan and his politics, and we found the idea of this demon-like child carrying a Ron and Nancy lunchbox incredibly funny. Afterward, we told Savage what a great satiric touch it was.

To our astonishment, Savage admitted it really wasn't satirical at all; more of a tribute, really. He liked Ronald Reagan.

Savage? A Reagan supporter?

I was shocked. Of course, I had no right to be. He had never talked politics with either one of us. I guess we just assumed he hated Reagan as much as we did, which is ridiculous in retrospect. In Hollywood, Republicans of our generation existed. The fact that we didn't personally know any of them wasn't Savage's fault. The fact that we had spent many weeks in close proximity to a Republican and hadn't been turned to stone or something was a lesson, at that point, we were incapable of learning.

I had been raised not to discuss other people's politics and religions, so I was able to swallow my instinctive revulsion and just say, "Oh, okay, that's cool," or something equally inoffensive. But for John, this was absolutely the last straw.

"You are kidding. You are kidding me," he said in an even, cold voice. He may even have removed his sunglasses to get a better look at this changeling. It seemed, as far as John was concerned, that if he was being forced to act in a stupid comedy with a man for whom he had no respect as a director, he could deal with it. But when that man reveals himself to be a supporter of someone he regarded as the worst president ever, that was simply too much.

He stormed off, leaving me to talk to Savage about the weather.

From that time on, John made no bones about his unhappiness. In Wodehouse's immortal phrase, he may not have been disgruntled, but he was very far from being gruntled. While we remained friendly, I found myself spending more time with other cast members, like Bobcat Goldthwait and Demi Moore.

Bobcat had only just moved to L.A. He was new enough that he had to take a bus to his audition for *One Crazy Summer*.

For Savage, that kind of determination might have been enough to cast him right there, but his audition was weirdly brilliant on top of it. Bobcat invited Savage to see his act that night; he went and that clinched it. He had already cast Tom Villard in the film as one of the group of local oddballs. But he had to have Bobcat in his film, so he wrote him in as Villard's twin brother.

People who only knew Bobcat from comedy clubs were always shocked to discover what a smart, politically progressive person he was, which always surprised me. His politics seemed obvious to anyone who looked past the persona he presented, and just the way his act was structured spoke to his intelligence. I liked him immediately.

Bobcat really became the center around which everyone else on the picture revolved. Everyone was drawn to him: John, Demi and Joel Murray because of his coolness, Savage because of his humor and the energy he brought to the project, and I because Bobcat shared my politics and feminism, which few men on the films I was making did at the time. It was his first film and as he told me many years later, "Yeah, when I first met you I thought, Oh, good, this is what these Hollywood people are like! This'll be easy! Then you wound up being the last one I met like that for a long time."

And it wasn't just energy he brought to the process. In at least one case, he brought a perfectly formed scene, in its entirety, to the film that both Savage and I wound up benefiting from. One day at lunch, Bobcat took me aside and said he had an idea he wanted to pitch to Savage, but he wanted it presented in full, which required my help. We went to the garage set where it was to take place, rehearsed it and, after lunch, presented it to Savage, who just kept exclaiming, "Oh my God! Yes!! Oh my God!!" Whatever we had been intending to shoot after lunch, this was what we shot in its place.

It was the scene, well loved by fans of the film, when Egg Stork, played by Bobcat, takes Ack Ack, my character, aside to tell a story about a lonely little boy who nobody ever liked; everyone thought he was weird and he was bullied and beaten up by everyone in school.

It is a weirdly touching moment. Ack Ack, going through a rough patch himself in the film at that point, thinks he understands. He gives Egg a shy, sympathetic smile.

"And were you that little boy, Egg?" he asks gently.

"Ahh, no!" screams Egg in Bobcat's inimitable strangled delivery. "But I really used to love beating the crap out of him, though!"

The one drawback to Bobcat's presence on the set was that John, Demi and Joel, to varying degrees, started talking like him on camera. Not like Bob talked; how *Bobcat* talked. It was completely unconscious but unmistakable. It was sort of like an American being with someone English or Australian. If you are sensitive to these kinds of things, you find yourself aping the accent.

In this case, it was obvious enough that Savage actually had to talk to Demi and John about it, which irritated John even more. Every time Savage approached John on the set, the temperature would drop fifteen degrees and the rest of us would all huddle together for warmth.

Demi and I became set buddies. She was seeing Emilio

Estevez at the time, but the relationship was rocky and I was happy to provide an ear. We had dinners, went to movies—she even took my sister to AA meetings when she was in town for a visit. We were both up for the film *About Last Night* and helped each other run lines before the quick flight to New York for the audition. (She got it. I didn't.) It was nice having a calm, normal, platonic relationship with a woman on a set that was becoming increasingly testy as the shooting went on.

Then, I got a call from Demi late at night. She apologized for the lateness of the hour but said there was something that had been on her mind for a while and she really needed to talk to me about it.

There was something funny about the way she said it. I told her to fire away. There was a pause.

"It's not really something I can tell you over the phone. It's . . . complicated. Could you come to my room?"

I stared at the wall, listening to the blood in my ears. So this is how it starts, I thought. I emphasize that there had been nothing on either side of this relationship that would have given anyone the slightest indication that it could be going in a different direction. And yet here we were.

I told her I'd be over directly. I hung up the phone and took a few minutes to collect my thoughts. This had the potential to be an extremely delicate situation. But it really wasn't something I had instigated. These things happen between sophisticated people, I said to myself. It was no one's fault. But we had been thrown together in a beautiful place, far from home, and now, thanks to the mysterious workings of this talented, beautiful woman's heart, she felt the need to take it to the next level. How I handled it was of the utmost importance.

I took a quick shower, brushed my teeth, dressed and passed across to her room, my heart pounding. I have never considered myself an attractive man, certainly not to someone like Demi. But attraction is a complex and unpredictable quality. I found myself wondering if I'd overdone the Old Spice behind my ears.

She opened the door and I stepped in. We exchanged a couple of brief hellos, then the room got very quiet.

"So," I said, "what's up?"

Demi backed away and then nervously started moving around the room, adjusting things. Books were moved, glasses taken from a table to a bedside stand, a jacket taken off a chair and hung in the closet.

"I . . . just wanted to talk, you know. I mean, we've been spending a lot of time together . . . and you're someone I feel I can really trust . . ."

"Of course," I said, stepping toward her. "Anything." I uncorked an encouraging smile and she did a startled backward loop, positioning herself against the wall with a big black chair between us. Clearly this was proving very difficult for her.

There was another silence, broken by the distant crash of the ice machine. She couldn't seem to get the ball rolling and I realized it was going to be up to me. I took a deep breath.

"Demi . . ." I began.

"Well," she said, "here's the thing. Everything is kind of taking off for me right now and I'm doing a lot of press. Like, really a lot of press. People are starting to ask me things about important issues and I'm fine with most of them, but the one thing I just can't get a handle on is this whole Central American war."

"The . . . war in . . . ?"

"Yeah," she said. "People are asking me about it, what my feelings are about it, and I can't keep it straight. I know it's Nicaragua and El Salvador, but which side are we on? And who are the contras? You seem to know a lot about politics. Could you explain it, 'cause I just find it really confusing."

Nothing solidifies a calm, normal, platonic friendship quite like a late-night chat about the history of the CIA and American military intervention in Central America, and Demi and I remained friends over the course of the filming.

The same could not be said for John and Savage. John wouldn't speak to Savage if he didn't have to and openly resisted whatever he suggested on the set. Conversely John would come up with ideas that he would insist on using whether Savage liked them or not. One was the scene at the drive-in when Hoops (John's character) was on his clandestine date with Cookie, during which Hoops, terrified of being spotted by Cookie's boyfriend, is watching the film wearing sunglasses and a pith helmet, literally hiding behind bushes inside the car. Kimberly Foster, who played Cookie, told me afterward how awkward and embarrassing the whole evening was.

"He didn't want to be playing the fool," Savage said. "Which is too bad, because there's a lot of falling down and silliness in the script, which he knew going in. But he just didn't want to be that guy."

Even years later, Savage remembers John's cold contempt with pain and hurt. He was already insecure about his abilities in general and *One Crazy Summer* in particular. If he had felt he at least had John's support it would have been easier. But faced with the innate challenges of shooting a film, the additional stress created by John's intransigence and what Savage referred to as his "emotional disengagement" made him feel like he was losing the thread completely.

"I mean, I liked John," Savage told me. "I thought he was a really cool guy. I respected his opinion. I liked talking about movies with him. But now I was thinking, how could I have been so wrong about something that I thought was funny? Suddenly it . . . it was almost like I should be ashamed of myself. It just became so disappointing because I did respect his opinion and then it became one of those things, 'Maybe I really *don't* know what I'm doing.' You know, you start questioning yourself. And that's how the poison got into the thing."

If John had just been an asshole from the beginning it would've been one thing. But he was really a funny, charming, down-to-earth person at the time we did *Better Off Dead*; and even on *One Crazy Summer*, unless he was dealing with Savage, he was much the same person. But he also had an insecure side. One evening we were at the hotel watching Savage, Bobcat and Joel—three brilliantly funny people—riffing off of each other. When they were on a roll, nothing short of live ammunition could slow them down. Individually, they were effortlessly funny people, but when you put them together they were like a single, well-oiled joke machine. After a while, Bobcat started shooting off fireworks in the hotel (as was his wont) and John and I left them to it and went to sit outside.

John glanced back to the room, where the screams of laughter could still be heard. "I don't know about you," he said to me after a few moments, "but sometimes I just can't keep up."

I gave a weary laugh. "I gave up trying weeks ago," I told him. John and I were both straight-men in *One Crazy Summer*, both on screen and off. It wasn't a role either of us was accustomed to and neither of us was really equipped to compete with the others. It was worse for John, of course, who didn't want to be there in the first place.

There were times of unadulterated joy, but they were few. One was the night John, Bobcat, Joel and I spent on a Nantucket beach watching the inimitable Joe Flaherty, as Ack Ack's crazed Patton obsessed father, giving a training speech to a group of clueless, increasingly frightened Boy Scouts. Joe had a script but clearly regarded it more as a list of well-meant suggestions. A kind of comic jazz soloist, he knew when to come in, how long to let loose and how to always go out on a top note. No two takes were the same. When he found a riff that worked, it stayed in. One that didn't would be discarded automatically. He went on for hours. The four of us sat in the darkness just outside the bonfire-lit location, laughing in silent delight, conscious of what a treat it was to be able to watch a real master at work.

But oddly for a film so suffused with sunshine and silliness as *One Crazy Summer*, most of my recollections of the time were tinged with melancholy. John, ranting on about some forgotten injustice, while Savage stares at him with a bewildered half-smile of sadness. Tom Villard on a beach in Falmouth at sunset, on his knees, facing a young man none of us had ever seen before, also on his knees, the two staring wordlessly into each other's eyes, within arm's reach but with chasms between them. Demi and Emilio, famous, celebrated and envied, sitting across from each other at a restaurant, silent, awkwardness and impending dissolution radiating in great hopeless circles around them. And I, more and more aware of my own weaknesses and failings, befriending a waitress who was struggling in an abusive relationship, offering what support I could, which could never be enough. The last time I saw her, she asked me for a kiss. I gave her one. As I pulled away, her eyes were wet.

"No," she said. "A real one."

Savage had returned to L.A. from Cape Cod to oversee the editing of *One Crazy Summer* and the release of *Better Off Dead* only to find that people weren't answering his calls. Something was clearly amiss and Savage couldn't get anyone knowledgeable or honest enough to tell him what it was.

It was *Revenge of the Nerds* all over again. The preview screenings of *Better Off Dead* had been off the charts and yet the studio had inexplicably gone stone dead on the project. The number of theaters set for the film's release were cut back. There was no press. Suddenly, Savage Steve Holland had become the loneliest man in Hollywood.

The final indignity was reserved for the day *Better Off Dead* opened. Reviews were bad, box-office terrible, and when Savage called his agents that morning, he was told he was being dropped.

He still had *One Crazy Summer* to release, but the writing was on the wall.

It was 1985 and I was thirty-two years old. I had been working almost without a break since 1979. I had been married since 1981 to Cynthia Carle, though we had been spending increasing amounts of time apart and the separations were starting to take a toll.

After *One Crazy Summer*, my old mentor, Terry Kilburn of Meadow Brook Theatre, offered me a part in Noël Coward's brilliant farce *Present Laughter*. He offered Cynthia a role in it as well, which settled the matter and shortly after wrapping the film, I found myself back in Detroit again, onstage at the theater where my professional career had begun and acting with my wife for the second, and final, time. For now, the circumstances felt very much like a circle closing.

The production also starred Jayne Houdyshell, my old classmate from the Academy, and Carl Schurr, a fine actor and director whose day job was artistic director of Pennsylvania's Totem Pole Playhouse, where I would find a second home in the years to come doing summer stock. The show was a great success but by the time Cynthia and I had returned to Los Angeles, it had become clear that change was in the wind.

Since *Revenge of the Nerds*, I had really been a man without a country, or at least without a home. The roles on stage and film had been pretty much constant, for both of us. We had the apartment in New York but were also renting a place in Hollywood, because we had both been working there. But Cynthia was from L.A. and living there was something she had no interest in doing. It had reached the point where we had to make a choice—did we want to put our efforts into salvaging a failing marriage or did we want to cut our losses and focus instead upon saving our friendship? There were no children to consider and eventually the solution seemed inarguable: I would stay in Los Angeles and she would move back to New York. I would keep her beloved cat, Butch. She couldn't bear to take him back to the apartment, when he had grown so used to the California life of basking in the courtyard, dodging coyotes and killing things.

The decision was very civilized and logical, and ultimately correct, but it was a damaging period for me. I didn't have many friends in Los Angeles at that point, but those I did have knew how to have a good time and so did I. A life of pretty much unbridled debauchery followed, made easier by the fact that I never really had to get up in the morning, because the work that had been flowing so freely for the last few years suddenly went dry.

Part of this was due to the fact that the films I had done, with the exception of *Risky Business* and, arguably, *Revenge of the Nerds*, had not exactly set the world on fire. They had all been received tepidly, and while the first two had done well at the box office, the rest had been unmitigated disasters. It seems hard to imagine that films like this and *Better Off Dead* could have been seen as anything less than successes given their legendary status now, but that was the reality.

There had been loose talk about doing a sequel to *Revenge of the Nerds* ever since it opened. But the company who owned the rights to make that happen, Interscope, was blocked by 20th Century Fox, whose new administration had a strict no-sequel policy and hadn't been a fan of the movie in the first place.

The end result for me personally was that I had been working steadily but not in what you might call prestige motion pictures. *Clan of the Cave Bear* had been a disaster. (My favorite bad-review headline was from *Time* magazine: "When Is a Bear a Dog?") I don't even remember *Bad Medicine* opening in theaters at all, though it wasn't in them for long and I may just have missed it. I was auditioning for things but not being cast in them. I was beginning to think I'd lost the knack of auditioning. It was like the early days in New York, when I was just starting out, struggling to find who I was as an actor and what I had to offer. I did something I had never done before. I started turning down *auditions* because they frightened me. I would only go in on jobs for which I was perfect. I would reject anything that seemed against type at a time when those were the very roles I should have been working hardest to get.

Months passed like this. I was living on my savings and those were dwindling to a pretty alarming degree. I was seriously considering moving back to New York and trying to pick up where I'd left off in the theater. I was feeling that my initial instincts were being daily proven correct: I was never meant to be a film actor, it was wrong for me. I should've stayed in the theater, where I belonged. The following spring, while Cynthia was working out of town, I went back to spend a few weeks in our old apartment.

John Cusack was in New York, too, renting a two-bedroom

apartment on University Place in the Village with his friend and one-man entourage Jeremy Piven. We spent weeks together, culminating in a night at the Bitter End where Bobcat Goldthwait, who was rapidly becoming the hottest comedian walking, was doing his act.

Bobcat, as usual, was brilliant, but as the show was winding down and we were headed backstage to congratulate him, John spied Savage Steve in the crowd. That was enough for him and he fled the place without a word, Jeremy in tow. I went and greeted Savage and we went backstage together.

It was crowded with Bobcat's fans, including Richard Belzer, with whom I sat while Bobcat dealt with the mob. Finally, Savage approached him and the two started an intense conversation. It turned out that Savage was there to try to persuade Bobcat to publicize *One Crazy Summer*. "I'm desperate," we heard him say. "John's not talking to me, Demi wants nothing to do with it. You steal the movie. If I can't get you to do press, it's not going to have a chance."

Bobcat was polite but regretful, and Savage could look for no help from him. I don't know what his reasons were: whether he didn't want to publicize a movie that the film's stars wouldn't touch, whether his own burgeoning movie career made it impossible or what. But he wasn't buying.

"God," Belzer murmured to me, "this is just painful."

Savage left dejected and so did I. I returned to L.A. shortly after that. As much as I loved New York, I didn't have enough money to come back to try to start over. Things weren't looking promising in L.A. but I had to try.

Then one day, shortly after my return, I was submitted for

three auditions in the same day. Unprecedented! With a new-found energy and enthusiasm born of desperation and looming poverty, I flung myself into all three.

One was a television movie starring Ed Asner. I liked Ed Asner! I remember nothing about the role I was reading for, but it was young and quirky and who did young and quirky better than me? The second was for John Hughes's new film with Kevin Bacon. I don't even remember which movie it was, let alone what the part was, but John Hughes made total sense to me. This was right in my wheelhouse! Having done a string of cult youth-oriented pictures, I figured it was only a matter of time before John Hughes came calling. These were the two auditions that I put most of my focus on. The third was certainly the least promising of the bunch. The potential love interest of a regular character on a television show that I had never seen, but a lot of people were talking about. Love interest? I remember discussing this with my agent, who was very excited about the audition. I hastened to assure her that there was no use in my even showing up for it. I had never played love interest to anyone. No one would buy me as a love interest to anyone. I was feeling particularly dumpy and unattractive and felt we should just stick to dumpy, unattractive parts, like Booger and Charles De Mar.

For once, my agent wouldn't take my bullshit and demanded I do the audition.

So I went into the Ed Asner project and blew the audition. For once, my youthful quirkiness wasn't enough. It was one of those times where you've prepared for the thing and then you start in on it in the room and it's like an out-of-body experience. Almost like the classic actor's nightmare where you're on-stage opening night and realize you don't know the lines and missed all the rehearsals.

But I wrote that one off, pulled myself together and went on to read for John Hughes and Kevin Bacon. Honestly, I was completely taken aback to see I was actually reading *with* Kevin Bacon. The two men were welcoming and very nice and clearly were familiar with my work: in short, a love fest. Then I started reading. It began badly and went downhill from there. At some point during the audition I swear it got so quiet in that room I could hear Hughes's watch ticking. Their faces were frozen masks of encouragement.

Then, as the sun was setting, with despair and humiliation overwhelming me, I went in to read for the part of Herbert Viola on *Moonlighting*. The love interest one; the one I had no business reading for.

That one, I nailed.

MOONLIGHTING

LOS ANGELES, 1987–1989

When I came in to read that day, I wasn't reading for the part of Herbert Viola. I was reading from a script that had already been filmed and broadcast, an episode that had featured Allyce Beasley's poetry-spouting receptionist Ms. DiPesto prominently. They always had at least one of these episodes—called "DiPesto episodes"—every season, usually around Christmas so Cybill and Bruce could get their parts shot in a day and then get a long holiday. Though I didn't realize it at the time, this particular episode had featured Allyce's then-husband, Vincent Schiavelli, with whom I had worked on *Better Off Dead*.

The current episode, called "Yours Very Deadly," introduced my character, Herbert Viola, specifically as a temp. The reason for this, obviously, was to see how I came off. Did I work well with Allyce, and did I get along with Bruce and Cybill? And there was one other element that needed to be sorted out. Was I going to be "difficult"?

Maybe the despair and hopelessness I was feeling the day I auditioned helped. It does sometimes. There are times when, overcome with anger or sadness, actors can read with a depth or energy that they could never have brought to it on a good day. Whatever. I read well. But in this case, it wasn't just a good audition that saved the day. It turned out I also had *Risky Business* to thank for *Moonlighting*.

Moonlighting had already been on for a season at that point. The show's creator and mastermind, Glen Gordon Caron, had put together what was later described as a "placebo detective show." It had nothing to do with cops or crime or solving mysteries. The mysteries, often as not, made no sense at all. The crimes were mainly there to showcase the talents of its two mismatched lead characters, Maddie Hayes and David Addison. But there was a problem. There was no ensemble cast to shoulder the work on *Moonlighting*. There was just Shepherd and Willis getting the lion's share of the screen time every week, and it had become clear that another character was going to be needed to work with DiPesto, to be part of a B story and provide a secondary, less sexually charged relationship for viewers to follow and to take some of the pressure off the two stars. Once Glen started thinking about who would be a good choice for this, he started thinking about me because, like Jeff Kanew and Savage Steve Holland before him, he was a fan of *Risky Business*. It struck him that the "what the fuck" guy might fit the role perfectly.

Cybill Shepherd already had a long reputation as a diva and after a brief honeymoon period on *Moonlighting* was reverting to type. Bruce, on the other hand, was as funny, laid-back and casual off screen as he was on . . . for now. That would change. But Glen wanted to make certain that whomever he brought onto the show was going to be easy to handle and "professional." So he called Jon Avnet, producer of *Risky Business*, and asked what I was like to work with.

Fortunately, I received a stellar recommendation from Jon, who again told the story of how I was able to repeat a performance exactly over a period of three months, as if I had been able to turn water into wine. While I wasn't aware of it at the time, I was in.

Being cast as Viola on *Moonlighting* was the beginning of a remarkable phase in my career. It marked the end of almost a year of unemployment. Exciting, gratifying, infuriating, exasperating, exhausting and, finally, heartbreaking, it was a job that lasted two and a half years: a blink of an eye to actors who land television roles that can last ten years or more, but to me it seemed like a lifetime. I divorced my first wife shortly after it began and met my future second wife shortly after it was over.

With one exception—*Revenge of the Nerds II: Nerds in Paradise*, which will be dealt with in it's own chapter, out of order—I didn't make another feature film for almost five years. Having gone so long without ever having appeared on television, my career now basically became about being on television. Except for our summer breaks, when I would flee to Fayetteville, Pennsylvania, to do summer stock at Totem Pole Playhouse, my professional life consisted exclusively of playing Viola on a critically acclaimed and enormously popular television show.

On the day of the reading—having already twice proved that auditioning is an art, not a science—I went to the production office in the "Blue Building" on the Fox lot to read for Glen Gordon Caron, Jay Daniel, and the other executive producers. The show's casting director, Karen Vice, was going to be reading DiPesto's lines. Entering the room, I was faced with a long table, Glen seated in the center and the others arrayed on either side of him. It looked strangely like Da Vinci's "Last Supper," with Glen in the role of Christ, which on *Moonlighting* was an apt analogy. At the conclusion of my reading, he looked down the table, right and left, and to my utter amazement, everyone nodded in unison. Glen then told me I had the role, but they were going to put me in another room, because there were still actors waiting outside to read for the part and they had to go through them as a courtesy.

Everything after that was a blur, and I eventually headed home, enjoined to show up the following morning to shoot my first scene: a passionate kissing scene with Allyce Beasley.

My phone rang the following morning at about 6:00 a.m. It was my agent. Someone had called from *Moonlighting* with a question. Was it true Curtis was gay? If so, there was a possible problem. This was 1987, AIDS was rampant and still misunderstood, and since I was going to be—ahem—exchanging bodily fluids with Allyce Beasley, they wanted to know up front which way I swung.

I was speechless. There was no overt threat in this astonishing invasion of privacy. They would not be foolish enough to fire me because of my sexuality—or perceived sexuality—but they could presumably rewrite the scene to excise the passionate necking and the role that had been described as "recurring" could very possibly become "not recurring." My agent was aware of my heterosexuality but had been put in a position of having to have me confirm it, which I didn't do. I went to work as scheduled, the subject was not referred to and Allyce and I spent the morning rolling around on a desk as planned. I began to think I'd dreamed it. It was only later that the truth came out.

"I don't know if you ever knew this," Allyce told me in an interview in 2016, "but that was Vincent [Schiavelli, her husband at the time]. He really wanted to play that part. He'd already been on the show once, and I think he just thought the part was his. When he found out you got it, he got angry. He called his agent and that whole thing happened."

Vincent had told his agent that he was pretty sure I was gay. At that time, it was believed by many that AIDS was transmitted through saliva and since I was going to be kissing his wife, he demanded that they intervene and find out first.

Roger Director was fresh off the game-changing hit *Hill Street Blues* when he was brought by Glen Caron into the *Moonlighting* fold. In those early days the writing staff consisted of Debra Frank and Carl Sauter, Roger, Jeff Reno and Ron Osborne, shortly followed by Kerry Ehrin, Barbra Hall, Chic Eglee and others. Roger Director had been tasked with creating the character of Herbert Viola.

"Viola was introduced," Roger told me during a 2016 interview, "because we couldn't make twenty-two episodes. Bruce and Cybill had to be in every shot. The schedule was so tough.

There was a strain on everyone." Viola's relationship with Agnes DiPesto, Director said, "was a logical evolution. But of course we had to wait and see how that played out. You and Allyce turned out to make a good team, so in addition to furthering your own story, you could sort of comment about what, you know, the King and the Queen were doing. And I think it was just thought it might be a good idea if we could have a few scenes in which Bruce and Cybill were not on screen together.

"It was clear that you and Bruce were working well together. Working *really* well together. It always tickled us to watch dailies when you two were in a scene because he always had such a great manner, always throwing stuff away, whereas you were just super-earnest. He could always impress the shit out of [Viola] with some scheme he'd come up with, or some observation about the workings of the universe that [Viola] found fascinating. You just had this enthusiasm—pure enthusiasm. There was clearly room to develop that."

I don't think I had seen a single episode of *Moonlighting* before the day I showed up for work. Cybill's work I was familiar with, of course, but Bruce was just another name I didn't know. That first morning I was on the Blue Moon office set, talking awkwardly with Allyce Beasley, when Bruce and Cybill made their entrance at the same moment.

That was a rule, by the way, even then: Bruce and Cybill were called to set at the same moment so that one would not have to wait for the other. Later, as the relationship deteriorated, a couple of Teamsters were instructed to measure the exact distance between their two trailer doors to the stage entrance, so one actor wouldn't have to walk even a foot farther than the other. In subsequent years, I would work on two different shows—*Lois and Clark* and *The Chronicle*—both of which featured two stars who boasted to me of having even worse relationships than Bruce and Cybill. *Lois and Clark*'s Teri Hatcher and Dean Cain even had their trailers measured from the stage door, just as they'd heard *Moonlighting*'s trailblazers had.

Someone introduced me to them. Cybill was in wardrobe, a shiny blue creation that was mostly shoulder pads. Bruce was barely dressed at all and appeared hungover. As he explained it, he'd been in a club most of the night and overslept. Rather than shower, he just fell naked into his swimming pool, threw some clothes on and actually arrived at his call time, give or take an hour or so. They were both polite and welcomed me to the set. We blocked the scene and then Cybill vanished. Bruce, looking blearily at me, said, "So what the hell are you doing here?"

Funny question, really, and I was a little unsure how to respond to it. *Moonlighting* was a critical darling and its followers were passionate and rapidly becoming legion. I responded with the caution of a man crossing an unmarked minefield, little dreaming that that was what I was going to be spending the next three years of my life doing.

"Well, I don't know," I said. "It's a good show. . . ."

"Hmm," he said. Noncommittal. "But you do movies."

"Yeah," I said.

"That's the thing," he said. "If I could do movies, I'd be outta here so fast . . ."

Well, of course, that was a little peep into the future if there ever was one. I had never done television before, but it seemed to me as the weeks went by that this really was a great show. And for a comic actor, David Addison was just a gift from God. What I didn't realize was that Bruce was already tired of the David and Maddie schtick and wanted the show to move in a more serious direction that would give him a chance to show off his dramatic chops. The reason that Viola became the role of a lifetime for me was because Bruce was rapidly reaching the point where he would just refuse to do the comic stuff that Glen and the writers wrote for him. All those comic ideas had to go somewhere. So if they needed someone to pop out of a cake in full drag and sing "Lady Is a Tramp" or to be thrown down the length of a laden banquet table and smash into an ice sculpture or lip-sync "Wooly Bully" or do an extended Humphrey Bogart impression, I was their man! It would be a bumpy ride during the next couple of years, but *Moonlighting* was the last of the four jobs—following *Risky Business, Revenge of the Nerds* and *Better Off Dead*—that would establish my career for the next three decades.

First, though, I'd have to survive it.

The first exposure I had to the multifaceted force of nature that was Cybill Shepherd was just a couple of episodes after my arrival. We were doing a clip show at the time. Clip shows are what TV shows do when they are short on story ideas so they come up with some conceit which will allow them to string together various clips from past episodes. This system requires relatively little in the way of new filming and gives everyone—crew, cast and writers—a chance to catch their breath.

Well, the idea for this episode, "It's a Wonderful Job," was that Rona Barrett, the famous gossip maven, comes with her camera crew to do a story on the Blue Moon Detective Agency, because of all the "rumors" about David and Maddie not getting along. An amusing idea, twisting reality in that *Moonlighting* way to counter all the rumors about problems on the set with Bruce and Cybill, which were, of course, all true. The cold opening was particularly funny. Rona barges in after David and Maddie have had a fight and bangs on Maddie's door. The door opens to reveal a distraught Maddie, eyes red and swollen, hair disheveled. She is visibly shocked at the appearance of Rona and the cameras. "Oh, Rona! Just a minute." Closes the door. Stage wait. Then the door is opened and there stands Maddie, with a big fake smile, holding a sheet of scrim in front of her face.

"Hi, Rona!" Cut to opening credits.

This was really a marvelous inside joke. The scrim was a great gag, representing the camera filters that old-school cinematographers like our own Gerry Finnerman used on their actresses. They were intended to "soften" the features of actresses who were not, shall we say, in the first flush of youth. The effect, one of Gerry's specialties going back to his work on the original *Star Trek*, was pretty dated by the time we were doing *Moonlighting*. The end result was risible, but some stars of a certain age still swore by it and Cybill was no exception. I was actually kind of impressed that Cybill would go along with a joke like this.

Well, we had finished this shot and Cybill was sitting there while cameras were moving around, apparently lost in thought, the scrim sitting on the desk in front of her. Suddenly her face darkened. She snatched up the piece of scrim and stared at it.

"Hey!" she yelled. Everyone froze.

She held up the scrim and her voice took on a menacing tone. "I just got it!"

My position as the new kid on *Moonlighting* was a peculiar one. The politics of the set were complicated then and they were rapidly to deteriorate as time went on. But everyone I was dealing with on a day-to-day basis—Bruce, Cybill, Allyce, Glen— all looked at me as someone as yet in no particular camp but who could, with a little care, be annexed into their own. I felt at times like a comet being pulled into one planet's orbit, and eventually flung out again straight into a different planet's orbit and on again.

I understood fairly quickly that there was friction between Bruce and Cybill—long before I witnessed any personally. That had happened some time after my arrival, when I was standing outside Maddie's closed office door waiting for my cue to enter, while David and Maddie had a scene inside. Then the scene broke down and some sort of dispute began. It escalated rapidly, ending with Cybill flinging a briefcase against the door with a force that shook the set. The two disappeared (probably for the day) while the rest of the Blue Moon employees were hustled off the stage.

I realized there was a problem between Cybill and Glen during a visit to Glen's office shortly after I had become a regular on the show. There had been problems roiling the set and we were having a cautious conversation about them. Glen, at one point, gestured behind me.

"I mean, look at that," he said.

I turned and saw a dartboard on his office wall with Cybill's face on it. I looked back at Glen with wild surmise, not sure what I should say.

"Does that help?" I asked.

"No!" he said, sadly. "That isn't mine. That was her Christmas present to me. What do you do with a person like that?"

That was a question I was asked often by different people, about different people. I do honestly believe that Cybill struggled with a "boys' club" mentality on the show. Glen had gone on the record as saying he created David Addison as a reaction to the so-called "Alan Alda–sensitive-feminist-male" type of character that was allegedly flooding the culture following the success of *M*A*S*H*. As a feminist myself, I hadn't been struck by this phenomenon, but some swore it existed. Bruce and Glen were obviously close, which seemed natural enough, but whether Cybill's outsider status was a result of that or whether it was an attitude she had brought with her, I was never able to determine.

The first time I had a real encounter with Cybill was shortly after I started on the show. It was a late-night shoot—we frequently shot fourteen- or even sixteen-hour days—and I had left the soundstage on my way to my trailer. Cybill was also outside and we practically ran into each other. I had never actually had a private word with her at that point. The night before, I had seen a recent episode in which her work was well done and this seemed like a good time to tell her so.

"Oh, Cybill," I said, "I saw you in the episode the other night and—"

"Stop. Just stop," she said, turning abruptly to me. "You'd better not say anything nice to me. If you say anything nice to me, I'll probably cry."

There was a brief pause while I considered what my next move should be. On the one hand, she didn't seem remotely upset, so maybe she was just kidding. But you couldn't know with Cybill. I thought about saying, "Okay, never mind!" and just continuing on my way but that seemed wrong. Or I could've tried the jokey route and said, "Something nice? You kidding?" but again, that seemed to strike a wrong note. As we stood there in the darkness, it was clear we were at an impasse. She wasn't going anywhere and it was my line.

"Well," I said carefully, "no, I was just going to say that I thought you did some wonderful work in it." And with that, there was a gasp and a rush and the next thing I knew, she was in my arms, sobbing into my neck.

It probably didn't last for more than ten seconds or so, but for the time being my world consisted mainly of unusual tactile sensation. She was dressed in some sort of shiny, satin-like fabric that felt to my hands like a prom dress. Her hair was coated in some kind of aromatic product that guaranteed a completely unmussed look no matter how many character actors she threw herself at. I was considerably shorter than she was and was conscious of her having to sort of bend over to reach my shoulder.

And there we were. It seemed a little like a tableau in a Victorian melodrama in which the ingénue flings herself into the arms of her estranged lover at the Act 3 curtain. I felt I should say something, like "There, there," but again that seemed like an impertinent thing to say to Cybill Shepherd. I could imagine her pulling back suddenly and snapping, "How dare you say 'There, there' to me! Do you know who you're talking to?!" So I contented myself with a couple of cautious pats on her shoulder pads. It was like patting a box of books I was shipping somewhere.

After a few moments, without another word, she pulled herself away and ran into her trailer. The Teamster whose job it was to sit outside her trailer on guard whenever she was there had seen everything that had transpired. I stared at him as if begging for confirmation that what I thought had happened had, in fact, happened. He merely stared back at me, his face totally void of expression. I figured he'd seen way odder things.

Later, I was called back to the set to finish the scene we had been shooting. Cybill was of course not called until the rest of us were *in situ*, and ready to roll. I had to admit to a little uneasiness. What would happen when she got there? Cybill was tough, she'd been around and people who crossed her did so at their peril. And yet, in a moment of vulnerability, she had revealed her innermost self to a mere character actor. What would happen when she saw me? Would I get a meaningful glance that would speak volumes? Perhaps a discreet brush of her hand upon my arm? Maybe even a softly murmured "Thanks?"

I was prepared. After all, we had just shared an emotional moment and I would let her know with a wink, a warm smile or a squeeze of her hand that she could count on me. I would always be there.

Then she came sweeping onto the set, laughing with her

makeup and hair people, beautiful, unaffected, her old self—
and looked through me as if I wasn't there. From that time until
the last day I ran into her coming out of an elevator years later
in Vancouver, there was never a hint that she had ever revealed
anything to me that night. She may not have.

At the point that Glen Gordon Caron created *Moonlighting*
for Cybill Shepherd she had already enjoyed a career spanning
almost two decades. She had worked with Peter Bogdanovich,
Elaine May, and Martin Scorsese among many others. I had
gazed at her nude scene in *The Last Picture Show* at the Berkley
Theatre in Michigan with a kind of awe. But by the time *Moonlighting* came around I frankly admired her as much for her resil-
ience as her talent or her beauty. After all, beauty can fade and
having talent is no guarantee of anything but a multi-decade
career in Hollywood demands respect—especially for someone
who started out dismissed as a model who got lucky. She had
had a couple of career turnarounds and simply refused to allow
anything to slow her down. Bruce was my age when she stepped
out on that diving board in *Last Picture Show*, and I was in high
school. She may have been tough and often impossible, but that
kind of behavior isn't created in a vacuum. When it came to
casting the show, Glen had essentially two fights on his hands:
he had to fight for Cybill because of her reputation and he had
to fight for Bruce because he didn't have one yet. Despite some
off-Broadway and episodic television appearances, Bruce was
mainly known as a bartender in New York at the same place
John Goodman used to hang out.

Bruce had started out on the show as one of the boys. I wasn't there at the very beginning, but everyone on the crew told me about it. Cybill was always impossible, they said. Cybill, they said, was always a bitch. (The men in particular told me that.) But Bruce—BRUCE!—BRUNO!!—he was one of us, whoever the "us" was they were referring to. In those early days, it was really difficult to tell where Bruce ended and David Addison began. Bruce partied. So did David. Bruce joked. David had a wisecrack for every occasion. Bruce was a swinger in the old-fashioned, pre-feminist, New Jersey–born-and-bred definition of the word. (One of his favorite jokes: "Why did the feminist cross the road? To give me a blowjob.") He was a one-man Rat Pack. When he was in a good mood, it was as if the sun shone on Stage 20 exclusively. When he was in a bad mood, everyone else got in a bad mood, too, and then blamed Cybill for it. When he finally sobered up, later in the show's run, he was generally considered a lot less fun. Everybody told me that, too.

He rapidly amortized his success on the show into a quirky and briefly notable venture into rock and roll as a fictional character named Bruno. This is pretty much the dream of every actor everywhere who isn't satisfied just being an actor. As a rock star, Bruce was as highly qualified as any actor in the world who was pretending to be a rock star. *Moonlighting* showcased him in the famous "Atomic Shakespeare" episode, in which he performed a creditable cover of the Rascals' old hit "Good Lovin'." He got a band together eventually and did a highly publicized concert at the Paramount Theatre in Hollywood. The concert, which was attended by the crème de la crème of hip Hollywood, was turned into a *Spinal Tap*-like documentary called *The Re-*

turn of Bruno, which featured painful cameos by legends like Ringo Starr, who claimed that without "Bruno," the Beatles would still be electrician's apprentices in Liverpool.

By then Bruce was riding high with *Moonlighting,* as high as he could get with a mere television show. Movies, as he had said to me that first day, were now his goal. His first two films, which no one remembers, were both directed by famed director Blake Edwards. Sadly, *Blind Date* and *Sunset* were two of Edwards's weakest films, and the light comedic touch that served Bruce so well on television did not transfer successfully to the big screen. One more flop, and Bruce would've been relegated to television for life. At this point, fortunately, Joel Silver entered the picture and the third time was the charm. *Die Hard* buried Bruce's false starts in movies forever. Unfortunately, it buried *Moonlighting* along with them.

I was never part of Bruce's inner circle. I probably had two lunches with him in three years. He had a nickname for me ("Curt-eye") but he had nicknames for everyone so I don't think that meant much. I don't believe I ever saw the inside of his trailer. My position with Bruce as a person was really similar to Viola's with David: that of hapless sidekick.

An example: not many people remember this but Bruce started out as a Democrat. It was only when he reached the Joel Silver period and started hanging out with guys like Schwarzenegger and Stallone that he came roaring out of the Republican closet. But in the H. W. Bush campaign against Mike Dukakis, Bruce was still decidedly on the side of the angels. Most of young Hollywood at the time were going to be stumping for Dukakis all over the state by bus and plane. People like Robert

Downey Jr. and Rob Lowe, Katey Sagal, Michael Gross, Moon Zappa, Elizabeth Perkins, Hart Bochner, LeVar Burton, Morgan Fairchild . . . it went on and on.

But Bruce Willis, Cher and Sally Field weren't going to get stuck on a smelly bus with a lot of mad young actors for three days. So they just showed up before we all boarded to give statements to the press and *look* like they were boarding the bus. Then as the bus left they were sneaked off back to their cars and back to Malibu in time for brunch and a quick swim.

Bruce and I were sitting together before the scrum started. "Good to see you here, Bruce," I said.

Bruce nodded, squinting off into the distance. "I'll tell you, Curt-eye," he said, "people might think people like us don't have a right to get involved, you know, that we just take everything for granted. We make our money and go home. But it's really time everybody wakes up to the direction we're going in this country . . ."

And more and more in the same vein. Don't recall the exact words, but it was stirring stuff and I was impressed. This election clearly meant something to Bruce. I was surprised, as I didn't think I'd ever heard him speak at such length on any subject that didn't have a dirty punch line. Finally the press were all brought up and the A-listers, like Bruce and Cher, were put through their paces.

As Bruce started to talk I had a feeling I'd heard what he was saying somewhere before:

"You know, people think that we just take everything for granted," Bruce was saying into the mikes. "We make our money and go home. But it's really time everybody wakes up to the direction we're going in this country . . ."

As he went on and on I was thinking how funny it was that some actors can always find gullible schmucks like me they can run their lines with, while at the same time giving them the illusion of a personal moment!

For Christmas at the end of my first year on the show, I gave Bruce an album of pornographic thirties-era blues recordings called "Copulatin' Blues" and Cybill a new book about Rodgers and Hammerstein. Both gifts were accepted without comment. The closest I got to having actual quality time with Bruce consisted of one night when we were shooting extensive scenes driving around Los Angeles together. The episode was called "Blonde on Blonde" and we wound up being stuck in this car until at least three in the morning. It was during this interminable night that he intimated to me that there had been one disastrously ill-conceived "thing" between him and Cybill, early on in the show's run. While not going into explicit details (for once), he made it clear that that kind of mistake was one I should be sure never to make. I told him I didn't think it would be an issue.

We were setting up at a little park just off of La Cienega and I was wandering around, waiting to be called to set. It was one or two in the morning and the neighborhood was deathly still—no one around. Then I saw a young woman walking toward me. When she saw me, she came up and asked what was going on. It seemed odd that anyone who lived in Los Angeles could mistake a location shoot for anything else, and it turned out that she had indeed just moved here. We started chatting.

She was very pretty and was apparently just getting off work and had been driving home when she saw our trucks. She asked what show we were working on and I told her *Moonlighting*. She had heard of it but never seen it. I was getting coffee and offered her one and we wound up having an in-depth conversation about what it was like being transplanted to a strange city, and I was thinking how strange it was that I should come across someone like this in an empty part of town in the middle of the night. Sometimes my naiveté astonishes me.

We were strolling along when suddenly, Bruce appeared out of nowhere, walking past us on his way to his trailer. I was in the middle of saying something to my new friend when I realized she wasn't beside me anymore. I looked back just in time to see her walking with Bruce into his trailer.

Whatever happened in his trailer that night took long enough that we were considerably delayed. Finally, about forty-five minutes later, Bruce emerged with her, she disappeared into the darkness and he slipped into the car beside me. As we were pulled into traffic to start filming our scene, he looked at me with that sly Bruce Willis smile, his eyes looking a little glassy.

"I'm tellin' you, Curt-eye," he said with a sigh of satisfaction. "I am *never* gettin' married!"

Allyce Beasley, from the beginning, was something of an angel. She and I had become close almost instantly. At that point, she was beginning to struggle with the success of *Moonlighting*. It had all started so well, a show in which she had been cast as one of a colorful, unique threesome. It's important to remember that, in American television, there really never was a character on a show quite like Allyce Beasley before *Moonlighting*. Afterward, there were as many as you could shake a stick at, all of them variations on the cheerful, sympathetic, sincere, loyal, quirkily attractive DiPesto. Now, as it progressed into its first season, she was finding her role being steadily diminished as Bruce and Cybill became the topic of conversations at water coolers all over the world and she was stuck doing her signature rhymes when she answered the phone. In addition, though I was unaware of it at the time, she was also struggling with a doomed marriage, which gave us something in common other than the sense that we were two children in a dysfunctional family, covering our ears and crying out "Mommyand-Daddyloveeachother!! MommyandDaddyloveeachother!!" while Mommy and Daddy screamed at each other and threw briefcases.

Coincidently, Allyce and I filed for divorce from our respective spouses on the same day, and we didn't plan it that way. It had been awhile since we'd been at work and when I saw her I said, "Hey, how was your week?"

"I filed for divorce," she said.

"So did I!!!"

I then suggested that under the circumstances we should probably have an affair. She was polite enough to say she'd consider it, but ultimately declined on the grounds that it was probably too soon for both of us, plus she was pregnant with her soon-to-be-ex's child, which would certainly have complicated matters. It turned out that the rumors of our affair spread without our help. Allyce and I were photographed together arriving at a pro-choice rally in West Hollywood and the *National Enquirer*, tired of printing the same old "Bruce and Cybill Hate Each Other" story, printed a "Curtis and Allyce Love Each Other" story instead. It didn't sell anywhere near as many copies as the Bruce/Cybill issues, but it was awfully sweet and I'm sure they meant well.

In 2016, Allyce confessed that as early as the pilot episode she found working with Bruce and Cybill a trial. When I asked if she had a sense in retrospect which of the two had led the way into difficult behavior, she put it succinctly.

"For her," she said, "it was really a thing where no one had ever said no to her. She'd started out as a model and went on to have all those big connections, and had just come to expect that she would get her way no matter what, you know? If anyone ever said no to her, they were gone. It happened on the show all the time. That's why she was the way she was. Bruce was just an asshole."

Like me, Allyce found herself in the middle of everyone else's dysfunctional relationships.

"I'd be on the set with Cybill," she told me, "and Glen would walk onto the stage. And she'd freak out. She'd grab me and start dragging me off the set. She'd say, 'I have to get away from him! Please! I can't talk to him! Come with me!!' and drag me into her trailer to keep from facing him.

"With the two of them [Bruce and Cybil]," she said, "I

really think it wasn't professional jealousy so much as sibling rivalry. Like two spoiled children and Glen was Daddy. Constantly fighting for his attention, each of them thinking, 'He loves me more.' But there was no competition. Bruce was Glen's favorite. Glen loved Bruce."

Allyce's recollections confirmed for me that sense of a twisted family dynamic at work on *Moonlighting*. She had been the "middle child" before I arrived and when I got there I shared that position with her.

One of the residual effects of this was the bewildering yet inevitable way that Allyce and I enabled everyone else in their behavior. One notorious aspect of working with Bruce and Cybill was understanding that there were certain basic things that professional actors gave other professional actors that we would never get. Like getting their lines read off-camera. For those who've never worked on a film set, I must explain: the way that filming works is involved and complicated. When we shoot what's called the master shot, everyone is on-camera at once. When we then come in for coverage, the camera may be on just two or three people, and when doing close-ups, obviously, there will be only one person. But when doing, for example, close-ups, it is considered a professional courtesy to stand next to or behind the camera and read your lines to the actor in close-up, just as you did in the master shot. Many of the greatest, most famous actors do this every day.

Not Bruce and Cybill. It had started with Cybill refusing to do Bruce's off-camera. Bruce hung in for a while, continuing to do her off-camera even knowing she wouldn't do his. Then he stopped, too. He would still do my off-camera, but eventually quit even doing that. It was the guest stars, though, who really suffered.

Every episode of *Moonlighting* would have the client sitting in David or Maddie's office explaining what the problem was they wanted them to solve. The client would usually be seated in the chair, David or Maddie sitting facing them across the desk. These were very long, sometimes emotionally difficult scenes to do, and the onus was always on the guest star to deliver. But the rule on *Moonlighting* was all of Bruce's or Cybill's coverage would be shot first. Then as the cameras were turned around to face the guest star, they would disappear, leaving it to the guest star to get through the scene however they could with only the script supervisor to feed them lines.

Allyce and I were so ashamed of Bruce and Cybill's behavior, we would show up on the set and read *their lines for them*. I remember the look on some of these people's faces when they realized that they were being left in the lurch. We couldn't stand it. In all my years in the business I don't recall ever hearing of a supporting cast volunteering to read the stars' line's off-camera because the stars were so inconsiderate as to leave before the scene was finished. I honestly don't know, now that I think of it, whether it helped the guest stars or whether it just made an awkward situation worse. But just like "good" children, we did whatever we could to mitigate our rebellious older siblings' unconscionable behavior.

Both Allyce and I learned quickly how to act to a piece of tape on the camera just to survive. One morning I came into work thrilled because our guest star that week was the great American stage actor Colleen Dewhurst, who had started filming the day before. I went to the makeup trailer and found her sitting in the next chair.

"Miss Dewhurst," I said. "Hi. My name's Curtis Armstrong. I'm on the show. It's really a pleasure to meet you."

She looked at me through her cigarette smoke and growled, "You on this show?"

"Yes," I said.

"Okay, then maybe you can tell me something," she rumbled. "Just who do those two assholes think they are?"

Even Colleen Dewhurst didn't warrant an off-camera.

In our 2016 interview, Allyce also told me a story I had never heard before, which occurred during the filming of "Atomic Shakespeare." It's a harrowing example of how bad working on that set could be.

Allyce had shot a scene with Bruce in a master and they were coming in to do Bruce's close-up. Bruce liked to act without other actors there, perhaps because it could allow him to justify not being there for other people. But on this day, for some reason, the director, Will Mackenzie, sought Allyce out and asked her if she would come and do Bruce's off-camera. She was sort of surprised.

"Really?" she said. "Are you sure he wants me? He doesn't usually . . ."

"Yeah," said Will. "It's fine. Come do your lines with him. It'll help."

So Allyce stood by the camera and they started the scene. Then Bruce stopped in midline.

"Cut, cut, cut!" he said. "Allyce isn't close enough to the camera." So Allyce got closer and they rolled again.

"Cut, cut, cut!!" he snapped again. "Allyce isn't close enough to the camera!!" She made another adjustment, now with her face against the mat box. They rolled again. This time, Bruce cut again midsentence and stormed off the set.

Allyce felt that somehow this all was her fault, so she went to his trailer to apologize. When he opened the door to her knock and saw it was she, he grabbed her by her costume, pulled her to him and snarled, "Do you have any idea how hard it is to be that funny?! Do you?!!! DO YOU??!!!' His voice raised to a near-shout. "DO YOU HAVE ANY IDEA HOW HARD IT IS TO BE THAT FUNNY???!!!"

As the spirit flagged on the show, Cybill chose to make a stand and told ABC at the end of season two that if they wanted her back on the show, Glen Caron would have to be fired. And ABC, amazingly, caved. Suddenly the creator of the show was gone. While many of the other executive producers, including Jay Daniel, Chic Eglee, Jeff Reno, Ron Osborn, Kerry Ehrin and Roger Director chose to stay, naturally the feel of the show changed, since virtually every page of every script, regardless of who wrote it, was rewritten by Glen himself. This was one of Cybill's primary complaints, as every night new pages would be delivered to everyone's house at 4:00 a.m. for their shooting call at 7:00 a.m. the same morning.

Admittedly, this was tough sledding, especially for Bruce and Cybill, who had massive amounts of dialogue to learn every episode. The rewriting—and the resistance to the rewriting—also contributed to delays in shooting. On one memorable occasion, we had shown up on set and had just finished shooting the master of the first scene on the schedule when new pages were handed to us on set. The master was basically trashed as a result and the editors had to piece the scene together using only coverage.

The stories of *Moonlighting*'s adventures in filming are legendary. There was the Whoopi Goldberg episode, famous among fans for making absolutely no sense at all. Then there was the episode we were filming up against the deadline for the writers' strike in 1987. The strike was called, and we hadn't finished the episode. As usual, we were down to the wire on delivering the episode for broadcast. We couldn't hand it in seven minutes short. What to do?

I got a call the evening before giving me a call time and telling me we couldn't shoot scripted material, but we were going to do "something." "Bruce," I was told, "had an idea."

We didn't even try to wrap up the episode. The show just cut to Bruce and Cybill walking among our writers, who were all seated at desks holding strike placards. Bruce explained that there was a writers' strike so we couldn't finish the episode, but instead, he was going to have "Bert" Viola come out and sing the Sam the Sham and the Pharaohs' hit "Wooly Bully." No reason, really, just a way to fill up the remaining time. Under protest, Viola does.

It was one of the most famous *Moonlighting* episodes, even if no one can remember what the rest of the episode was about. We were able to get away with it because it was, literally, unscripted.

Nevertheless, Glen got in trouble with the Writers Guild for breaking the strike by filming anything, scripted or not.

There was the episode that featured an introduction by Cybill's friend Orson Welles (in his last filmed appearance before his death); the episode shortly after the premiere when a critic for *TV Guide*, who had given the show a vicious review, appeared in the cold open of the show recanting his review, after which he was handed an envelope of money on screen; the black-and-white *noir* episode; the musical episode; and most famously, the Shakespeare episode.

"Atomic Shakespeare" was written by Jeff Reno and Ron Osborne and is based on Shakespeare's *The Taming of the Shrew*. Amazingly, it's still used to introduce middle and high school students to Shakespeare. It took almost three weeks to shoot, primarily utilizing Universal's Court of Miracles for exterior locations, and was, I believe, the first single episode of an hour-long network television show to cost over a million dollars to produce. It was directed by Will Mackenzie. I was the only member of the cast to have actually played Shakespeare and this was the first episode in which I had a chance to do some real work. That, the "Bogart" episode ("Here's Living With You, Kid"), "Blonde on Blonde" and "Sam and Dave" were probably my favorite episodes on the show.

These were the high points. The low points were so low that it may explain why now, after decades, no one has written a real history of the show. As Bruce and Cybill's relationship deteriorated—and there seemed to be, literally, no bottom to its devolution—the show's producers did pretty much everything they could to diffuse the situation except say "no," and it was way too late for that. To minimize the time the two would have to work together, they brought in recurring women guest stars (Brooke Adams and Virginia Madsen) to work with Bruce and male guest stars (Mark Harmon and Dennis Dugan) to work with Cybill. All four did sterling work and were fine examples of how professionals can display grace under pressure. Dugan wound up staying on as one of the only directors that both stars could work with, but the show, once a critical darling and ratings success, became the target of vitriol and plunging numbers. Weirdly, as things got worse, Bruce and Cybill seemed more and more like two sharks smelling blood in the water. Each for their own reason appeared determined to see the show crash and burn and they finally got their wish in 1989, when ABC canceled it.

The last few weeks of *Moonlighting* seemed, even then, like we had shifted into an alternate reality. At one point, we were actually shooting three episodes at one time. Strangely, it was not all horrible. In some ways, I guess, the pressure was off and we were faced with a finite future. But Allyce, now a single mother, was suffering a kind of combat fatigue following the years of both personal and professional stress. "Here's Living With You, Kid," the only episode ever on the show that could rightly be called a "Viola" episode and the only one in which neither David nor Maddie made an appearance, was a dream come true for me and a kind of professional hell for her. After struggling through years of DiPesto episodes being farmed out to spec writers and B directors, here was an episode that was written by our staff and directed by one of our producers, Artie Mandleberg. That kind of respect had never been shown to Allyce's episodes. It was a difficult shoot for everyone. Even our friendship, usually proof against anything this show could throw at it, suffered from the stress and never completely recovered.

But as we approached our finale, "Lunar Eclipse," the sadness was sometimes overwhelming. I took to stocking my trailer with booze and having regular Friday-night bacchanals with the crew and other actors. Fridays were usually late nights anyway and I often didn't make it home until dawn, drunk and miserable. But at the same time, there would be Curtis Armstrong Day . . .

Given what a significant event it was during my *Moonlighting* years, it's amazing how much of Curtis Armstrong Day I don't remember. I do know that it came during a difficult time on the show. I do remember everyone was kind of stupid with exhaustion and tension and Curtis Armstrong Day was probably partially a means of releasing some of that tension. It definitely wasn't the product of just one person's inspiration. Many contributed and put an amazing amount of effort into making it happen. But my recollection is that it started with Bruce Willis.

First, though, I should mention that Curtis Armstrong Day is a bit of a misnomer. It was officially known as Curtis Armstrong Week and it began with Bruce's arrival on the set one morning—certainly a Monday—making the announcement, absolutely out of nowhere, that "It's Curtis Armstrong Week, ladies and gentlemen!" This was greeted with the somewhat bewildered applause and polite laughter that greeted Bruce's occasionally perplexing pronouncements, which were not uncommon. But he was in a good mood and that put everyone else in a good mood and I thought nothing more about it, other than bowing and thanking everyone for their support. It was forgotten pretty much as soon as it happened. Except that later on in the day, Bruce made the announcement again, for anyone who missed it the first time. And then again. And again. He asked Cybill on her arrival on the set if she was excited about Curtis Armstrong Week. Cybill displayed the feigned enthusiasm of a real pro. She had no more idea what he was talking about than anyone. And so it went on. For days. Now it was no longer just Bruce's thing. Everyone was talking about it. Crew, writers, staff, actors—everyone wanted to know how I was enjoying Curtis Armstrong Week and the answer was, at that point, not very much. I was starting to look pale and nervous and would start noticeably at sudden noises. Something was definitely up. Now comments about "my week" were greeted with a stony stare. People thought *that* was funny.

By the end of the week I was a shadow of my former self. We had been on the set all morning, though I don't remember what the episode was we were doing. The morning seemed interminable. Finally, just as we were breaking for lunch, someone came up to me and said I had a call on the set phone. This was almost never good news. As the rest of the crew and cast went to lunch, I went to the phone.

"Curtis! It's Glen!" I hadn't heard from Glen since his departure from the show sometime before. But he was at Warner Bros. at that point, doing *Clean and Sober* with Michael Keaton.

"Curtis," he said, "I'm kind of up to my neck here, but I just had to call to say congratulations on Curtis Armstrong Week! Having a good time?"

"Glen," I wailed, "what's going on? I have this feeling of impending doom . . ."

"Don't worry about it. Sorry I can't be there. Have fun!"

He hung up. The huge door of Stage 20 had opened for the lunch break and I walked out to head to the commissary, and that's when the cheering started. Outside a crowd of maybe seventy-five people had gathered. Actors, crew, staff, friends, friends of friends were massed around two open cars and several studio golf carts, all festooned with balloons and signs reading "Curtis Armstrong Week." A huge banner had been plastered over the door of Stage 20. Everyone, bizarrely, was carrying masks of my face, so it appeared that everywhere I looked I saw me. Throughout the crowd were extras and artists clearly hired for the occasion, including a group of amateur rappers and a gold-painted one-man band. A camera crew from *Entertainment Tonight* filmed as I was hustled into the front car, next to a costumed beauty queen, whose ribbon described her as "Miss Pacoima." Bruce walked next to the front car. Cybill waved to the crowd from the second car as we set off on a trip around the 20th Century Fox lot. Savage Steve Holland was there, as was Brian Tochi. As we passed the *Hooperman* stage, there was John Ritter, waving and cheering. As we passed the building that housed the editing rooms for the show, our editors dumped huge hampers full of waste film on us like ticker tape. Bruce's stand-in, Randy Bowers, and a couple of our crew followed along with their own cameras filming everything, eventually turning it into a pseudo-documentary, a copy of which I still cherish. It was all dreamlike and completely ridiculous at the same time. It was so chaotic that resuming work after lunch seemed pointless and Curtis Armstrong Day wound up being a half-day holiday, which I suspected was Bruce's idea all along.

The last day of filming was focused primarily on Bert and Agnes's wedding, the ceremony being performed, for some reason, by Dr. Timothy Leary. At one point, the legendary acid guru said to me absolutely out of the blue, "You know, there are three results of long-term hallucinogenic use. One is long-term memory loss. Another is short-term memory gain!"

There was a pause as he gazed into the middle distance. Finally, I said, "And what's the third?"

"Oh," he said. "I don't remember."

Meanwhile, another amateur video was being made, which had been in the works for some time. It was called "What Does the End of *Moonlighting* Mean to Me." Everyone connected to the show was asked the titular question and had come up with their answers. But this sequence would be the last chance they would have of getting responses from Bruce and Cybill, who would be moving on to shoot their final scene together, which no one was looking forward to. Cybill had already given her response. Bruce had been putting them off for days. Now, as he arrived on the scene, when he was asked on-camera what the end of *Moonlighting* meant to him, he mouthed his answer: "Blow me."

The final scene shot with Bruce and Cybill was in keeping with the whole. Shot in a church, the elegiac tone required the two actors to look at each other, but they were past that. They finally shared a reluctant glance—which the editors had to artificially slow down to give the impression that they were looking into each other's eyes. Cue the montage of clips of happier days and the Ray Charles recording of "We'll Be Together Again."

The cast and crew of *Moonlighting* gathered the following week at the fabled Coconut Grove at the Ambassador Hotel in Hollywood for a wrap party. It was quite a night. The nightclub itself, legendary for decades as a glamorous watering hole for the Hollywood elite, was on the verge of being closed. Within a few years, the entire hotel would be history. But for this one night, the place actually resembled its former self, which is more than I could say for me. I was desolate at the loss of the show, glumly facing an uncertain future as an actor at the start of a new decade. I spent most of the night drinking with the crew and doing lines with ubiquitous eighties scenester Rodney Bingenheimer.

Suddenly, in the middle of the crowd, I felt a hand on my shoulder. It was Bruce.

"Hey, Bruce!"

"Curt-eye!" Bruce said, with his familiar sideways smirk. I wasn't really sure what to say to him, as most of the season he'd had little to say to me or anyone else unless it was absolutely necessary. But now, here he was: the last night before parting, probably forever, and he was reaching out. He put his arm around my shoulder and started to walk me across the dance floor.

"Well, it's been some year," he said, gazing off into the partying throng. "Hasn't all been good. We've had some challenges, too. It's a roller coaster, sometimes, you know? Good times and bad. But, hey, the work was good, good for all of us and I'll never forget it . . ."

He turned to me, gave me a quick smile. "See ya sometime. Good luck." And then he disappeared into the crowd. I allowed myself a moment of amazed reflection. Bruce was clearly at the start of an amazing career and whatever he had done or not done during the last few years, I did appreciate that he had taken the time to seek me out, among all these people, for a final, private word.

And then, there was a roar of applause and I turned to see Bruce there on the bandstand, waving to the crowd. Then he stepped up to the microphone.

"Hey," he said. "Well, it's been some year. Hasn't all been good. We've had some challenges, too. It's a roller coaster sometimes, you know? Good times and bad . . ."

I went off in search of another drink. I had just played my last scene with Bruce Willis.

REVENGE OF THE NERDS II: NERDS IN PARADISE

FT. LAUDERDALE, FLORIDA, 1988

Toward the end of my first season on *Moonlighting*, I started hearing rumors about a sequel to *Revenge of the Nerds*. This was something that had come up from time to time as the first film had become more popular thanks to repeated showings on cable and following its release on home video. Bobby Carradine had been a strong proponent of the idea, as the film's star and a man who expected to have a piece of any nerd property to come. I'd get calls from Bobby every time there would be a new flurry of speculation in the trades. I was always supportive of the idea, though obviously, *Moonlighting* was my prime concern. Viola had become a character that the producers liked to write for and I was going to do nothing to endanger my position on the show. Anthony Edwards, in the meantime, had become a desirable commodity thanks to *Top Gun*, which had made Tom Cruise one of the biggest stars in the world at the time. Luring him back to a nerd sequel—for nerd money—was going to take some doing. But Bobby was convinced all it would take was a little pressure from him and Tony would come around. Sadly, Bobby's boundless optimism about the prospect of future nerd projects would often end in disappointment.

For a while, it was a moot point. As long as the current administration at 20th Century Fox held sway that would never happen. Fox still considered *Revenge of the Nerds* a misstep and, in addition, had implemented a strict studio-wide no-sequel rule as part of their new "quality control" policy. As far as quality control went, it was successful in eliminating sequels but it didn't stop them from continuing to release plenty of inferior product. But it was "original" inferior product, so that was okay.

Suddenly, everything changed, starting with the administration at the studio. Leonard Goldberg came in and the no-sequel policy went out. According to Bobby Carradine, a sequel to *Revenge of the Nerds* was the first project green-lighted by the studio. Goldberg allegedly claimed a sequel to *Revenge of the Nerds* was "a no-brainer."

Truer words were never spoken.

We were receiving updates on *Nerds II* almost on a daily basis, and none of the news was good. Jeff Kanew had gone on the record as saying that he couldn't fathom why anyone would want to do a sequel to the film. "It's done," he said at the time. "The nerds won. What are you going to do? Have them win again?"

It seems that at least when it came to the nerds, Jeff's integrity always ran counter to his own best interests, since in Hollywood the whole idea of a sequel was to have them win again.

But it isn't clear that the studio ever considered Jeff to direct the film. Joe Roth, a director with no more experience under his belt than Jeff had in 1984, had been selected to helm the film. He was an insider with the new studio heads and had a reputation for being an "efficient" filmmaker. What he didn't have was much of a sense of humor, which is kind of essential when you're directing a comedy, even a sequel.

The script was given to Dan Guntzelman and Steve Marshall, a writing team then best known for the television show *Growing Pains*. I have no idea how much time they were given to knock out the *Nerds II* script, but it wasn't enough. There was really no indication from reading it whether they had even seen the original film.

I hated the script. Some of it may have had to do with working on *Moonlighting*, which boasted some of the best writers of the day. I did remind myself that I had also hated the original script of *Revenge of the Nerds* and that had turned out all right. But I had a nagging suspicion that lightning wouldn't strike twice when it came to a potential *Nerd* franchise. In addition, the shooting schedule would mean my missing the season finale of our current season of *Moonlighting* and the premiere episode of the next one. Bobby was on the phone daily, begging me to do the picture. Without Anthony, who, unsurprisingly, was still holding out, it was more important than ever that I be in the film. He was genuinely concerned that the whole project would collapse if I weren't on board.

But I turned it down. Even the prospect of a summer playing with nerds and doing it for more money than I'd ever been offered for a film wasn't enough for me to take it. Twentieth came back with another offer: more money. I turned it down again. My agent nearly wept with frustration, but I was adamant.

Then I got a call from the agency. The executive in charge of production at 20th Century Fox wanted to meet with me.

We were shooting *Moonlighting* on Stage 20, which was directly across from the old executive office building at Fox. I was going to be filming all day, I said, and the only time I would have would be my lunch hour. "They will accommodate you," she said. "You must take this meeting."

I am afraid that this executive's name is lost in the mists of time. I'm sorry not to know it, because he gave me one of my first really great Hollywood lessons, as well as a good story.

I went to his office and sat for a while in his waiting room. He was on the phone behind a closed door and he was not happy. He was screaming at someone about something, and whoever was on the other end of the line would've needed a hollow chisel to get a word in edgewise. Every once in a while I'd catch his assistant's eye. She gave me nothing. Her face was utterly expressionless.

Finally, I heard the phone slam down and the door to the office was flung open.

"Curtis!" he said, his arms spread wide, an easy smile on his face. "Sorry to keep you waiting. Come on in!"

Seated opposite him, he faced me and leaned forward. He gave me a confidential, sympathetic shake of the head.

"Curtis. Curtis. What's the problem? Why don't you want to do our movie?"

I wasn't quite sure how to respond. "Well, you know, I'm a regular on *Moonlighting* now—"

He cut me off. "I know. I know Glen."

"Okay," I said. "Well, the schedule—" He cut me off again.

"We can fix that. Come on, tell me. What's the problem?" He leaned forward, his eyes widening. "Is it the money? Is it not enough money?"

"Oh, no!" I assured him, like an idiot. "No, no, no! No, the money is fine!" (My agent hadn't shown up for this meeting, obviously.)

"Well, then," he said, brow furrowed and eyes full of baffled concern, "what's the problem? Please tell me. I mean, if you're not doing it I think I deserve to know why."

The conversation was starting to take a weirdly personal tone, as if I'd just told this guy we should start seeing other people.

"Well, okay," I said finally. "It's the script. It's a kind of . . . a script . . . problem."

"What do you mean," he asked, "a *script problem*?"

"Well," I said, "the problem is it's just a terrible script. It should be better.

"And . . . it isn't. It's really not very good and I just feel like not . . . doing it." It could've been more artfully expressed but I considered myself lucky at that point to have gotten anything out at all.

"Wait!" he said. "Wait!" He spoke carefully, as though making his way through a jungle thicket without stepping in a nest of vipers or something. "You think . . . you think were going to be shooting"—he held up a copy of *Nerds II*—"this script?"

"Well, yeah," I confessed. "That's the script they sent me. I guess I thought that was the script they were shooting."

He smiled. He shook his head. Relief seemed to flood the room like sunshine after a storm. His expression spoke volumes. *It's going to be okay*, his expression said. *Just a little misunderstanding, but everything is going to be okay.*

"Curtis," he said, "we're not going to be shooting this script!"

"You're not?"

"NO!" he said, with a kind of disbelieving laugh. "Do you think we're crazy? We've just been through this with Whoopi's movie!" (Whoopi Goldberg's *Burglar* had just escaped into theaters and everyone was in the process of assigning blame for the catastrophe.) "We learned our lesson! We're not shooting . . . this!" His disgust was almost beyond words. He tossed the script on his desk.

"We are bringing in someone to do a rewrite. I shouldn't tell you this . . ." He paused for a moment as if wondering whether he could chance telling me whatever it was. I watched him give himself permission.

"We're bringing in a script doctor. And would you like to know who it is we're bringing in?"

"Yes."

"We're bringing in Larry Gelbart."

For those who don't know, Larry Gelbart was creator of the legendary television show *M*A*S*H*, the coauthor of *A Funny*

Thing Happened on the Way to the Forum and was widely regarded as the greatest script doctor since Neil Simon. In Hollywood in the eighties, Elaine May was his closest competitor.

I was flabbergasted. "Larry Gelbart is rewriting *Nerds II*?" I gasped.

He nodded solemnly. "*That's* how much we care. Now what do you say? Will you do the picture?"

"Hell, yes," I exclaimed. "I'm in!!!"

Needless to say, as I was shortly to discover, Larry Gelbart never rewrote a word of *Revenge of the Nerds II*. Nor was he ever approached to rewrite it. By the time we reached Ft. Lauderdale the script's obvious shortcomings necessitated immediate work, so a young writer—now extremely successful—was flown down to write whatever he could to save it. I can't imagine what they paid him, but compared to Gelbart's asking price, it would've been a deal. Robert Carradine, Tim Busfield and I visited him once to talk about the script and it was terrifying. He hadn't showered or slept since his arrival, and was pretty much living on room service and raw nerves. He was babbling incoherently, grinding his teeth and pacing around his room. The curtains were drawn and the place looked like an animal lived in it. Periodically one of us would knock on his door just to make sure he was still alive. One day he had just disappeared.

In the days leading up to filming, there were some other truly disturbing developments regarding *Nerds II* that gave me reason for concern.

To begin with, Anthony Edwards's Gilbert was nowhere to be seen. Anthony later told me that he had asked to read the script and been told that no one was reading the script until the deal was done. The producers claimed that Anthony had asked for too much money. Anthony, who didn't need a *Nerds* sequel at that point in his life, passed. Apparently, the powers that be just shrugged. The truth was, they said later, they didn't really feel they needed Tony in the film. According to them, Gilbert wasn't that funny a character anyway, and they would just give the other nerds more to do to compensate. This showed a total lack of understanding of what had made the original film work to start with. It was the chemistry between Bobby's balls-out nerd and Anthony's more gentle, sensitive character that gave the film the grounding it needed for all the broad comedy to work. The other nerds, Booger included, worked precisely because they weren't overused.

But that brought up another problem. Not only was Gilbert not in the film, Takashi wasn't either. Brian Tochi had been cast in the highly successful *Police Academy* series at Warner Bros., and Fox suddenly got cold feet about featuring the same actor in the *Nerds* sequel. I was finding myself increasingly concerned about doing a sequel with two of our characters missing in action.

There was another problem in the casting as well, in this case having to do with Julie Montgomery.

When Julie read the script of *Nerds II*, her heart sank. The writers, in order to free Lewis from a domestic relationship with Betty Childs and open up possibilities of hot young college students in Ft. Lauderdale, had included a scene at the beginning of the picture in which Betty is shown fucking an Alpha Beta. And Julie, to her credit, would have none of it.

"They sent me the script," Julie told me in 2016, "and I was aghast. Very upset. They had me in a hotel room with some jock—it wasn't Stan Gable—just some jock. But I was cheating on Lewis! It was upsetting because Betty was my character. She had fallen in love with Lewis and that was a big deal. This treated that like Lewis was a one-night stand or something. So I said no. As stupid as that sounds, I said no.

"Then," she added, "there was a conversation with Joe Roth and he said 'No, don't worry, we're going to rewrite it when you get to Florida.'"

I had reconciled myself to the idea that Julie was not going to be a part of the second film and frankly thought she was going to be well out of it, when Joe Roth showed up at my door one night, asking a favor.

"So," he said, awkwardly. "Julie Montgomery."

He left it there, waiting for me to take the bait.

"Yes?" I said.

"You know she's decided not to do the picture," he said. I nodded.

"I need a favor," Joe said. "I—understand you have a . . . kind of relationship with her?"

"We're friends," I said, already knowing where this was going.

"Yeah, but you're good friends?"

"We are friends," I repeated.

"I'd like you to give her a call. She has a problem with the script. Something about her character." His eyes started rolling, but he caught them in the nick of time. "Just call her and tell her what your experience has been. Tell her she can trust us."

I made the call, but I put his message in my own words. Julie stayed clear of *Nerds II* and never regretted it.

Revenge of the Nerds II was, I suspect, the last time Joe Roth was forced to do a movie he didn't believe in. He was in the inner circle of the new regime at Fox and it wasn't long after *Nerds II* was released that he was promoted to head of production—and it wasn't because he'd shot a classic film. We all suspected this had been an assignment. At that point, Joe had more experience as a producer than a director and it may have been felt that he needed a little more set experience before moving up the ladder at the studio.

Whether that was true or not, it was clear that *Nerds II* was not really a good fit for Joe's talents. I liked him from the start because I found him intelligent and interesting. He had an interesting personal history. As a boy in New York, he had been at the center of a landmark case involving school prayer—his parents, opposed to school prayer, were the plaintiffs—which fascinated me. I was surprised to discover that this was not something he was proud of or even talked about much, as he had suffered for it in his youth. But there was much about Joe that I liked and I was hoping for the best as we started filming.

At the very least, I was hoping to see something of the instinctive genius we'd seen with Jeff Kanew as far as creating an environment conducive to the kind of movie we all wanted to make, despite the script problems. I was quickly disappointed. The absence of Kanew, Jeff Buhai, Steve Zacharias and Peter Macgregor-Scott was felt from the first day until the last. Joe's main objective was to get the film done fast and cheap. That wouldn't have been a huge problem, but he was missing a couple of key components essential in the making of a nerd movie: empathy and a sense of humor.

Joe was not a nerd. Of course, neither were Bobby, Tim or
Larry B. Scott. Of the primary cast of *Revenge of the Nerds*, I'd
say only Anthony, Andrew Cassese, Brian and I could really
self-identify as nerds. But as long as we were good actors that
didn't matter. Jeff Kanew was such a nerd that he did the original film for that reason only. Joe struck me as sort of an intellectual jock. He was also born for the executive suite. He had
been bullied as a child due to the unwanted attention he received
because of the school prayer case, but that hadn't seemed to create a sense of empathy in him, at least in so far as these fictional
nerds were concerned.

That wouldn't have been an insurmountable problem if we'd
had a decent script. But that combined with his lack of sense of
humor was a real problem.

Tim Busfield said, "Joe was neither funny as a person nor was
he funny as a director. He wasn't a person, like Kanew, who
could get a real chuckle out of it when anyone said something
stupid. Joe would just get this kind of quizzical look on his face.
He took the experience of making *Nerds II* a little lightly. That
would've been my impression. In hindsight I think he thought if
he could deliver that movie by a certain date, they'd make him
president of Fox.

"That's what it felt like, anyway," Busfield continued. "It felt
like a guy rushing through a movie, to get it in, to get it into the
can. He kept saying, 'Come on, come on, we don't have time.
We gotta release this thing.'

"I had a good relationship with Joe," said Busfield, "and I
was never afraid to go to him and sort of represent the actors
and say, you know, what are you doing? You're breaking every-

thing down into camps, you're making this divide between your guys [at the studio] and us. Us against them. I'd say, look, we want to contribute and help you play, but whatever it is you're doing, it's not making us *feel* like we can contribute and play. I said, it's like you're a pitcher on the mound. You got nine guys behind you helping out. Just relax and throw strikes. He understood that. But he still couldn't do it."

Bobby Carradine recalled, "All through that movie I remember wishing we had Jeff Kanew, you know? Then Joe becomes president of Fox and leaves *Nerds II* off his resume."

Andrew Cassese was only fifteen when he played Wormser the second time, but his reaction to Joe was surprisingly perceptive for his age. "He kind of seemed like a fish out of water," Andrew said. "It was like he wasn't a director, but he was directing this movie. He wasn't really a director but he was cutting his teeth on it. I had the impression he was in the studio system, but they gave him the movie because they thought he needed to know more about that part of it. But he was kind of like a father figure to me, or older brother figure. I remember him trying to do a magic trick for me but I was too much of a smart ass for that. I saw the trick and called him on it. I think he was a little frustrated with me."

"*Nerds II* was really crazy in terms of the input," Larry B. Scott says. "Joe and I didn't really get along so well. I mean, we were okay, but he wasn't really about anything. He just wanted you to do everything his way. I think he thought he knew how this should be done. The musical number was really the only time he left us alone. Other than that, it was a couple takes and move on."

It didn't take long for tensions to rise on the set. I knew Richard Chew, the Academy Award–winning editor who was cutting our film and who had also edited *Risky Business*. To speed up the process, he was flown out to Florida and his editing bay was set up in a room in the hotel that was one of our main locations so he could do rough cuts as we shot. I dropped in on him one day to find him staring, frozen, at his monitor, his hands literally pulling his hair.

"What's he doing?" he said to me, without preamble. "What is he doing?"

"Who? Joe?" I asked.

He looked at me with desperation and said, "He's not shooting coverage. He's not shooting coverage! How am I supposed to cut this?!"

My relationship with Roth, having started well, soured quickly. At one point fairly early on, he came up to me on the set and took me aside.

"What is your problem?" he said. "You are supposed to be part of a team here and you're contributing nothing."

I was speechless. He continued, "I think I know what the deal is. You're on a big, popular TV show and you feel you don't have to do your part. Well let me tell you, I expect everyone on this film to bring something to the table and that includes you." With that, he turned and walked away.

Certainly my "big, important TV show" had had an effect on me when I started filming *Nerds II*, but it wasn't the one Joe imagined. On the first day of filming, we were shooting the nerds on an airplane on their way to Ft. Lauderdale. We had shot the master and were coming in for my close-up. I was in my seat waiting when the first A.D. called for the other nerds to come onto the set to deliver my off-camera lines. My reaction was instant.

"No, that's okay!!! They don't have to! Don't bother them! I'll be fine!!"

The A.D. looked at me with a knowing smile.

"It's okay, Curtis. I'm sure the guys won't mind doing your off-camera. Where do you think you are? On *Moonlighting*?"

It startled me to realize that my relatively short time on *Moonlighting* had me reacting to normal set behavior like that. At no time, however, had I felt that I was "too good" for *Nerds II*. All of us were disappointed with the way it had been seemingly thrown together and we missed Tony, Brian, Julie and the rest of our cast. But I had thought I was doing my job to the best of my ability.

In retrospect, it may have been that Joe suspected I hadn't done all I could to lure Julie down. Protracted negotiations had resulted in bringing Anthony in for just a couple of days: one in Ft. Lauderdale and one on the nerd-house set back at Fox. In an attempt to "replace" Tony, and to add some "youth" to an already aging franchise, Barry Sobel, a popular stand-up, was introduced as the orphan nerd who is brought into the fold by Lewis. Barry was extremely funny as a stand-up and a nice man, but even he would admit he wasn't an actor. All of us were working on bits, coming up with ideas and *rehearsing*. Rehearsing was anathema to Barry. The idea of working as part of an ensemble was a completely alien concept to him. The lack of connection was felt on screen and was definitely felt on the set. This was nothing against Barry, who was brilliant at what he did. It was just not the same thing that we were doing. But when he surprised us by showing up when we were appearing together thirty years later at a *Nerds* tribute at the San Francisco Sketchfest, we were delighted to see him.

Nerds II did boast a great supporting cast: Ed Lauter and Bradley Whitford were superb as our Alpha Beta nemeses, and Priscilla Lopez and James Hong were wonderfully over the top in what were basically stereotypical eighties racist comic roles. Courtney-Thorne Smith, as the embodiment of male nerd fantasy, was funny, professional and a delight to have around.

We had shot an extensive scene that included U. N. Jefferson (Bernie Casey), Mr. Skolnick (James Cromwell) and Dean Ulich (David Wohl). It was cut. There appeared to be less and less a sense of continuity and more a feeling of desperation about the whole project. As our fictional incarnations would do, the nerds clung to each other for support. We rewrote scenes, improvised when we were allowed and basically did everything we could to make the movie work.

We were thrilled to have Andrew Cassese back as Wormser, though he was unrecognizable; no longer the tiny, adorable boy from the first film. While Andrew isn't that well known in films outside of the *Nerds* franchise, he had an extensive career on the New York stage, including on Broadway in the musical *9* and had been working pretty much nonstop since the first *Revenge of the Nerds* movie. He was, though, at fifteen, still a virgin and that was a problem that Tim Busfield and Larry B. Scott decided needed fixing.

Fortunately, they had someone at hand who was both philosophically and biologically accommodating.

"I got a phone call at the hotel," Andrew told me recently, "and it was Tim and Larry and they were inviting me up to hang out. No idea of any funny business. I go up there and there's Larry and Tim and this girl. Everyone's hanging out. Tim and the girl disappeared into the bathroom for a while and I'm thinking, 'What's goin' on in there?' Anyway, they come out and then there's stuff going on between them, just sort of sexy stuff, you know. Larry B. said something privately to me, like, 'You like her? You find her attractive?' And, yeah, I mean she was beautiful. Well, next thing I know Tim and Larry leave us alone. They just left me in the room with her. She was very much in control of the situation, trying to help me relax. I didn't really know what was going to happen or what was coming next. I was just sitting there, trying to be cool. She offered me a joint, but I turned that down. You know, 'No, I don't do that.' A real prude.

"She was talking sexy to me and being physical and I wasn't sure how it happened but suddenly, my pants were down and she was giving me a blowjob. Ultimately, I've told the story a little differently, but the truth is, I didn't have sex with her. I would've loved to, but finally, I just chickened out. I really regret that."

With the accumulated wisdom of a quarter century or so, Tim's recollection was a little more circumspect.

"Well, it was just Larry B. and I arranged to have somebody spend a little time with Andrew. There was no money involved. She was someone we were hanging out with, you know, 'Would you consider spending a little time with our buddy Wormser, just help him get this out of the way? You, know, he might be able to focus better at work a little bit.' I think I made it about how it would improve the movie. Just tried to help the lad score. I mean, they were both teenagers, we figured just leave 'em alone for a while, they'll figure it out. Actually, she wasn't a teenager, she might have been in her forties. That's the problem, I think she was maybe fifty years old."

Larry B: (laughing) "She wasn't any fucking fifty years old!! You could not believe how beautiful this girl was. She was in her twenties or something. And generous! Generous *and* fine? That's like ringing the bell twice!"

There was plenty of blame to go around for *Nerds II* winding up the way it did. Primary responsibility probably lay with a studio eager to do a sequel fast and cheap so they could get a strong opening weekend out of it. They hired writers who had to write a script on their hiatus from their day jobs, and who had no real sympathy for the project anyway. Joe was not the right director for the project but Kanew was probably right in his assessment that there was no real future for a *Nerds* franchise anyway. We told the story the first time and all we could do was to retell that story indefinitely.

For all the difficulties between the cast and Joe, Tim Busfield points out something else to be considered.

"I'm really proud of what I contributed to the second movie. That we went forward with some of those ideas and that some of them wound up in the movie. More than anything, looking at the movies now, is realizing what you can get when you allow actors to play. That's the thing about Kanew. He let us create and he never got in the way. When you don't allow actors to play you're never going to get inspired, stupid stuff. But it's tough, 'cause nobody makes those kinds of movies anymore.

"With *Nerds II*, though, if I had been Joe, I don't know what I would've done. It was the eighties and we were young and in Ft. Lauderdale at Spring Break, doing a sequel to a big cult movie. And what would you do if you had your cast rolling in drunk from judging wet T-shirt contests at two in the morning?"

I left the set of *Nerds II* to return to a *Moonlighting* set even more bitter and dysfunctional than the one I had left in the spring. My marriage was ending, so the endless days on the Fox lot were a welcome respite. But soon, even that distraction had come to an end. The response to the end of *Moonlighting* was almost as toxic as the environment in which it had been filmed. I saw *Revenge of the Nerds II*, when it was finally released, as an embarrassment. I felt unmoored and directionless.

During the months that followed I sank deeper into an overwhelming sadness and a sense that I had thrown away whatever potential I had started my career believing I had. It was as if I were coming out of a decadelong dream. As an actor, I had come further than I ever could have imagined back at the Academy. But I couldn't help feeling that I'd sacrificed something at the same time, and not just my evangelical devotion to live theater. I dove into a series of doomed relationships with wonderful, accomplished women, all of whom deserved and eventually got better. The combined income of *Revenge of the Nerds II* and *Moonlighting* made the year 1988–89 the most lucrative year I had ever had and I wouldn't make that kind of money again for another quarter century. But now my professional life, by the beginning of the decade, was becoming a blur of uninspired jobs in which I delivered lackluster performances. The change in my fortunes in every respect was sudden and bewildering. I never imagined ever doing anything else but acting, but I had come to a point that I couldn't fathom what my next step would be.

And then after a few years it was announced that someone had green-lighted a television film pilot based on *Revenge of the Nerds* called *Revenge of the Nerds III: The Next Generation.*

There really isn't very much to say about the final entries in the *Nerds* franchise but I'll say it anyway. The first, as advertised, was a pilot for a proposed television series featuring a whole new batch of nerds at Adams College. Here, the freshman Tri Lambs are under siege from the Alpha Betas, under the leadership of Stan Gable (Ted McGinley) and the Big Bad Alumni character, played by then notorious right-wing talk show host Morton Downey Jr. The former nerds come to the rescue: Lewis, Booger, Lamar, Takashi, Ogre and Betty Childs (now married to Lewis, who has become a yuppie and is ashamed of his nerd roots). Booger, in this telling, had become a personal injury lawyer. Written and executive produced by original *Nerds* scribes Zacharias and Buhai, the screenplay was a cross between an essential rewrite of the first film in the first half and what amounted to a kind of *Nerds* fan fiction in the second. Most of the "next generation" of nerds was played by stand-up comics rather than actors, and Robert Carradine got co-producer credit on a *Nerds* film for the first time.

Nerds III had a few things to commend it: the introduction of women into the fraternity, the return of James Cromwell and Bernie Casey (not cut out this time) and Ted McGinley's dramatic breakdown at the conclusion when he reveals that he too is a nerd. McGinley was a revelation to me in this film. From the moment he's first seen as the adult Gable, now a bullying, smarmy traffic cop, to his final moment of coming out of the nerd closet, he gives a performance that frankly shames everyone else's. Julie Montgomery was cool and professional as Betty Childs but was given, predictably, little to do but be patient with her man-child Lewis in the time-honored tradition of male comedy writers uncomfortable with the concept of women as characters.

All of this, though, was overshadowed by Buhai's and Zach's decision to bring in "Poindexter," "Wormser," "Dean Ulich" and "Gilbert" at the end of the film, but played by other people. I thought it was a horrible mistake and begged everyone to rethink it, but Zacharias, Buhai and Robert were convinced "the audience would love it." Anthony, obviously, had had to be begged to do the second movie. Nothing would've possessed him to do this one. Tim Busfield had also—wisely—jumped ship at this point. As for Andrew, when I asked why he was not brought in, I was told by Zach and Buhai that they had "tried to find him, but he'd, like, disappeared." I told them I thought he lived in New York, and we should either get him or cut his character out of the sequence. They went ahead as planned. I found the whole thing acutely embarrassing as a creative decision and insulting to the actors who had created those roles.

Andrew himself said in a recent email to me: "Regarding *Nerds III*, I was never contacted. I wasn't that hard to find, either. I imagine they just didn't want to go to the expense of flying me out and putting me up just for a walk-on cameo, so they just said they couldn't find me. I did feel a little sad that someone else was playing my role. I would've loved to have seen everybody and to have been a part of it."

Possibly as a result of Andrew's "disappearance," a rumor started around this time that he was dead. From a pop culture point of view this was a win, putting him in a very small club with people like Paul McCartney and Mark Twain. The version I heard of Andrew's demise was that he'd been killed in an adult bookstore in Phoenix. The version he heard was he'd been shot in a nickelodeon in Westwood, California. In fact, he was attending NYU Film School at the time, which isn't the same thing at all.

One unique, if pointless, aspect of *Nerds III* was that some scenes in the film were shot in 3D. You could get your 3D glasses at any participating 7-Eleven store and experience the nerds in the magic of a gimmick briefly popular in the 1950s and which was enjoying an even briefer surge of popularity in the 1990s.

Revenge of the Nerds IV: Nerds in Love saw the sun finally setting on the Tri Lambs as they reunited to celebrate the unthinkable: Booger's nuptials. The script was again written by Buhai and Zacharias and the film was directed by Steve Zacharias. *Nerds IV* was given a jolt of energy by some of its gifted guest stars, including James Karen, Robert Picardo, James Gleason, Christina Pickles, Joseph Bologna, Jessica Tuck and

Corrine Bohrer as Booger's beloved. Legendary comic character actor, the late Marvin Kaplan, played Booger's father. Apparently, previous to filming, Zacharias, with all the enthusiasm
of a first-time director, told Marvin—also a playwright—to
feel free to add anything he wanted to the script, so on his first
day of filming Marvin showed up on set with a sheaf of papers
covered in gags and jokes that he expected to be incorporated
into the script. The suggestions were mainly of the "You say
this, so I can say this" variety and were generally unusable. Out
of respect for the man, though, we were obligated to try all of
them.

More shocking, and a fact only revealed to me recently, is
how the producers treated Larry B. Scott. "I almost didn't do
that last one," Larry told me. "They low-balled me. Shameful.
Like, a couple thousand dollars to do that movie."

There was probably no better indication of how far we had
fallen since 1984 than the idea that the company was low-balling
the one black member of our original cast. As I drove back into
Hollywood after the last day of filming, I struggled to come
to terms with the sloppy and cynical process that had gotten
us to this point. That night when I got home, I poured myself a Scotch and watched the original film again and made a
promise to myself that I wouldn't be a part of this anymore. I
was done.

Periodically, Robert would get in touch, talking with manic
enthusiasm about the possibility of something else: a *Nerds* feature or another TV movie. I had reached the point where I knew
sand castles when I saw them and I would just make noncommittal noises as he sketched out our future. So accustomed

was I to this that when he came up with another new idea—a reality show based on *Revenge of the Nerds*—I wrote it off just as I did everything else.

It would be a while before our first group of nerds moved into Nerdvana, but Bobby's idea turned out to be the inspiration we were looking for.

ENTR'ACTE
WHAT IS A CAREER?

What is a career?

Everyone now knows Malcolm Gladwell's theory, from his book *The Outlier*, about the "10,000 hours of practice." Using the Beatles as his example, Gladwell posits that in order for an artist, say, or a musician to truly master her craft, she must put in 10,000 hours of practice. The artist who reaches that landmark can look back and feel every hour.

Ringo Starr—a man who knows something about the 10,000-hours rule, even if it had never occurred to him when he was doing it—had a theory of his own. Everyone, according to Ringo, has about ten years in which to do his best work. There will be good work leading up to that and there might be plenty of work after it, but ten years is generally the period during which the best work is produced.

Based on my own experience, I think they're both onto something.

Ringo may have been talking about musicians, particularly rock-and-roll musicians, but the same could be said for actors. While there are always exceptions, I think what I call Starr's Theory of Creativity is pretty sound in general, and certainly true for me.

My decade *mirabilis* really began in 1979 with that gradual, unbelievable mass of plays, beginning with regional, off- and off-off-Broadway productions, including my first tour, with Moliere's *Adventures of Scapin*, which gave me my first introduction to life on the road. It was exhilarating and I wanted more. More road. More old theaters and opera houses. More bad food and lousy accommodations. More smelly buses. More loneliness. More applause.

It was being in this cluster of plays and working with the actors, playwrights, directors and designers that filled in the gaps in my education that the Academy of Dramatic Art didn't fill. There isn't a school in the world that can prepare anyone for a life as an actor. They can give you technique, impress upon you the importance of learning how to move and how to use your voice; they can even give you a sense, through their experience and their stories, of the history of the craft you've chosen.

But from there on, you're on your own. If you're lucky, and determined, you keep learning. "Education never ends, Watson," says Sherlock Holmes. "It's a series of lessons with the greatest for the last."

One of the most important lessons I had yet to learn—and the point of this chapter—was some years away and I'll get to it in its place. In the meantime, as I stepped into the 1990s, and the decades beyond, the lessons were coming over the plate too fast for me to get any wood on them. Not to say I wasn't learning things. Anyone in my line of work will tell you that your worst professional experiences are the ones you learn the most from. And in the nineties, I was in for some intense higher education.

I don't think I ever really stopped working. But once I started working in television, as well as film and theater, the amount of dross exponentially increased. It wasn't even that the jobs I was taking were all bad. Some of them were wonderful. But many of them involved episodic appearances on shows of varying quality or low-budget independent films or festival "shorts" that were seen by few. I did many pilots for shows that never made it on air. In one case, I was cast in a CBS pilot—*Almost Perfect*—from which I was fired immediately following the first table read.

I returned whenever possible to do summer stock at my beloved Totem Pole Playhouse. The purity of just disappearing into the bucolic surroundings of south-central Pennsylvania to do plays like *Dracula* or *Charley's Aunt* or *The Nerd* was a glorious respite from what was becoming sometimes a grind of uninspired, hackneyed half-hour comedies or hour-long procedurals. At Totem Pole there was, despite the serious work involved, an almost Zen-like serenity to it: living communally, all the men in one dressing room, all the women in the other. And always, there was the magic of the woods, the oppressive summer heat, the cool of the evening under an impossible expanse of stars. I continued doing plays in Los Angeles, but Totem Pole was the last time I had a theater that I could call my home. Anyone curious about this period would be well advised to check out a lovely little movie, written and directed by John Putch, called

Route 30, which I filmed many years later, but which is a love note to Chambersburg, Pennsylvania, and environs, and to Totem Pole Playhouse itself. It includes scenes filmed in the theater, and the house used as my character's home was the one I lived in while working at the theater. Talk about being frozen in time: while filming in the house, I found some of my books were still on the shelves. Home indeed. Of all the films I've made it remains my personal favorite.

I look back on the period following the cancellation of *Moonlighting* and even I'm amazed at how much work I did. It had the pleasure of diversity, if nothing else. But I'm amazed, too, at how much repetitive, joyless, laborious work I did without ever seriously questioning whether I had made the right choice in picking this path. Amazed at toting up the days, months, probably years spent unemployed completely. And missing in this book is any kind of accounting of the literally countless auditions that led to nothing. This is an essential part of what makes up an actor's life. Obviously, the time it takes to prepare an audition and then go through the process of auditioning, sometimes numerous times for the same role over a period of days or weeks, is part of our 10,000 hours. The jobs you don't get, the pilots never seen, the films never issued, the plays on nights when your cast outnumbers the people in the seats—those are all part of it, too.

All of this is important to impress on people interested in an actor's life, but frankly it doesn't make for compelling reading, which is why a couple of decades here will go largely unaddressed as to specifics. But there were jobs that stood out: Shooting Disney's *Adventures of Huck Finn* on the banks of the

Mississippi with my hero Jason Robards, Robbie Coltrane, Courtney B. Vance and Elijah Wood. Recurring roles in wildly different shows: Eunetta T. Boone's *One on One*; J. J. Abrams's *Felicity*; David E. Kelley's *Ally McBeal* and *Boston Legal*; Mara Brock Akil's *The Game* and James Duff's *The Closer/Major Crimes*. The quirky and occasionally brilliant SciFi series, courtesy of Mark Sumner and Javier Grillo-Marxuach called *The Chronicle*, in which I played Sal the Pig Boy—literally a man who was half pig, half person, and who worked at a *Weekly World News*–type tabloid.

Savage Steve Holland brought me into the cast of *Terrible Thunderlizards*, the much-mourned cult animated comedy that had spun off his equally beloved *Eek! the Cat*, co-developed with Bill Copp. That would lead to virtually a second career in voice work for shows such as Disney's *Emperor's New School*, Nickelodeon's *Robot and Monster* and my particular favorite, *Dan Vs.* created by Dan Mandel and Chris Pearson in which I played one of the great antiheroes of my career. Dan, the angriest little man in the world who was abetted—or more often rescued—by his best friend, Chris (voiced by Dave Foley) and Chris's secret agent wife, Elise (Paget Brewster). For more than a decade as of this writing, the voice job that keeps on giving is *American Dad*, Seth MacFarlane's enduring satire. My character on the show, Snot, was created by MacFarlane for me as a tip of the hat to Booger, a character he had loved as a boy. Another benefit of longevity.

Among a dozen or so films during this period, two remain remarkable for the very best reasons: *Ray*, Taylor Hackford's Academy Award–winning biographical drama of the life of Ray

Charles. Cast in a straight dramatic role as the legendary head of Atlantic Records, Ahmet Ertegun, I was given some of the best reviews of my career. The film starred Jamie Foxx, Kerry Washington and Regina King. Then there was *Akeelah and the Bee*, written and directed by Doug Atchison and starring Laurence Fishburne, Angela Bassett and Keke Palmer. Despite the Academy Award for Foxx, both films were criminally undervalued and will stand the test of time.

Sometimes when you're deep in this kind of soup of experience it can surprise you how other people view what you do from a distance. While I had been pretty sure for decades what a nerd was, and what an actor is, it took another, younger actor, with far less experience than I at that point, to teach me what a career was.

This happened sometime in the early nineties, during a conversation one day on the set of the Fox/CW series *Grounded for Life*, which starred Donal Logue and Kevin Corrigan. Kevin, who had grown up with the *Nerds* and Savage Steve Holland films, was asking me what I'd been doing lately. The truth was, I'd been doing quite a lot. A pilot that hadn't sold, a recurring part on one show, a guest spot on another—but somehow at that point I was discouraged about the grind of doing one substandard network piece of shit after another and never apparently getting anywhere. So as I recounted what I'd been doing as a working actor, I did so with some bitterness and, weirdly, shame. Shame because I was looking at myself through the eyes of a younger man who had grown up admiring my work and what did I have to show for it? Well, at that stage, I'd had about twenty years of near-consistent employment, but I guess I didn't see it that way at the time. I don't think I actually used the words "usual rubbish" to describe what I was doing at that point, but the tone I was using was unmistakable. I considered myself someone who sold out a career in the theater for good movies and television and now I had sold those out for crap movies and television. Kevin was looking at me with a curious expression during this litany of self-flagellation before saying, "You know, you do have a career that most actors my age would kill for, right?"

He said it quite seriously and it got my attention. I give you my word that until that moment I had never thought of myself as having had a *career*. I got that I was an actor who had spent a couple of decades acting (except when I wasn't) and then I was trying to start acting again. But somehow I never made the connection that if you continue to do that, over and over, for years, without quitting and going into another line of work, then you have what people call a career. What Kevin was pointing out, without saying so in so many words, was that few people have careers that are composed exclusively of "career highs." A career is much more a quantitative thing than a qualitative thing. Your "career" will start down and then go up and then down again and then up again. Unless you only do that up-and-down thing once: in that case "career" is probably the wrong word. "Dabbling" might be a better word. I had gone far, far beyond dabbling. I was a lifer. An actor whose decades of work have left him, finally, with something to show for it: a career.

SUPERNATURAL/ NEW GIRL

VANCOUVER/LOS ANGELES

Strange that I should have at my fingertips the date and time of my audition for the Academy of Dramatic Art back in 1974 and yet be unable to retrieve the day or even month in 2012— May, possibly?—that *Supernatural* first tugged on my coat.

It was an auspicious day, at any rate. I had two auditions, one in the morning and one in the afternoon. At this point in my career, more than one audition a day was an extremely rare occurrence. In this case, I had already booked an audition in the early afternoon for Liz Meriwether's show, *New Girl*, which starred the inventive and adorable Zooey Deschanel.

I was having some little difficulty with the audition for *New Girl*. There wasn't a lot to the role of Principal Foster and the only clue I could get as to who this man was came from the fact that he was described in the script as being a notorious "slow talker." *A slow talker?* I wasn't even sure what that meant. Surely they didn't mean he just talked slowly. What was funny about that? For a while I wondered if that might have been a sort of snarky code for something else, like someone who has really eccentric sexual tastes. No, it appeared that that was the joke about Principal Foster. He talked very, *very* slowly.

Talking slowly is actually harder than you'd think if it doesn't come naturally, and I was having some trouble nailing down this person. And it was just at that point that the second appointment came in for the morning of the same day, for a character on *Supernatural* called Metatron.

The idea of reading for two such wildly different and possibly recurring roles on the same day was remarkable enough. To have landed both of them was unprecedented in my experience. It was the start of a very busy four years.

Of the two shows, *New Girl* was definitely the least complicated from a scheduling point of view. I was usually required only one day per episode and virtually all my scenes were with Zooey, which no one in their right mind could describe as hard labor. The first time we rehearsed a scene and I looked into those eyes of hers, I forgot what stage I was on, let alone what my next line was. I have since learned that all was not sweetness and light on the *New Girl* set, but everyone seemed to make it their job to keep the unpleasantness away from me, like a couple whose marriage is breaking up but manage to hold it together when friends are over. Zooey was always unfailingly charming and extremely funny and very clear—in the politest but firmest of ways—when she was done with a take. In the early days, we would always complete the scene as written and then improvise it to see what else we could come up with. That would change. Toward the end of my tenure as Principal Foster on the show, I would come in to find that alternative lines—as many as five "alts"—had been written for virtually every line in the scene. This meant, practically, that a half-page of dialogue would be two pages of dialogue by the time we were finished. Almost invariably, in our scenes at least, the take chosen was the original scripted one. I have enjoyed my time on *New Girl*, a job that continues as of this writing, despite Principal Foster's retirement from the school he had overseen so ineptly for so long.

As it turned out, the lightness of my schedule on *New Girl* was a lucky thing, because *Supernatural*, which I began within just a few weeks of *New Girl*, would prove to be a much more involved commitment.

When Metatron, the Scribe of God, a hermit armed with a shotgun and surrounded by hundreds of thousands of books, made his first appearance, I thought I had died and gone to heaven. Given everything I had seen on the page, I could see this fallen angel—eccentric, violent, articulate, unpredictable and hilarious—as being an unexpected gift to any lucky actor, even if he only lasted three episodes, which it turned out was the intention of the show's writers at the time.

At the same time, as I flew up to Vancouver, British Columbia, to shoot my first episode, I was a little concerned about the kind of set I'd be walking onto. I had only seen a couple of episodes of *Supernatural* at that time, but I knew that the show's stars, Jensen Ackles and Jared Padalecki, had been playing these parts at that point for over eight years. Misha Collins, who played the angel Castiel, had been on since season four. These, I was thinking, are young men. I imagined them bitter, bored and exhausted. I recalled countless long-running shows I'd worked on in the past and the insufferable behavior of those lucky actors whose regular employment on popular programs seemed to be the worst kind of cross to bear. Contractually obligated to play the same role for sometimes unimaginable amounts of money, they seemed to feel, was a kind of wretched suffering that people like us—mere supporting players—would never know. I knew nothing personally of these men who were already international stars thanks to *Supernatural*, but under the circumstances, I was prepared for the worst.

When they turned out to be professional, supportive, thoughtful and funny men who came to the set on time and prepared to work and were welcoming and generous to boot, I was flabbergasted.

More astonishing still was realizing that the absolute believability Jared and Jensen brought to playing brothers Sam and Dean Winchester extended to their real life as well. I would say that they are as close as brothers but I understand from people who have brothers, like my sister, that you really want to kill your brother most of the time. One of these men and his wife actually moved to Texas to be closer to the other man and his wife. During my final episode on the show, we had a four-day weekend and the two of them took off with a friend of theirs into the wilderness to fish and shoot at exploding targets. ("Yep," said Jensen to me when they returned, "a real redneck holiday.") They don't argue, at least not publicly. They are two good-natured, even-tempered Texas men who found themselves on a show that appears to be running forever and who are smart enough to realize a good thing when it's handed to them. And it is their warmth and generosity of spirit that sets the tone for the remarkable *Supernatural* conventions. These are not Comic-Con–like conventions where there is a booth and panel dedicated to *Supernatural*—these are three-day *Supernatural* conventions, attended by all of the series stars, plus assorted guest stars and occasionally writers and producers as well. Thousands of people attend them, and they are held not just domestically, but internationally. And the actors appear at these conventions ten times a year, all over the world. And what makes all of that possible—the money, the travel, the private jet—is the fandom.

I refuse to believe that a relationship exists between a television show and its fandom anywhere else in the world like the one *Supernatural* has with its fans. A company exists to facilitate the unique alchemy that occurs when the *Supernatural* Family, as they are known, meet up every few weeks with the objects of their worship. There follow three days of highly structured interaction between the actors on a stage—accompanied by Louden Swain, an excellent band led by one of the actors, Rob Benedict, and MC'd by yet another actor, Richard Speight—as one star after the other is brought out to deafening cheers and are then put through their paces: chatting with fans, answering questions, interacting with the band and each other. Then that star is played off while another takes his place. The love and adoration rushing over the stage in deep, religious/erotic waves is heady and humbling at the same time.

By this time there is a compact between adoring and adored that has become as predictable and reassuring as a Catholic Mass, an appropriate choice of words, as *Supernatural*, with its mix of family, angels and demons—and God himself as a character—is a show that relies heavily on Christian tradition and biblical characters, without ever accepting any sort of Christian orthodoxy that would exclude any fans from partaking of the service. The strong LGBTQ presence at these conventions assures that, whatever trappings or traditions are absorbed from actual religions, there is always a sense that the people attending these services are there not just to adore and to be thanked and acknowledged for their constancy, but to heal themselves, to rejoin a community that relies on itself and its untouchable icons to fill the emptiness within themselves and the gaps within their own families and relationships, which have proved less reliable or fulfilling than the Church of *Supernatural*. Here, judgments are left at the door rather than regularly levied upon parishioners. There is music and laughter and the sharing of stories and parables. The men and women onstage will give talks about the importance of believing in oneself and the helping of others in the community and, most importantly, how here, within this community, in this place, they can feel safe and loved. Those who suffer from depression—an important element within the *Supernatural* community—take part in various charitable initiatives led by some of the actors themselves.

If this all seems a little heavy for what people might naturally assume is just another Comic-Con type of event, well, it is. I've been to many conventions of all sorts all over the country and in other countries as well, and there is simply nothing to compare to this. Books have been written about this fandom, as well as the usual exegesis about the *Supernatural* characters and world that are a regular and wonderful part of every fandom everywhere. But it isn't entirely a religious experience. One component the *Supernatural* conventions have in common with others is that of sheer joy, and it is difficult to be in the midst of it without feeling it oneself. But almost as important, the sexual element is inescapable as the show features in its four stars men who are impossibly, devastatingly attractive to the fans who pack their ballrooms. The physical stress that the fans endure during the brief moments they are allowed to meet, talk with, touch or take pictures with Jared and Jensen or Misha or Mark Sheppard is palpable. At the end of a photo session with hundreds of palpitating women, these men return to their dressing rooms to strip off shirts literally drenched with the sweat of the Believers.

It is a Traveling Salvation Show that plays to hundreds of thousands of fans in hotels around the world. These conventions are expensive. The company that organizes this and other TV-related conventions is a profit-making enterprise. Many fans simply don't have the money to afford even the least expensive of the tiered-priced tickets at the events. For those who can, even the most fleeting of contacts is worth every penny. And as a fan of many things myself, and as one who grew up in a time when this sort of artist-fan contact would've been unthinkable, I get it. If I could've met the heroes of my youth and adolescence—or adulthood, for that matter—in this kind of organized weekend, I would've done it in a heartbeat. The differences between us notwithstanding, I see myself in them.

Unfortunately, most of them saw me as Metatron, the troll among far more attractive men, the forever unforgivable, most hated of the show's numerous "Big Bads," the smirking slaughterer of their most adored darlings. Thankfully, most fans are able to differentiate between actor and role, but even those who can make the distinction had little time for the Scribe of God. After Dean Winchester referred to Metatron in one episode as a "douchebag," the Internet gleefully bestowed the nickname "Metadouche" on my character. It is a sobriquet that has become almost as ubiquitous as "Booger," although always said with a lot less affection. For the four seasons that I appeared on *Supernatural*, the fans prayed for my extermination—and that it would be slow and painful.

I embraced it all. In my relatively few encounters with the *Supernatural* fandom *en masse*, I affected bewilderment as to why everyone should be so angry with a character who really wasn't evil, per se, just misunderstood. I took to social media myself, posting funny, occasionally perverse posts, allegedly from Metatron to the fandom. These were almost always answered with a barrage of invective and hate, though the more thoughtful would include an added "Love U, tho, Curtis!" to let me know it was all in good fun.

And it mostly was. Then came what was to be my penultimate show as the character, though no one had told me that at the time. Titled "Don't Call Me Shurley," it was written by Robbie Thompson and directed by Robert Singer, and is now considered by some fans to be one of the best episodes of the show. Thompson created what was essentially a one-act, two-character play in which Metatron, down on his luck and desperate, is brought to an empty bar to meet with God, played by Rob Benedict, who has written his autobiography and needs his scribe's help to punch it up. Metatron realizes that God, tired of his creations' failings, is going to allow humanity to be destroyed by his sister, Amara. Metatron, once regarded as the most inhuman of villains, is given the extraordinary task of defending humanity in the face of an uncaring, unfeeling God.

It is a truly remarkable script and those days that Rob Benedict and I spent together were some of the most rewarding I have ever experienced anywhere—TV, film or stage. The episode was not just an extraordinarily vivid and complex discussion of some large issues, but it had the additional surprising effect when it aired of literally changing the fandom's opinion of Metatron overnight. They had watched as the reviled Metadouche, in tears, had fought for them, pleaded for them. They realized that finally, in a totally unexpected twist, Metatron had become one of them. Perhaps he had been one of them all along. If we go far back enough in anyone's story, we can find the moment that made them into the saint or the monster that they ultimately became. Metatron may have been no different. But it was too late, in any event. Having made the fandom, in spite of themselves, love and embrace Metatron, the writers killed him in the very next episode, "All in the Family," in which the scribe sacrifices himself for the good of the universe.

Supernatural the TV show, as opposed to *Supernatural* the touring show, boasted some truly remarkable talent behind the scenes. With writers like Robbie Thompson, Nancy Won, Andrew Dabb, Jeremy Carver and Jenny Klein; directors like John Badham, Phil Sgriccia, and Thomas R. Wright; designers like Jerry Wanek; editors like Nicole Bayer; and the great cinematographer Serge Ladouceur with a top-notch camera crew, the show has creative talent to spare. The makeup, wardrobe and hair departments show continual invention (and re-invention). Care is taken by everyone. To name them all is impossible, but for an actor to be able to work with those people, and to be given those words to speak season after season, makes it difficult to imagine it *not* being fun. It was also work—sometimes remarkably hard work.

And yet there I was, in the center of it all, with Metatron as my splendid alter-ego, working in and sharing a popular spotlight with such evolved and generous actors. And despite their unfailing kindness and courtesy—or perhaps in a way, because of it—I never, from beginning to end of my time on *Supernatural* became a *part* of it. I observed being on *Supernatural*. Even when being a guest at *Supernatural* conventions, I came away imagining what really being a part of those conventions would be like.

So, strangely enough, as a creature of fandom, as one who was present at the creation of modern fandom as we know it today, I, the most obsessive and giddy of superfans in my own right, found myself but tepidly welcomed by some of those organizing these events. It may have been just a matter of getting off on the wrong foot, I don't know. But when I first showed up at a *Supernatural* convention in Chicago, I was never told that there were after-hours events at which the cast could perform for the fans. At another I was put alone in a separate room from the rest of the cast for an entire afternoon between events. Once I was told by the staff they were going to have to move me into a hallway to sign autographs because I wasn't doing it fast enough. In this case, it was a question of me not understanding the rules. I was accustomed to conventions where I could engage with people one-on-one while signing. I had never gotten complaints before but this kind of interaction at a *Supernatural* convention was, due to the sheer volume of people, not possible. I just hadn't known. But it was an awkward situation and I felt it. After three conventions in the U.S. the phone stopped ringing and my relationship with the *Supernatural* conventions discreetly ended.

"It isn't that they don't want you," one of my castmates told me later. "They just don't *need* you."

Because I was not on the road with the cast, I found myself by the end of my final season on the show about as close to them all as I had been the first day. I had been told at one point by Misha Collins that attending the conventions was really how everyone became friends on the show. When filming in Vancouver, there just isn't time. Being cut out of the conventions meant that kind of interaction was lost to me, which made me sad. Most actors are, I think, social creatures and crave support and community as much as anyone. We tend to be nomadic and travel in herds, whether it's touring a play or on location for a film. To see a clan as close personally as the *Supernatural* cast is was a beautiful thing, but it was one Eden, to use another biblical analogy, that I found myself cast out of forever.

Of course, by that time, I was a man in my early sixties who had been acting for decades. This sense of being considered disposable wasn't unknown to me, either as an actor or a nerd.

It was just a strange thing, after all these years, to feel like I was back at the Spazz Table again.

KING OF THE NERDS

LOS ANGELES, 2013–2016

When Robert Carradine and I would get together for dinner from time to time, the conversation would inevitably turn to two subjects: Nerds and Money. I tended to focus on the nerds, while Robert obsessed about the money, in a way a man with two children on the cusp of entering college tends to do.

Over the years, we had seen *Revenge of the Nerds* only grow in both influence and popularity. We had been invited— separately and together—to be guests at various screenings around the country, after which we'd do question-and-answer panels. I was always struck at these events, and from even just talking with strangers on the street, how much the movie meant to people when they were young and still struggling with their nerd identity. The subtext of *Revenge of the Nerds* was not lost on any of these people. Bullying and oppression are universal scourges, more so today than ever, and that fact was an essential part of the nerd legend. Over the course of the four movies, blacks, gays, Jews, women, Asians, Kurds and Sikhs were all represented in the Tri Lamb house.

The universality of the connection always struck me, too, when I would be approached by some white, middle-aged jock who wanted to talk about the effect that *Revenge of the Nerds* had on him. There he'd be, all muscle-bound and buzz-cut— the kind of guy who, at the frat house, would've been nick-named "Crusher"—getting all misty-eyed about how important the movie was, because it was *his* story. He'd been picked on when he was young and seeing *Nerds* made him realize there were others like him. And I'd be listening to him and thinking, "You fucker! People like you beat up people like me!"

But with age comes experience and with experience comes wisdom, or what passes for wisdom in my case, and over time I've realized that this guy was probably telling the truth: his truth. He may have been the most vulnerable jock in the house— someone had to be—so the bigger jocks picked on him. Which made him pick on the nerds even more. In this game, someone is always dealt the low card. Who am I to judge?

But even Robert, a former nerd abuser himself, could see the influence our little movie was still having on people of multiple generations, and, being Robert, he figured there had to be a way we could cash in on that. Obviously a feature or TV movie was out of the question. A feature "reboot" had been attempted at one point and was apparently so bad that 20th Century Fox actually pulled the plug on it while they were filming. A sequel with the original nerds at our age would just be an embarrassment for everyone. But during one dinner, Robert came at the thing from another angle.

"You know what's killing us, man?" he said, leaning across the table, his glittering eye fixing mine like he was the Ancient Mariner. "It's that reality shit!" This was a common lament for actors and writers at the time who were seeing networks throwing huge chunks of prime time over to these insipid creations. "But ya know what? Can't beat 'em, join 'em! What we need to do is create one ourselves! Base it on *Nerds*! That's where the money is, man."

It would be nice to say, "So, that's what we did!" The actual process, though, took about seven years. We would start talking about it and then get jobs and drift apart for a few months or a year, and then have another dinner and the whole procedure would begin again. Neither of us had ever produced a reality show or any sort of show, though Robert had some experience with production on the later *Nerds* films. We didn't even know what, in those days, would constitute a pitch for something like this. We came up with an overall approach and somehow wrangled a meeting with one of the prominent reality show houses at the time. Their subsequent offer was so discouraging that we dropped the idea for another couple of years.

But after numerous twists, turns and disappointments, we wound up with Ben Silverman and Jimmy Fox (Electus) and Craig Armstrong and Rick Ringbakk (5×5 Media). Armstrong (no relation) and Silverman were the nerds, with Ringbakk serving as a kind of jock ballast. We pitched the show to TBS, at that time the home to reruns of *The Big Bang Theory* and not much else; they bought it and they mainly left us alone for three seasons.

Armstrong and Ringbakk gently but firmly moved Robert and me through the thickets of development. Fortunately, Robert and I had no passionate commitment to any of the ideas that we had brought to 5×5, because most of them were jettisoned entirely, or drastically reworked. It was essential that any direct connection with *Revenge of the Nerds* be avoided, as Fox was uninterested in leasing any rights to the original film or characters.

Finally, the three ideas that we brought to the table that did become part of the show were that there be a "nerd house" (Nerdvana, as it was dubbed by someone), that there be approximate gender parity among the cast, and that philosophically, the show, in whatever form it took, would never mock nerds.

The show (*King of the Nerds*, as it was named by someone) was to be a celebration of all aspects of nerd culture and I made myself kind of a bore on the subject. Over the three seasons that the show was in production, whenever I felt instinctively that the tone was off, I would remind everyone to get out the *Revenge of the Nerds* DVD and run through the pep rally scene at the end of the film. That, I would say, is the spirit of this show and we must never veer from it.

Everyone was very patient, and to give our producing partners all their due, they really made every attempt to stick to the nerd ideal. Hunter Thompson once said about the medium,

"The TV business is uglier than most things. It is perceived by some as a kind of cruel and shallow money trench . . . a long plastic hallway where thieves and pimps run free and good men die like dogs." In my experience, that's a fair assessment but in the main the people we worked with were of a different breed. We were never deliberately cruel, there were certainly no actual thieves or pimps on the payroll, and by television standards the money trench idea is laughable. We noted every mistake made during the season and attempted to fix it in the subsequent one. We weren't perfect, but we tried.

The idea went like this: Comb the continent for eleven top-notch, geeky nerds, from all areas of the culture, and put them in a house. Allow them to pick opposing teams. Every week, the episode would begin with a Nerd War, a team-against-team battle royale focusing on some aspect of the nerd world: cosplay, robot building, debate, etc. Then, two members of the losing team—one picked by the winning team and one picked by the losing team—would enter the Nerd-Off. This could involve a massive chess game, or dance-off, or superhero trivia competition. The loser of the Nerd-Off would be banished from Nerdvana until the final episode, when only two nerds remained. Then all the banished nerds returned and picked a nerd to support in the final Nerd-Off, which would determine who would sit upon the fabled Throne of Games, win $100,000 and be crowned King of the Nerds.

I had a problem with the idea of calling the show *King of the Nerds* because of the gender focus. It confused people. What would happen, people wanted to know, if a woman won?

Would she be Queen of the Nerds? Would the title of the show be dependent upon who won every season?

When Robert and I first appeared at the Television Critics Association event to introduce the show, I made a point of noting that there have been historical cases where women ruled as kings, not queens, including the Egyptian pharaohs Merneith and Khentkawes. This may have been a stretch, but no one else connected with the show seemed concerned about it so I doggedly stuck to my explanation.

As co-executive producers in that first season, Robert and I were generally kept on the sidelines. Many actors get executive producer titles for shows without ever having anything to do with the creation, casting or running of the show, and our producing partners took it for granted that we would be happier simply collecting our fee and doing our "real" job, hosting the show as heightened versions of ourselves, Curtis and Bobby. Robert was happy with that but by the time pre-production for the second season rolled around, I had forced myself into the entire process, attending challenge meetings, budget meetings and casting sessions. When the show was in production I would be one of the first producers in the monitoring room in the morning, and one of the last to leave at night. To me the show had become far more than just a handy source of additional income.

By the end of the first season, despite a disastrous climax in which the final Nerd-Off was decided by what could only be described as a popularity contest, I was hooked. It wasn't that I was interested in the idea of producing for a living. If anything, I realized I didn't really have the ice water in my veins that is necessary to be a successful producer. It was *King of the Nerds*, and more importantly, the individual cast members that made up those three magic seasons, that had hooked me.

Here I was—a successful actor—approaching sixty, married to Elaine Aronson, the love of my life and my best friend; I was the father of Lily, an accomplished, beautiful, brilliant daughter. At a time when my personal life couldn't have been more happy and stable, I found myself falling helplessly in love again.

With a bunch of damned nerds.

There were eleven of them in the first two seasons, and twelve in the third: gamers, mathematicians, computer geeks, scientists, comic book nerds, cosplayers, rocket scientists, puppeteers, writers, vloggers. They swore by *Star Trek* or *Star Wars*, by DC or Marvel, by Dr. Who or Harry Potter. They played traditional board games, console games, tabletop games, computer games, video games. They LARPed, sang, played musical instruments, spoke HTML/CSS. Their casual conversations, sometimes caught on camera, sometimes not, were a baffling delight. They communicated on an elevated level, regardless of the subject, that appeared to be beyond the comprehension of mere mortals. They understood one another, which didn't mean they always got along. They flirted, disputed, argued and laughed. They ate shitty pizza till it was coming out of their ears and drank themselves into stupors. They plotted and schemed and manipulated, celebrated and debated. A couple of them may have hated either other nerds or us for putting them through constant challenges and inevitable failures.

Two of the three kings were women. I loved that.

But there were problems during that first season, one of them involving Robert.

King of the Nerds was an unscripted show, but there were parts of it, particularly when we were required to lay out parameters of the game, where we had to be word perfect. On the first day of filming, Tuesday, July 15, 2012, we stepped out to address the nerds for the first time and Bobby froze. The lines were just gone. Fortunately, we were hooked up to the production room through earbuds, a necessity for this kind of show in case the show runners wanted us to repeat a line or give direction in our questions. Now, this system was called into service to feed Bobby his lines.

It was a traumatic start for everyone, especially Bobby. At the time, he didn't really give any kind of explanation for his situation. Only that he was finding it hard when he didn't have a script to fall back on, though improvising wasn't that difficult when we were supposed to do that: it was the scripted material he was having problems with. Admittedly, the script changed constantly during the course of the day, sometimes with new pages handed to us at the last possible moment. My *Moonlighting* schooling had prepared me for this kind of eventuality, but it was clearly hard on Bobby. Separately, our show runners would approach me during the course of the day, eyes filled with concern. "Is he always like this?" they would say. "What can we do to help?" The truth was, I had no answers for them. I tried to remain calm, feeling that that was the best approach with him at this point. I privately asked Edie, his Swiss-born wife, if she knew what the problem was.

"What problem?" she asked, with a stony expression. "Everything's fine."

Everything was not fine and it didn't improve much that season. His wooden, tentative delivery was cause for concern and had to be tweaked constantly in post-production. I was beginning to think this could cost Bobby his on-camera job and, as we were a team, maybe mine, too. Edie seemed to make a point of being at his side at all times and virtually every question or comment directed to him had to go through her. When I could get Robert alone I would try to talk with him about what was troubling him but there was no getting through, no communication. By midway through that first season, I had started writing, unofficially, some of the scripted material on the show, particularly my farewell speeches to each of the nerds. One of the producers, Rebecca Hertz, and I, along with Armstrong and Ringbakk, started subtly reworking how Robert and I "presented." Bobby played the quiet, reserved nerd and I became the loud, voluble, talkative one, which was pretty much what we were like anyway. We got through that first season, but it seemed that from now on, the weight of the hosting duties would be on me. If we got a second season at all.

In a conversation for this book in 2016, Robert was candid about his struggles in the first season of *King of the Nerds*.

"For me, the first season was enormously uncomfortable," he said. "They kept changing the script at the last second and I found that really annoying. I just couldn't find my comfort level in that environment. I think it was what I was going through personally at the time—not professionally, because there was nothing wrong with the production. They were perfectly capable people, doing everything they were supposed to do. So it was my inability to leave my problems at home.

"By the second season, having done it once, it was just a little less terrifying."

Indeed, by the second season, Robert had leveled out to the point that Charles Wachter and Antony Carbone, who were coming more to the fore as show runners, were giving him more to do. To everyone's relief, on-camera Bobby was recognizably the Bobby of old.

Off-camera, Robert had always had a thing for speed. He was a car nut, a gear head, a speed freak. He loved cars, powerful cars, and he loved driving them fast.

He also was a passionate race car driver and had only quit— at Edie's insistence—when he was involved in a serious crash on the speedway. But, no matter how reckless he was, Bobby always seemed to be able cheat death and disgrace.

The morning of the third-season finale of *King of the Nerds*, I was up early and preparing to head to Las Vegas for a *Supernatural* convention when I got an email from Kayla LaFrance, the winner of the second season of *KOTN* and a friend. She wanted to know if I'd heard anything about Bobby having been in a car crash, and provided a link to the TMZ site that showed Bobby's car crumpled at the side of a highway in Colorado.

I started by trying to contact Bobby by every means at my disposal. I called his phone, Edie's phone, his two younger children's phones. I tried texting, DM, emailing. I tried the hospital that had been named in the TMZ article, but at that point it had been ten days since the accident and if Bobby was still in the hospital, the hospital had figured out how to deny it. Meanwhile, I was trying to figure out whether or not I should board the plane to go to Vegas for the *Supernatural* convention, or cancel at the last minute. I decided finally to go, thinking if Bobby were still in Colorado, it would be as easy for me to get to him from there as from L.A. My agent had already been contacted by the press wanting me to comment, which I didn't do. This had all the ingredients of a classic Hollywood Dynasty Tragedy in the making: Robert's older brother, David, had died just a few years earlier, found hanging in a hotel room in Thailand. The details surrounding David's death were still a matter of dispute—suicide, sexual auto-asphyxiation gone wrong or murder, with Bobby believing the last—but clearly the press was going to be all over this.

But as I boarded my plane at Burbank airport, I got a call from 5×5. Both Rick and Craig were on the phone. At 5×5, they were juggling calls, not just from TMZ and other organs, but from TBS as well.

"We've heard from TMZ again," Craig told me. "They're now saying that according to the information they have, Bobby's in a coma, and if they don't get some comment from us, they're going to go with that story. They're kind of panicking in Atlanta. They've seen the picture of his car and they're starting to get cold feet. They say they don't want to air the finale if . . . you know, the worst has happened."

"We have to be careful, though," said Rick. "This could be just a ploy to get an official statement outta somebody. If they ask to comment on the accident and we stonewall, they come back saying he's in a coma, which makes us say, 'No, it's just a bad accident!' That's how they get their quote."

TBS wasn't interested in discussing the finer points of tabloid strategies. They didn't want to run the risk of running the *KOTN* finale if one of its stars had just died in a car crash. They wanted to pull the episode.

All I could think of was Bobby's children. Ever, the little girl I'd met all those years ago in Tucson, was a grown woman now and a gifted actress herself. But there were Marika and Ian, Bobby's children with Edie. And Edie had been in the car as well. What was her condition?

We finally decided that they should call TBS and suggest that they run the episode but that *KOTN* would add a card at the end that would acknowledge the accident and send him our love. The network felt that would answer their concerns and the show aired as scheduled.

As *King of the Nerds* went out on the East Coast, I was on a stage in Las Vegas talking to *Supernatural* fans. Someone in the audience asked how Bobby was. The lights blurred and my voice faltered as I answered he was fine.

I was finally texted by Bobby, or someone using his phone, and basically told to "cool it." Meanwhile, Edie Carradine was talking and texting extensively to anyone who contacted her, as long as his name wasn't Curtis Armstrong. Our relationship, never close, had deteriorated dramatically during the course of the show, essentially ending in the second season during a furious argument on the telephone, during which she told me that *King of the Nerds* "was Bobby's show. You're only on it because he wants you on it."

Once it became evident that Robert Carradine hadn't died in that pile of mangled metal on a Colorado highway, the story faded away. The following year, Robert filed for divorce from Edie.

The fate of *King of the Nerds* itself dragged out over months. The third season, both from a critical and a ratings perspective, had been the most successful yet. Yet with a new broom at TBS, headed by Kevin Reilly, *King of the Nerds* was canceled on June 26, 2015. I was in Vancouver, shooting the latest episode of *Supernatural*. Thanks to Craig and Rick, who gave me a heads up, I was able to break the news of the cancellation on social media. None of us, including the executives at 5×5 Media or Electus, were ever told by TBS that the show was being canceled. Craig and Rick found out through a journalist who had interviewed Kevin Reilly about the future of the network. Reilly told him, only in answer to a direct question, "We won't be doing any more episodes of *King of the Nerds*."

Under his administration, only cheap knock-offs of *King of the Nerds*, like *The World's Greatest Weatherman* (right down to the gender-specific title), would be considered.

A little light winked out inside me when *King of the Nerds* was canceled, but even when the wound was still fresh I realized that what was really important about the show were the new friends I was fortunate enough to have made on it. Of the thirty-five nerds who appeared on the show, I have remained in touch with all but three and have become close friends with a surprising number of the rest. In addition to Kayla, who had always dreamed of a future in space, and is now employed by the Johnson Space Center in Houston, Genevieve Pearson has become one of my best friends. The smarts, creativity and energy she brought to season one of *KOTN* weren't enough for her to win the crown, but they were enough for her to be snapped up by a production company to work for them developing other reality shows: the company was 5×5 Media. Elaine and I have periodic nerd bashes at our home; we put nerds up when they come to town; we've been to two nerd weddings (Moogega's to Derek and Ben's to Colleen) and one baby shower (Ivan and Cassandra's). One Christmas, as a surprise gift to me, Xander brought his professional Christmas carol group to give a private performance for my ailing mother. Amanda Liston, in a polyamorous relationship, mother of two boys (with Chad) and triplet girls (with Jeremy) moved to Los Angeles after the show and Elaine and I have become unofficial godparents to the children. The connections span all three seasons and are deeper than I can express.

Happily, Robert completely recovered from the accident and is back at work making one movie after another. Every few months we get together at Musso and Frank Grill in Hollywood for steaks and martinis, rehashing thirty-plus years of memories and talking about our children. It's unlikely that we'll ever again play the roles for which we are most famous, but the friendship that came out of *Revenge of the Nerds*, unlikely as it might have been, endures.

AFTERNERD

One of the advantages of being an American-born nerd of my generation is to have been able to reach this stage in my life and look back and realize how much our lot has changed, most of it unquestionably for the better. It's easy to say that nerds have it a lot better today than they did in the sixties because, strictly speaking, we didn't have nerds in the sixties. We had nerdy individuals, or pairs—even small packs, if you were really lucky. In the sixties, the culture as such was still years away. But people found each other in schools or each other's basements or garages. We existed; we just weren't a force yet. Wherever any kid kept a bunch of comics in a cardboard box, we were there. Wherever monster kids gathered at some supermarket opening to meet Forrest J. Ackerman, Vampira or Tor Johnson, we were there. We were learning folk songs, watching Buck Rogers serials at the cinema or sci-fi films on TV on Saturday afternoons. We collected dolls and action figures. We cosplayed our favorite fantasy characters or cowboys without even having the word "cosplay" to define what we were doing. Of course, our parents knew what we were doing: we were playing make-believe. My sister and I did that; most people do at some point. It's the make-believe characters played in childhood that help cement our identity as a person. Sometimes as a people.

Some screamed their heads off at Frank Sinatra concerts; their children did the same for the Beatles. There is a strong argument that the thousands of "silly girls" screaming as one person at the four boys from Liverpool actually found unimagined strength in their voices, in their power and unity, and it was that power, the sheer glorious noise they made, that laid some of the foundation for the second-generation feminist movement in the late sixties and seventies and beyond. In 1977, George Lucas created *Star Wars*, a thrilling pastiche of a very traditional sort, but in doing so created what could only be described as a nerd cultural watershed. In 2015, J. J. Abrams created a new Star Wars, *Star Wars: The Force Awakens*, which featured two actors, Daisy Ridley and John Boyega, who gave young black and female nerds new heroes they could cosplay. Of course girls had Princess Leia to emulate from the earlier film. But she was a princess. Rey was a warrior.

All of these hobbies, pastimes or avocations—we call them passions or obsessions, now—were tolerated by others as long as they remained the province of childhood: as long as they were things we grew out of. These days, one of the ways we identify as nerds is by accepting a higher truth—that we don't have to grow out of these things as we grow older. It may be Nancy Drew or Sherlock Holmes, Batman or Pokémon, *The Twilight Zone* or the *Twilight* movies: when we bring them along with us on our path, it only enhances the journey. One of the true signs of maturity is realizing that *not* gracefully surrendering the things of youth actually make us better grown-ups. If more people embraced their inner nerd, the better off everyone would be.

For everyone who looked on nerds with disapproval or hate, there were thousands who got it. The ones with sympathy and imagination always got it. They, too, were nerds, whether they called themselves nerds or not. Nerds always get it.

As long as there have been nerds, there have been those who hate them, bully them.

In *Revenge of the Nerds,* it was the jocks, the Alpha Betas, who were the bad guys, and that was easy because, in their red and white football jerseys, they were instantly identifiable, like black-hatted cowboys or brown-shirted fascist thugs from a previous generation. But say what you will about the Alpha Betas, they at least had to actually face their victims. The Internet has given Nerd Culture much—you could even say it created it. But it also gave a powerful tool to those who would like to see us humiliated and scorned and vilified. It gave us a chance to find ourselves at a time when we were wandering in the wilderness with no connection. But it also gave our enemies the platform to attack us and to do it completely anonymously. *#Gamergate* revealed that the problem with Internet fandom wasn't that we were spending too much time at it, as our parents feared, but that its truly dark forces were not imaginary. They walked among us.

But the Internet and gaming culture didn't invent trolls. The creatures who abuse and bully the innocent are not a sign that Nerd Culture is corrupted. They are an indication of the failure of modern culture writ large. They are everyone's problem, not just gamers', not just nerds'. We're doing our bit, though. Every time you see #*Gamergate* or #NoBullying, nerds are there. Every time you see a poster at a Comic-Con that says *Cosplay Is Not Consent* you are reminded that in the broader world, the Nerd Flag still flies.

Nerds have had the last laugh in many ways and that is evidenced by people like Steve Jobs and Bill Gates. They represent legions: the nerds who, early on, locked themselves in their rooms to play endless hours of Atari or spent months perfecting their Pac-Man game. The first to learn how to code have become the champions of the world. Comic-Cons—once attended by the fringe—have become, for better or worse, the place where advertisers and corporations go to take the temperature of nations.

Which brings me to dreams, which is a subject nerds know something about. When I was a boy I dreamed of being an actor someday. That's a pretty banal sort of dream, but it beat dreaming of being an auto company executive or a banker, which were my only immediate role models. I never dreamed of being a nerd. That's not something people aspire to. They're nerds already or they're not. They dream of other things because they're nerds and that's what they do.

But here's the amazing thing: I wound up actually becoming a successful actor, even if I only feel I'm a really *good* actor on very rare occasions. Whatever. It was still a dream that came true. And taking the big, broad view, my success as an actor was due to a string of movies that were recognizably nerdy and embraced by that culture. *Revenge of the Nerds* presented me with a huge break, but there was something ironic about it, too. Robert Carradine, nobody's nerd, gets the role of his career playing a nerd, while Curtis Armstrong, a dyed-in-the-wool nerd, gets the role of his life playing the one character in the nerd house who wasn't, by any but the loosest definition, a nerd.

I also dreamed of being a husband and father. Maybe a less common dream, and though my first marriage didn't work out, my first wife, Cynthia became one of my best friends ever anyway. And her husband, Christopher Reed, is another. They were to become Lily's godparents and share a relationship with her almost as close as Elaine's and mine. Lily refers to them as "my other parents." So, there's something to be said about that.

But the marriage/parent dream never died. I kept dreaming, and the second try took and then some. I met Elaine Aronson, a writer and producer who has worked on legendary half-hour comedies from *It's Garry Shandling's Show* to *Night Court* to *Roseanne* and many more. We met defending an abortion clinic in Los Angeles from the depredations of an anti-choice hate group called Operation Rescue. I was an organizer, she a volunteer, and I hasten to add we were on the same side. She introduced herself to me as the best friend of Clare Leavenworth, who I knew well as Bruce Willis's personal assistant. Elaine tried to set us up but figured after a while that I would be too much trouble for Clare, so she took me on herself. That's my version of the story. She can tell hers when she writes her book.

My eventual proposal of marriage—*very* eventual, to hear Elaine tell it; to me it seemed a little rushed—was kind of like *Revenge of the Nerds* itself: mixed reviews at the time, but now generally regarded as a classic. I arranged to take her to dinner one night at one of our favorite restaurants, but had secretly arranged to pack enough of her clothing and essentials for the weekend and spirited her away to San Francisco instead. The plan went perfectly, if I do say so myself. Tickets to that endlessly romantic city secretly procured, a room in a cozy bijou hotel, flowers and champagne on our arrival. We went to dinner at John's Grill, famous in *The Maltese Falcon* for being Sam Spade's favorite restaurant. (He had the lamb chops, but the steaks are good too.) It was here my perfect plan went a little awry. Having succeeded beyond my expectations in getting her to this point, I then realized I hadn't really worked out what my proposal of marriage would sound like. It came out sounding like someone with a brain injury, as I stammered and yammered endlessly through arguably the most important lines I would ever speak. She somehow interpreted this incoherent babbling as a marriage proposal (millions wouldn't) and accepted. We went off to City Lights Bookstore to celebrate because that's what nerds do.

My old mentor Terry Kilburn claims that in my Meadow Brook days I talked constantly about having children someday. I don't recall that, but when Elaine and I finally had Lily, I realized that all the dreams of a fevered imagination paled next to her reality. She, too, was a nerd, but that is not always a given. Often the progeny of two-nerd parents will reject nerd life entirely. Not Lily. Scholar, bibliophile and music nerd, she, too, has dined on the lamb chops at John's Grill.

And my nerd journey continues, even if it is now Lily introducing *me* to books, films and music, instead of the other way around. As I approach the autumn of my years, if not exactly the sere and yellow, I find myself surrounded by young nerds, barely older than my own daughter, who see me as an honored veteran in the nerd wars, and keep me up to date on what everyone's watching, listening to and playing.

Thanks to them, I'm getting younger all the time.

Nerds Rule.

ACKNOWLEDGMENTS

My editor at St Martin's Press/Thomas Dunne is Brendan Deneen, and my advice to anyone starting out in the memoir racket is, get someone like him. Thanks, Brendan.

This all began with my publicist, Laura Ackerman of AdvantagePR. It was she who said, "I think I know a lit agent in New York who might be interested in your book. . . ." Without her intervention, none of this would've happened.

There was a time when I thought the last thing I needed was another agent. Then Matthew Elblonk came into my life. He guided me through the painstaking, and sometimes just plain painful, process of writing this book. He's also very sound on The Beatles, which gave us something else to talk about when we needed it. To him and everyone at DiFiore, many thanks.

Leslie Bruce came to me through Matthew, and it was due to her perseverance and help that I was finally able to produce a book proposal that not only sold, but initiated a bidding war from three publishing houses. Leslie is a truly gifted guide and counselor for a first-time writer.

A lot of very dear and patient friends made this book possible. They spent a lot of time sitting with me, either in person or on Skype, recording hilarious, scandalous and sometimes tangled and contradictory recollections. The stories they shared were valuable, irreplaceable and sometimes unprintable. I hope to God I've done right by all of them:

Paul Brickman, writer and director of *Risky Business* not only shared fascinating facts about the making of that film, but graciously allowed me to reprint pictures taken from my first audition for the role of Miles Dalby. It's wonderful for an actor to have "behind-the-scenes" snaps of his first film, but I would say extremely rare to have extant pictures of him *reading* for it the first time. Thanks also to Paul for giving me my film career.

Robert Carradine, Tim Busfield, Jeff Kanew, Brian Tochi, Larry B. Scott, Andrew Cassese and Julie Montgomery shared at least one three-hour meal talking the ups and downs of the *Revenge of the Nerds* films. Thanks to Robert Carradine, too, for his recollections of our lamented TBS series *King of the Nerds*. I was very fortunate to have met and worked with you all. Love you.

Savage Steve Holland has, over the years, reminded me that it is possible to have friends in this business. Apart from *Better Off Dead* and *One Crazy Summer*, people have no idea how many times he's hired me for projects when jobs were thin on the ground. Thanks, little camper.

I flew to New York specifically to interview Allyce Beasley about our years on *Moonlighting*, and found her as funny and engaging and full of stories as ever. Our dinner at a little French bistro on the Upper East Side could've gone on forever as far as I'm concerned. Much love to you, my dear, as always.

Roger Director, writer par excellence, and creator of the character of Herbert Viola on *Moonlighting*, gave me invaluable behind-the-scenes stories on the show and did so with the wisdom of thirty-five years' perspective. I needed that. Thanks, Roger.

Bronson Pinchot gave me permission to share some of his correspondence and recollections, for which I am truly grateful. I'm also grateful for the years of laughter and good memories. Thanks, Bronnie.

Elliott Milstein has been my close friend, boy and man, for forty years or more. He makes an all-too-brief an appearance in this book, but as my unofficial editor, he was astonishingly helpful. He was the first to read the finished manuscript and the first to offer insightful suggestions on improving it. The bug has bitten us and we are now working together on a book about— who else?—P. G. Wodehouse.

Genevieve Pearson also read an early draft of the book and her suggestions made the inevitable word slaughter when it came easier to endure.

Every attempt has been made to assign credit to the photographs in this book. Many of them are from my personal collection. But I want to mention a few people whose help in tracking down some very early pictures was of enormous help: Photos of Meadow Brook productions came from the Meadow Brook Archive at Kresge Library, Oakland University, Rochester, Michigan. Ms. Dominique Daniel is associate professor of humanities, librarian for history and modern languages, and coordinator of archives and special collections at Oakland University's Kresge Library. Shirley Pacquette is the university archive assistant. Thank you for the trip down memory lane!

Very special thanks also to Charlene M. Kondrat, administrative assistant, principal's office, at Berkley High School, for her help in researching photographs and who very kindly gave me a tour of the old alma mater.

Thanks also to Rachel Lichtman, who leapt into the breech to supervise the photo session that produced the front and back cover of this book. Her expert advice and consultation was invaluable.

Most of all:

Special love and thanks to my father, Robert, my mother, Norma and my sister, Kristin, all of whom I suspect have been dreading this moment for years.

To Cynthia Carle and Christopher Reed, our dearest friends. It took a village to raise us and we were it.

I could write an entire book just on the subject of my daughter, the incomparable Lily Emma Armstrong. At the rate she's going, someone will have to. In the meantime, however fleetingly she appears in this book, I'll take this opportunity to say I love you and learn from you daily. Thanks for taking a chance on us as your parents.

And to my wonderful wife and the love of my life, Elaine Aronson, with thanks for all the times she told me, "Oh, for God's sake, the book's fine! Can we talk about something else for a while?" When I met you I realized I'd actually been waiting for you all along. Luckily for you, you didn't realize you were marrying beneath you until it was too late. Thanks for being my best friend.